STORY OF THE ASHES

Cricket's greatest rivalry as told by the writers who were there

Staff

Editor
Edward Craig

Designer
Zamir Walimohamed

Pre-press production
James Bunce

Photography
Patrick Eagar
Getty Images
PA Photos

Cover image
Philip Brown

Thanks to
Nicola Burrow
Jeremy Alexander
All the magazines' editors

Where to find us
Editorial, advertising and administration
The Wisden Cricketer, 2nd Floor,
123 Buckingham Palace Road,
London SW1W 9SL
tel 020 7705 4911
email twc@wisdencricketer.com

From the pages of

Foreword

I do not mind whether this is a book or a magazine (the term in the trade, I'm told, is 'bookazine'); the fact is that it is a joy. Goodness knows the total sum of books about the Ashes. There are classics among them but few can have given a flavour of the long and glorious rivalry between England and Australia better than this compendium of eyewitness reports, analysis and insight as written for *The Cricketer* since 1921 and in more recent years for *Wisden Cricket Monthly* and the healthy offspring of their union, *The Wisden Cricketer*.

Pelham – or 'Plum' as everyone knew PF Warner throughout a long life devoted to the game – should be the first of several editors to be celebrated. He was a missionary for cricket and, as founding editor of *The Cricketer*, he did an immense service to the sport in England. Praise is due, too, to David Frith, for bringing the standards of an exacting cricket scholar to his own rival publication, *WCM*.

Most of the great cricket writers have appeared in one or other of the magazines. Twice in every four-year cycle the Ashes series have acted as an inspiration for them as much as for generations of players. The differing styles of the likes of RC Robertson-Glasgow, Neville Cardus, EW Swanton and John Woodcock are as interesting as the deeds they record.

To produce this compendium of archive material from the magazines Edward Craig, *TWC*'s deputy editor, has spent countless hours delving through back issues. By shaking the dust that covered many a long-forgotten piece, and some of much more recent vintage, he has produced a publication to please both those with a deep knowledge of the Ashes and those for whom much of the story is new.

What a story it is, too; from Spofforth to McGrath; Trumble to Warne; Blackham to Gilchrist; Murdoch to Ponting; Grace to Pietersen; Barnes to Flintoff and more. This summer new heroes will be added to the saga and, with luck, there will be epic contests to rival those games of four years ago.

Among the pieces, I commend especially "Crusoe"'s brilliant illustration on page 36 of the way in which the familiar Ashes fever grips cricket followers. We know that it is all trivial really but, my goodness, how we care.

As Dr David Starkey proves with the Tudors, there are fresh ways of looking at old stories. But royal dynasties die out. With luck and wise governance Tests between England and Australia never will.

Christopher Martin-Jenkins edited *The Cricketer* from 1981 to 1991

Contents

4 A reduced history of the Ashes
Lawrence Booth's instant guide to the
133 years of England v Australia

1876-1912 **6 The beginnings** From the birth of
Test cricket to the end of the Golden Age

16 Hero No.1 Jack Hobbs

1920-1926 **18 The 1920s** The Big Ship's 5-0 win;
Hobbs and Sutcliffe

24 Hero No.2 Warwick Armstrong

1928-1948 **26 The Bradman era** The Don,
Sir Len Hutton and Bodyline

38 Hero No.3 Douglas Jardine

46 Hero No.4 Don Bradman

1950-1959 **48 The 1950s** Denis Compton, Jim Laker
and England wins

60 Hero No.5 Keith Miller

1960-1968 **62 The 1960s** Battling draws
and boredom

1970-1979 **70 The 1970s** The Chappells, pace,
pain and Packer

80 Hero No.6 Dennis Lillee

1979-1987 **86 The 1980s** Headingley '81,
bad behaviour and bad cricket

94 Hero No.7 Ian Botham

104 Hero No.8 David Gower

1989-2003 **106 The Aussie era** Domination
and the winning habit

114 Hero No.9 Allan Border

122 Hero No.10 Shane Warne

2005-2007 **124 Ashes fever** That 2005 series,
Flintoff and the second 5-0

132 Hero No.11 Michael Vaughan

1877-2007 **138 Why the Ashes matters**
Simon Barnes dissects

140 Facts in figures

The reduced history of the Ashes

Lawrence Booth on the start, what happened next and who whinged when. Updated by Edward Craig

In Affectionate Remembrance
OF
ENGLISH CRICKET,
WHICH DIED AT THE OVAL
ON
29th AUGUST, 1882,
Deeply lamented by a large circle of sorrowing
friends and acquaintances.

. . . R. I. P.

N.B.—*The body will be cremated and the
ashes taken to Australia.*

Old joke: The *Sporting Times'* obituary

Fair sailing: Australian Warwick Armstrong

Duck and dive: Bill Woodfull faces Bodyline

Spin king: Jim Laker after taking 19 for 90

1876-77

It's not the Ashes – they come later – but it's the first Test match at Melbourne. **Charles Bannerman** faces the first ball, scores the first hundred and becomes the first person to retire hurt. Australia win.

1882

England need 85 to win at The Oval but **Frederick Spofforth**, an early incarnation of Merv Hughes, skittles them for 77. The *Sporting Times* prints its mock obituary and the Ashes are born.

1882-83

England win at Sydney and captain **Ivo Bligh** is presented with a burned bail in an urn by an admirer. Reader, he married her.

1890

WG Grace leads England to an eighth successive Ashes victory. The crowd may or may not chant: "Can we play you every week?"

1894-95

The original uber-series – England win the first Test after following on and clinch the series 3-2 in the fifth and final match at Melbourne in front of thousands.

1902

Fred Tate's one and only Test cap: he crucially drops Joe Darling before being last man out with four needed as Australia win again. Don't call us ... Then at The Oval Gilbert Jessop played *the* great innings as Yorkshiremen George Hirst and Wilf Rhodes led England home by one wicket (but NOT in singles).

1920-21

Warwick Armstrong leads Australia to the first 5-0 scoreline in Ashes history (the second followed 86 years later). He then confirms that the last word of his nickname (The Big Ship) is indeed "Ship".

1928-29

Don Bradman begins his Test career with scores of 18 and 1. For the only time in his Test career the selectors drop him. He is recalled one game later and makes 79 and 112.

1930

Bradman registers scores of 131, 254, 334 and 232. Australia's selectors congratulate themselves on never doubting him.

1932-33

Bodyline – the start of the longest whinge in cricket history. The Aussies have always claimed they find the very thought of fast, short-pitched bowling morally repugnant. In truth, they were deeply irritated by **Douglas Jardine**'s Harlequin cap.

1936-37

An early example of English mental fortitude as **Gubby Allen**'s team take a 2-0 lead, only to lose 3-2.

1948

England shed crocodile tears as Bradman finishes his Test career with a second-ball duck, thus denying him a Test average of 100. Australians seem all too happy to accept the myth that Bradman couldn't pick **Eric Hollies**'s googly because he was so overcome by emotion.

'Knackered': Fred Trueman takes his 300th

Ray of light: Illingworth is carried off

Magic man: Botham at Headingley in 1981

Taylor-made: Australia win again in 1997

1956

Jim Laker, Old Trafford – the start of the second-longest whinge in Ashes history. Laker takes 19 for 90, thus proving incontrovertibly that the pitch has been doctored. Except that England had already managed 459. Oh, and Tony Lock, his spinning colleague, finished with 1 for 106.

1960s

The swinging 60s pass the Ashes by completely. Of 25 Tests in the decade, 15 end in draws. Still, at least **Fred Trueman** becomes the first man to 300 Test wickets, declaring that whoever beats him will be "bloody knackered". So far, just the 18 players have found the energy.

1970-71

Ray Illingworth's team triumph 2-0, despite not winning a single lbw decision in six Tests in Australia.

1974-75

Vicious seamer named **Lilian Thomson** batters England into submission in belated and transparent revenge for Bodyline. England call for Cowdrey.

1978-79

Mike Brearley leads England to a 5-1 win against a Packer-denuded Aussie side. Aussie captain Graham Yallop's book about the series, *Lambs to the Slaughter*, remains a masterpiece in melancholy.

1981

Not a bad little series. Chap called **Botham** has some fun. Annals of history, and all that. That's after he was axed as captain and couldn't buy a run or wicket. Don't forget Brearley, Willis, Dilley and others ...

1985

Tim Robinson's greatest moment. Jeff Thomson and Botham have their own private competition to see who can sport the worst mullet.

1986-87

Mike Gatting seals his place in history by captaining England to a 2-1 win – his only victories in 23 Tests as leader.

1989

England pick 29 players, each more incompetent than the last. **Terry Alderman** traps Graham Gooch lbw a lot. Steve Waugh is born as a Test batsman. Australia start to strut.

1993

Shane Warne stuns Gatting with a sleight of hand that leaves him open-mouthed and groping at thin air. After pinching his hotel fry-up, Warne then bowls Gatting with the Ball of the Century.

1997

Australia are 54 for 8 on the first morning of the series, and the Ashes are coming home. Except they're not. Again.

2002-03

Nasser Hussain invites Australia to bat at Brisbane on a hot day and flat wicket – and a nation groans.

2005

The greatest series ever, particularly if you are English. Top-quality cricket, drama, suspense, whingeing and celebration. At last the Ashes came home.

2006-07

Australia got serious, England were under-prepared and got smashed – a nation groaned again as loss followed loss followed loss. ◼ *The Wisden Cricketer, August 2005*

The Ashes did not start the great England-Australian sporting rivalry but crystallised it. Numerous Tests had been played before the Urn became the prize and symbol of sporting dominance. These matches created Test cricket as a whole and had plenty of stories and drama in themselves

Leading light: Australia's first captain Dave Gregory

Where it all began

In 1977 **Murray Hedgcock** revisited the 1876-77 Australian tour to celebrate Test cricket's centenary. England suffered injuries and Australia won ...

THANK HEAVENS for the Melbourne *Argus*, which, as far as can be determined, first used the word "test" on September 16, 1884, to describe the international cricket between England and Australia. Otherwise we should be celebrating not the Centenary Test, but the Centenary "Grand Combination Match", the unwieldy name first applied to the virtually impromptu but magnificently influential confrontation which began at the MCG [Melbourne Cricket Ground] on Thursday, March 15, 1877.

Visits by English teams were arranged by private promoters direct with local clubs: the first tour in 1862 had been sponsored by the Melbourne Cricket Club's caterers, Spiers and Pond. Money rather than prestige was the lure in those days, so that professional cricketers who needed the cash rather than amateurs who didn't were most likely to be attracted by invitations to tour Australia.

The fourth tour, in 1876–77, was sponsored by James Lillywhite junior, a good slowish left-arm bowler and solid left-hand bat whose place in history rests much more on his administrative and organising ability than his cricketing skills.

In 1873–74 the professionals of WG Grace's team had been unhappy at their terms from the money-minded Doctor – specifically that they travelled second-class. "A team of similar composition (mixing both amateurs and professionals) is not likely to be again attempted," said *Lillywhite's Cricketers' Annual* for 1878, mistakenly.

Lillywhite, who had been a member of WG's side, had the good sense to select his all-professional team of 1876 on the basis of first-class travel, which made for a much happier tour. The bowling was representative of the best in England but professional batsmen could not match the quality of the great amateurs, so that Lillywhite's team was below full potential.

The tourists normally played matches against odds: that is, against teams of 18 or 22 players who would all bat – and field. This

Pioneers: The first all-professional English touring team, with James Lillywhite Jr, the captain, pictured in the centre. The other players are: 1 H Jupp, 2 T Emmett, 3 HRJ Charlwood, 4 J Selby, 6 T Armitage, 7 J Southerton, 8 A Greenwood, 9 G Ulyett, 10 A Hill, 11 A Shaw, 12 E Pooley

made for amazing bowling analyses: Lillywhite himself took 18 for 42 when England beat 22 of Newcastle by 75 runs.

It was on the 1876-77 tour that the colonials began to feel it time to challenge England to a match on level terms, because in the 15 years since the first tour, the game had progressed rapidly.

Lillywhite's side were challenged to a match by a NSW XI which ended in a draw. The Victorians, eager then as before and since to better anything their neighbours could offer, decided a team combining the best talents of the two senior colonies might give the Englishmen a real battle.

Captaincy of the intercolonial team lay between the former English county bat Bransby Beauchamp Cooper, of Victoria – whose aristocratic Christian names alone must have just about disqualified him in egalitarian Australia – and the NSW skipper, Dave Gregory, first of a line of great Gregorys who were to play for Australia on and off for another 60 years.

Contemporary records said "no silly intercontinental rivalry was to be allowed to interfere with the prudent conduct of the match" – and Dave Gregory was Australia's first Test captain. The English team had problems: the team's brilliant wicketkeeper, Ted Pooley, was left in New Zealand, under arrest. He had used an old dodge by betting he could nominate the scores of individuals playing against the tourists in a match at Christchurch – and of course nominated a duck for everyone. Being paid one pound for every correct forecast and having to pay only a shilling for each incorrect one, he made a useful profit because of the certainty that a fair proportion of the opponents would actually get ducks. But the man with whom he made the wager, a local named Donkin, was livid, claimed he had been swindled, got into a shouting match and then a

scuffle – both Pooley and the tourists' baggageman were arrested.

Melbourne interest in the match was considerable although only about a thousand colonials arrived for the start at 1pm. The splendid new grandstand, just a year old and designed for 2,000 people at a cost of £4,700, had only a sprinkling of spectators: most preferred to stand on the lawn and embankment, or sit on the twin rows of wooden seats outside the fenced cycle-track.

Dave Gregory won the toss – whatever happened to that first vital coin? – and the wonderfully accurate medium-pace bowler Alfred Shaw, of Notts, aged 34, opened the history of Test cricket by bowling the first ball to Charles Bannerman, of NSW, aged 25.

The story of the match is there in the records: how the first wicket fell at 2 in the fourth over when Allen Hill of Yorkshire, fast right-arm, bowled Nat Thomson for 1.

Edward Gregory made the first duck in Test cricket – and Bannerman made the first century. He batted through the first day (to stumps at 5pm) and with 5,000 people drawn to the MCG on the Friday in the hope of seeing him carry his bat, he had to retire at 165 when the big Yorkshire allrounder George Ulyett cracked him on the fingers with a lifting delivery just after lunch.

After England had answered Australia's 245 with 196, Australia struggled to a modest 104 in the second innings and England were left to make 154. From two wickets for seven runs, the tired Englishmen never recovered. "The combined team worked together with the utmost harmony and goodwill," observed *The Australasian* of March 24. "On a Victorian ground, a NSW player was chosen as captain, and under him the whole team acted as if all ideas of rivalry were forgotten." ◪ *The Cricketer, March 1977*

Murray Hedgcock is a London-based Australian cricket journalist

1st Test, Melbourne, March 15-19 1877
Australia won by 45 runs

AUSTRALIA WON TOSS

C Bannerman	retired hurt	165		b Ulyett		4
NFD Thomson		b Hill	1	c Emmett	b Shaw	7
TP Horan	c Hill	b Shaw	12	c Selby	b Hill	20
DW Gregory*	run out		1	(9)	b Shaw	3
BB Cooper		b Souther'n	15		b Shaw	3
WE Midwinter	c Ulyett	b Souther'n	5	c Souther'n	b Ulyett	17
EJ Gregory	c Greenw'd	b Lillywhite	0	c Emmett	b Ulyett	11
JM Blackham†		b Souther'n	17	lbw	b Shaw	6
TW Garrett	not out		18	(4)	c Emmett	b Shaw	0
TK Kendall	c Souther'n	b Shaw	3	not out		17
JR Hodges		b Shaw	0		b Lillywhite	8
Extras	b4 lb2 w2		8	b5 lb3		8
Total	169.3 overs		245	68 overs		104

Fall of wickets 2 40 41 118 142 7 27 31 31 35
143 197 243 245 58 71 75 75

Bowling (1st) Shaw 55.3-34-51-3, Hill 23-10-42-1, Ulyett 25-12-36-0, Southerton 37-17-61-3, Armitage 3-0-15-0, Lillywhite 14-5-19-1, Emmett 12-7-13-0
(2nd) Shaw 34-16-38-5, Ulyett 19-7-39-3, Hill 14-6-18-1, Lillywhite 1-0-1-1

ENGLAND

H Jupp	lbw	b Garrett	63	(3) lbw	b Midwinter	4
J Selby†	c Cooper	b Hodges	7	(5) c Horan	b Hodges	38
HRJ Charlwood	c Blackham	b Midwinter	36	(4)	b Kendall	13
G Ulyett	lbw	b Thomson	10	(6)	b Kendall	24
A Greenwood	c EJ Gregory	b Midwinter	1	(2) c Midwinter	b Kendall	5
T Armitage	c Blackham	b Midwinter	9	(8) c Blackham	b Kendall	3
A Shaw		b Midwinter	10	st Blackham	b Kendall	2
T Emmett		b Midwinter	8	(9)	b Kendall	9
A Hill	not out		35	(1) c Thomson	b Kendall	0
J Lillywhite Jr*	c and	b Kendall	10		b Hodges	4
J Southerton	c Cooper	b Garrett	6	not out		1
Extras	lb1		1	b4 lb1		5
Total	136.1 overs		196	66.1 overs		108

Fall of wickets 23 79 98 109 121 0 7 20 22 62
135 145 145 168 68 92 93 100

Bowling (1st) Hodges 9-0-27-1, Garrett 18.1-10-22-2, Kendall 38-16-54-1, Midwinter 54-23-78-5, Thomson 17-10-14-1
(2nd) Kendall 33.1-12-55-7, Midwinter 19-7-23-1, DW Gregory 5-1-9-0, Garrett 2-0-9-0, Hodges 7-5-7-2

Umpires: CA Reid and RB Terry Australia lead the 2-Test series 1-0

1876-77
2nd Test Mar 31-Apr 4, Mel †Aus 122 & 259; Eng 261 & 122-6. Eng won by 4 wkts.

1878-79
Only Test Jan 2-4, Mel †Eng 113 & 160; Aus 256 & 19-0. Aus won by 10 wkts.

1880
Only Test Sep 6-8, The Oval †Eng 420 & 57-5; Aus 149 & 327. Eng won by 5 wkts.

1881-82
1st Test Dec 31-Jan 4, Mel †Eng 294 & 308; Aus 320 & 127-3. Match drawn.
2nd Test Feb 17-21, Syd †Eng 133 & 232; Aus 197 & 169-5. Aus won by 5 wkts.
3rd Test Mar 3-7, Sydney †Eng 188 & 134; Aus 262 & 64-4. Aus won by 6 wkts.
4th Test Mar 10-14, Melbourne †Eng 309 & 234-2; Aus 300. Match drawn.

1882-83
1st Test Dec 30-Jan 2, Mel †Aus 291 & 58-1; Eng 177 & 169. Aus won by 9 wkts.
2nd Test Jan 19-22, Mel †Eng 294; Aus 114 & 153. Eng won by an inns & 27 runs.
3rd Test Jan 26-30, Syd †Eng 247 & 123; Aus 218 & 83. Eng won by 69 runs.
4th Test Feb 17-21, Syd †Eng 263 & 197; Aus 262 & 199-6. Aus won by 4 wkts.

1884
1st Test Jul 10-12, Old Trafford †Eng 95 & 180-9; Aus 182. Match drawn.
2nd Test Jul 21-23, Lord's †Aus 229 & 145; Eng 379. Eng won by an inns & 5 runs.
3rd Test Aug 11-13, The Oval †Aus 551; Eng 346 & 85-2. Match drawn.

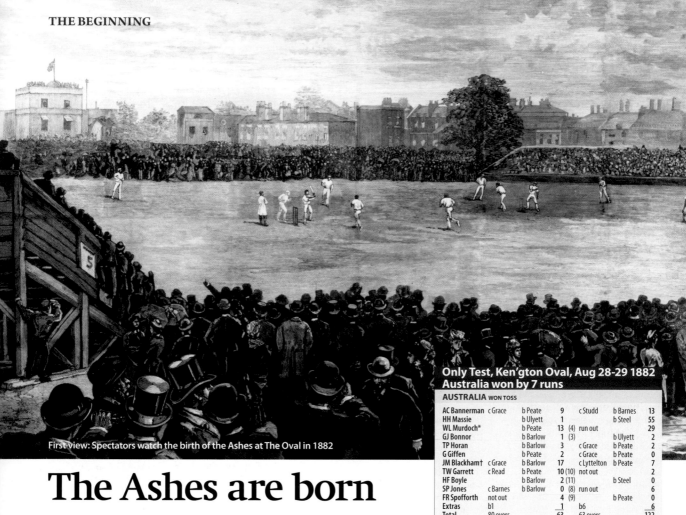

First view: Spectators watch the birth of the Ashes at The Oval in 1882

The Ashes are born

THE NOTICE [of the birth of the Ashes], as all students of the game know, was published in the *Sporting Times* the day after FR Spofforth, with match figures of 14 for 90, had bowled England out for 77 on a rain-affected wicket in the second innings of the two-day Test at The Oval in August 1882. It was only the second Test played on English soil and the home country's first home defeat. With WG making 32, England had needed only 34 to win with eight wickets left, but on a cold afternoon Spofforth and Boyle scythed through nervous English batting.

England had unwisely changed their batting order in the second innings. CT Studd, who had scored two hundreds against the Australians that summer, was dropped to No.10 and had not faced when the Yorkshireman, Ted Peate, swung wildly at Boyle and was bowled. "I couldn't trust Mr Studd" was Peate's unlikely explanation ∎

The Cricketer, August 1982

What is the Urn?

After The Oval Test the *Sporting Times* ran a mock obituary of English cricket, finishing with "The body will be cremated and the ashes taken to Australia". England set sail to Australia just weeks later, with captain Ivo Bligh out for revenge. While he was playing in a social match at Rupertswood Estate, a group of ladies presented him with the four-inch Urn, believed to have a burned bail inside, as a symbol of the Ashes. Bligh later married one of the ladies and took the Urn back to England.

Only Test, Ken'gton Oval, Aug 28-29 1882
Australia won by 7 runs

AUSTRALIA WON TOSS

AC Bannerman	c Grace	b Peate	9		c Studd	b Barnes	13
HH Massie		b Ulyett	1			b Steel	55
WL Murdoch*		b Peate	13 (4)			run out	29
GJ Bonnor		b Barlow	1 (3)			b Ulyett	2
TP Horan		b Barlow	3		c Grace	b Peate	2
G Giffen		b Peate	2		c Grace	b Peate	0
JM Blackham†	c Grace	b Barlow	17		c Lyttelton	b Peate	7
TW Garrett	c Read	b Peate	10 (10)			not out	2
HF Boyle		b Barlow	2 (11)			b Steel	0
SP Jones	c Barnes	b Barlow	0 (8)			run out	6
FR Spofforth		not out	4 (9)			b Peate	0
Extras		b1	1			b6	6
Total		80 overs	63			63 overs	122

Fall of wickets 6 21 22 26 30   66 70 70 79 79
30 48 53 59   99 114 117 122

Bowling (1st) **Peate** 38-24-31-4, **Ulyett** 9-5-11-1, **Barlow** 31-22-19-5, **Steel** 2-1-1-0
(2nd) **Peate** 21-9-40-4, **Ulyett** 6-2-10-1, **Barlow** 13-5-27-0, **Steel** 7-0-15-2, **Barnes** 12-5-11-1, **Studd** 4-1-9-0

ENGLAND

RG Barlow	c Banner'n	b Spofforth	11 (3)			b Spofforth	0
WG Grace		b Spofforth	4 (1)		c Banner'n	b Boyle	32
G Ulyett	st Blackham	b Spofforth	26 (4)		c Blackham	b Spofforth	11
AP Lucas	c Blackham	b Boyle	9 (5)			b Spofforth	5
A Lyttelton†	c Blackham	b Spofforth	2 (6)			b Spofforth	12
CT Studd		b Spofforth	0 (10)			not out	0
JM Read		not out	19 (8)			b Spofforth	0
W Barnes		b Boyle	5 (9)		c Murdoch	b Boyle	2
AG Steel		b Garrett	14 (7)		c and	b Spofforth	0
AN Hornby*		b Spofforth	2 (2)			b Spofforth	9
E Peate	c Boyle	b Spofforth	0			b Boyle	2
Extras		b6 lb2 nb1	9			b3 nb1	4
Total		71.3 overs	101			55 overs	77

Fall of wickets 13 18 57 59 60   15 15 51 53 66
63 70 96 101   70 70 75 75

Bowling (1st) **Spofforth** 36.3-18-46-7, **Garrett** 16-7-22-1, **Boyle** 19-7-24-2
(2nd) **Spofforth** 28-15-44-7, **Garrett** 7-2-10-0, **Boyle** 20-11-19-3

Umpires L Greenwood and RA Thoms   Test debuts JM Read, CT Studd (Eng)

Why it matters

TO ASK why the Ashes resonates so deeply for both England and Australia seems almost as absurd as wondering why the grass is green and the sky is blue. For Englishmen or Australians reading this, the answer will probably feel self-evident: the ancient rivalry between the Poms and the Cobbers simply is as it is – and that's that.

Yet, as with everything, there is a reason. And when it comes to England, Australia, and their desire to thrash each other at cricket, the reason stems almost exclusively from the idea – expressed in deliberately crude terms – that one team represents the mother country, and the other its distant, illegitimate sprog. It stems, in other words, from misplaced English feelings of superiority and Australian grievances that inevitably follow.

Australia have spent most of their sporting existence trying to get one over the snooty Poms, with their smug gags about yoghurt at least having a culture. England, for their part, have tried desperately, and often unsuccessfully, to prove that they are not an effete bunch of pansies. "We might not have Milton or Shakespeare," pointed out the Australian writer Thomas Kencally, "but by God we've got Don Bradman and Ray Lindwall."

The upshot of this Ashes rivalry, formalised when Australia beat England by seven runs at The Oval in 1882 and the *Sporting Times* newspaper ran a mock obituary of the English game the next day, has been some of the most memorable moments in the history of any sport, let alone Test cricket.

A potted history might run like this: Warwick Armstrong leading Australia to the only 5-0 win in 1921, the emergence of Bradman, Bodyline, the retirement of Bradman, England's catharsis in 1953, Lillee and Thomson, Headingley '81, Australian dominance, and finally – gloriously – 2005.

If Australia have the edge, winning 117 Ashes Tests to England's 95, with 84 draws, then it is probably because their players – revelling in their role of political underdogs – have generally been more motivated, more thoroughly prepared, and a bit better. But as the summer of 2005 showed, generalisations and predictions are only ever one wicket away from looking stupid. And that, more than anything, is what makes the Ashes so special. ∎

From *The Definitive Guide to The Ashes*, 2006-07 published with *The Wisden Cricketer*, Dec 2006

Captain's call: Australian and English skippers Warwick Armstrong and Johnny Douglas toss in May 1921

1884-85
1st Test Dec 12-16, Ade †Aus 243 & 191; Eng 369 & 67-2. Eng won by 8 wkts.
2nd Test Jan 1-5, Mel †Eng 401 & 7-0; Aus 279 & 126. Eng won by 10 wkts.
3rd Test Feb 20-24, Syd †Aus 181 & 165; Eng 133 & 207. Aus won by 6 runs.
4th Test Mar 14-17, Syd †Eng 269 & 77; Aus 309 & 40-2. Aus won by 8 wkts.
5th Test Mar 21-25, Mel †Aus 163 & 125; Eng 386. Eng won by an inns & 98 runs.

1886
1st Test Jul 5-7, Old Trafford †Aus 205 & 123; Eng 223 & 107-6. Eng won by 4 wkts.
2nd Test Jul 19-21, Lor †Eng 353; Aus 121 & 126. Eng won by an inns & 106 runs.
3rd Test Aug 12-14, T Oval †Eng 434; Aus 68 & 149. Eng won by an inns & 217 runs

1886-87
1st Test Jan 28-31, Sydney Eng 45 & 184; †Aus 119 & 97. Eng won by 13 runs.
2nd Test Feb 25-Mar 1, Syd †Eng 151 & 154; Aus 84 & 150. Eng won by 71 runs.

1887-88
Only Test Feb 10-15, Syd Eng 113 & 137; †Aus 42 & 82. Eng won by 126 runs.

1888
1st Test Jul 16-17, Lord's †Aus 116 & 60; Eng 53 & 62. Aus won by 61 runs.
2nd Test Aug 13-14, T Oval †Aus 80 & 100; Eng 317. Eng won by an inns & 137 runs.
3rd Test Aug 30-31, Old T †Eng 172; Aus 81 & 70. Eng won by an inns & 21 runs.

Start of the Golden Age

England dominated the 15 years that followed Ivo Bligh's inaugural reclamation of the Ashes in 1882-83, losing the series only once in 1891-92. Then came the first uber-series – England in Australia 1894-95. This was the start of a golden age of Test cricket where positive, exciting and high-quality cricket, played by well-loved (and hated!) players established the sport at the heart of Australian and British summers. **David Frith** rewinds to the first Test of that 1894-95 series, when England won after following on

A S ONE contented Australian put it, it was "a guinea to a gooseberry on Australia" to win: only 64 more needed, wise old Giffen and the brilliant youngster Darling in harness, and, if needed, Iredale (81 in the first innings) and Gregory (201) to follow, plus the two allrounders; Richardson was still below par, and all the other England bowlers had so far managed only six wickets between them in almost 200 overs.

The Australian cricketers went down to breakfast at the Baden Baden Hotel, Coogee with great anticipation. "It's all right, boys. The weather is beautiful!" roared Ernie Jones, who was first out of bed that morning.

Giffen was confident too as he looked through the window at the bright blue sky – until he bumped into his skipper. Blackham, who had worried about the weather throughout the previous day, had a face "long as a coffee-pot", and forecast bad things as they took off for the SCG [Sydney Cricket Ground], the carriage leaving deep furrows in the soft ground. It had rained heavily during the night. The uncovered pitch was saturated, transformed into a batsman's nightmare.

Some of Stoddart's men, feeling the match was lost, had got drunk on the Wednesday night, and it now fell to the captain to get the booziest of them all, Bobby Peel, sobered up for action. He was put under a cold

shower and told of the duty which lay before him now that a blazing sun on the wet pitch had given England an unexpected opportunity to fight back for a victory which had seemed utterly impossible for the previous few days.

Peel, as oblivious as any to the night's rainfall, at first thought somebody must have watered the wicket. As it gradually dawned on his befuddled brain that England were back in with a chance, he is supposed to have said to his skipper: "Give me the ball, Mr Stoddart, and I'll get t'boogers out before loonch!"

In his fresh excitement, the sandy-haired Yorkshireman forgot the lingering discomfort that was the legacy of the extraction of five teeth just before the Test match.

With the late arrival of Lockwood as well as Peel, the start was delayed slightly, with Blackham's generous forbearance, the pitch becoming more glutinous with every minute.

Stoddart placed a close-up field and entrusted Peel and Richardson with the first few overs. Under 2,000 people were present, making the SCG seem like "some silent cemetery" after the previous five days of large crowds and incessant applause. For the first time, a match had entered a sixth day.

Peel beat Giffen and Gay whipped off the bails, but the Australian had his back foot firmly anchored behind the crease. The Yorkshireman, despite his aching head, was pitching

a perfect length, spinning widely and variously and getting spiteful lift. Richardson too was making the ball leap, only at a disconcerting pace.

Giffen edged a four from one that kept low and Darling, recognising the dangers, bravely hit Peel out towards long-on and over the fence for a five. Bucketfuls of extra sawdust were brought to the middle and almost every ball saw the batsman walking out to pat down the disturbance in the muddy pitch.

With 53 to his name, Joe Darling lofted Peel into the deep, and saw Brockwell race in from in front of the two-and-sixpenny seats to cling to a very important catch.

Cruel luck: Australian captain Jack Blackham

Giffen was lbw to Briggs' first ball, slipping as he played at it: 135 for 4, last man 41; 42 needed. The tall Iredale and the short Gregory tried, with nimble footwork, to get to the pitch of each ball and another dozen runs came, with England experiencing some concern when Gay had a finger dislocated. The odds were still on an Australian win.

But Briggs lured Iredale into getting under a ball that climbed high before dropping into the bowler's grateful hands: 147 for 5.

66 Darling, recognising the dangers, hit Peel out towards long-on and over the fence for a five 99

Surely Gregory, the first-innings double-century hero, would see Australia home? He had moved on to 16 when, trying to run Peel backward of point, he touched the ball into Gay's gloves: 158 for 6: 19 only now wanted.

MacLaren, at second slip, dropped Reedman, but the miss was not costly, for Reedman now stepped out to Peel and missed. Leslie Gay had yet another accident, failing to take the ball cleanly; but his luck was in this time: it rebounded from his chest and broke the wicket. For ever more it would show in the book as "st Gay b Peel".

The slightly neurotic Blackham was now striding up and down the small players' balcony muttering "cruel luck" over and over. Behind him stood a stunned Giffen, singlet and shirt in hand, and Lyons, sighing at what might have been had his innings not ended so abruptly the evening before, and Harry Graham, head in hands, a helpless 12th man who had once survived for two hours against Peel on a wet pitch.

Still, Charlie Turner knew a thing or two about batting and could still carry Australia home with a few well-struck hits. He made two runs, but with 16 still needed, he hit a catch to Briggs at cover off Peel. Ernie Jones now had a go at finishing the match with some hard hitting on this near-impossible pitch, but with only a single to his name he belted Briggs back over his head only to be caught by MacLaren. Nine down for 162; 15 needed; Blackham, with his painful thumb bandaged, walking mournfully to the crease to join Charlie McLeod.

The two slow left-armers have almost completed the job for England. Will their nerves hold? Will the fielders be up to the task if catches go flying? The ball is dispatched unerringly towards off stump. McLeod spars; takes a single. Stoddart, England's captain, peers anxiously around the field, at the batsmen's rigid countenances, at Peel's round face, so recently florid with alcohol. Blackham pokes his bat forward and winces at the pain in his hand. Gay, fearful of letting through byes, gets his gloves over-deliberately in line.

Four of the 15 runs are banked. Then Peel bobs in again and drops the ball on a length. Bearded Blackham pushes out at it. It comes back towards the bowler. England, 261 behind on first innings, can now win the match if the resurrected Peel pockets the catch. He does. England have won by 10 runs, two minutes before lunch on the sixth day. They have won a match seemingly impossible to win.

Captain Stoddart congratulated the Australians on the manner in which they had taken their shock defeat but Stoddart was clearly moved by the efforts of his own men in this "uphill" game. Typically, he came back generously on the matter of Australia's ill-fortune with the rain, acknowledging that the weather alone had robbed them of victory. "There'll be a good deal said about this match," he predicted. And he wasn't wrong. ◪

Wisden Cricket Monthly, December 1994

David Frith is an author, historian and founding editor of *Wisden Cricket Monthly*

1st Test, Sydney, Dec 14-20 1894
England won by 10 runs

AUSTRALIA WON TOSS

JJ Lyons		b Richardson	1		b Richardson 25
GHS Trott		b Richardson	12	c Gay	b Peel 8
G Giffen	c Ford	b Brockwell	161	lbw	b Briggs 41
J Darling		b Richardson	0	c Brockwell	b Peel 53
FA Iredale	c Stoddart	b Ford	81 (6)	c and	b Briggs 5
SE Gregory	c Peel	b Stoddart	201 (5)	c Gay	b Peel 16
JC Reedman	c Ford	b Peel	17	st Gay	b Peel 4
CE McLeod		b Richardson	15	not out	2
CTB Turner	c Gay	b Peel	1	c Briggs	b Peel 2
JM Blackham*†		b Richardson	74 (11)	c and	b Peel 2
E Jones	not out		11 (10)	c MacLaren	b Briggs 1
Extras	b8 lb3 w1		12	b2 lb1 nb4	7
Total	172.3 overs		586	68 overs	166

Fall of wickets 10 21 21 192 331   26 45 130 135 147
379 400 409 563   158 159 161 162

Bowling (1st) Richardson 55.3-13-181-5, Peel 53-14-140-2, Briggs 25-4-96-0, Brockwell 22-7-78-1, Ford 11-2-47-1, Stoddart 3-0-31-1, Lockwood 3-2-1-0
(2nd) Richardson 11-3-27-1, Peel 30-9-67-6, Lockwood 16-3-40-0, Briggs 11-2-25-3

ENGLAND

AC MacLaren	c Reedman	b Turner	4		b Giffen 20
A Ward	c Iredale	b Turner	75		b Giffen 117
AE Stoddart*	c Jones	b Giffen	12	c Giffen	b Turner 36
JT Brown	run out		22	c Jones	b Giffen 53
W Brockwell	c Blackham	b Jones	49		b Jones 37
R Peel	c Gregory	b Giffen	4		b Giffen 15
FGJ Ford	st Blackham	b Giffen	30	c and	b McLeod 48
J Briggs		b Giffen	57		b McLeod 42
WH Lockwood	c Giffen	b Trott	18		b Trott 29
LH Gay†	c Gregory	b Reedman	33		b Trott 4
T Richardson	not out		0	not out	12
Extras	b17 lb3 w1		21	b14 lb8	22
Total	140.3 overs		325	181.4 overs	437

Fall of wickets 14 43 78 149 155   44 115 217 245 290
211 211 252 325   296 385 398 420

Bowling (1st) Jones 19-7-44-1, Turner 44-16-89-2, Giffen 43-17-75-4, Trott 15-4-59-1, McLeod 14-2-25-0, Reedman 3.3-1-12-1, Lyons 2-2-0-0
(2nd) Jones 19-0-57-1, Turner 35-14-78-1, Giffen 75-25-164-4, Trott 12.4-2-22-2, McLeod 6-0-67-2, Reedman 6-1-12-0, Lyons 2-0-12-0, Iredale 2-1-3-0

Umpires C Bannerman and J Phillips   England leads the 5-Test series 1-0
Test debuts J Darling, FA Iredale, E Jones, CE McLeod, JC Reedman (Aus); JT Brown, FGJ Ford, LH Gay, AC MacLaren (Eng)

1890
1st Test Jul 21-23, Lor †Aus 132 & 176; Eng 173 & 137-3. Eng won by 7 wkts.
2nd Test Aug 11-12, The Oval †Aus 92 & 102; Eng 100 & 95-8. Eng won by 2 wkts.

1891-92
1st Test Jan 1-6, Mel †Aus 240 & 236; Eng 264 & 158. Aus won by 54 runs.
2nd Test Jan 29-Feb 3, Syd †Aus 144 & 391; Eng 307 & 156. Aus won by 72 runs.
3rd Test Mar 24-28, Ade †Eng 499; Aus 100 & 169. Eng won by an inns & 230 runs.

1893
1st Test Jul 17-19, Lord's †Eng 334 & 234-8dec; Aus 269. Match drawn.
2nd Test Aug 14-16, The Oval †Eng 483; Aus 91 & 349. Eng won by an inns & 43 runs.
3rd Test Aug 24-26, Old Trafford †Aus 204 & 236; Eng 243 & 118-4. Match drawn.

1894-95
2nd Test Dec 29-Jan 3, Mel †Eng 75 & 475; †Aus 123 & 333. Eng won by 94 runs.
3rd Test Jan 11-15, Ade †Aus 238 & 411; Eng 124 & 143. Aus won by 382 runs.
4th Test Feb 1-4, Syd †Aus 284; Eng 65 & 72. Aus won by an inns & 147 runs.

1896
1st Test Jun 22-24, Lord's †Aus 53 & 347; Eng 292 & 111-4. Eng won by 6 wkts.
2nd Test Jul 16-18, Old Tr †Aus 412 & 125-7; Eng 231 & 305. Aus won by 3 wkts.
3rd Test Aug 10-12, The Oval †Eng 145 & 84; Aus 119 & 44. Eng won by 66 runs.

A hero away, forgotten at home

The Yorkshire pro and prankster, dashing batsman and bon viveur, lived too long ago and died too young to be well remembered but **Scyld Berry** believes Jack Brown played the finest innings ever for England against Australia – an innings that won the first great series

THE BEST individual innings ever played for England against Australia was by Jack Brown. There is no absolute measure of course but, given the circumstances, the case can well be made for Brown's achievement in 1894-95. With the series standing at 2-2 and England chasing 297 to win the final Test, Brown went in at 28 for 2 and scored 140 to win the match, and the Ashes, and with such panache that his first 50 was, and still is, the fastest recorded in Test cricket in terms of time.

Brown might have received more recognition if he had lived beyond the age of 35 but he died of heart failure when he had plenty of runs left in him. He was a bon viveur who drank and smoked even though he had asthma as well as heart trouble. As one prank on England's 1894-95 tour of Australia he and his fellow northern pro Johnny Briggs persuaded a couple of spectators to put on flannels during an up-country match. Then Briggs and Brown asked their captain if they could field in the deep – so deep that they disappeared into the refreshment tent while the spectators fielded in their place.

Short and stocky, he seems to have been mostly a back-foot player, renowned for his late cutting and a daring variety of leg-side shots. He was not a consistent batsman, especially on uncovered northern pitches, but was skilful enough not only to be the first batsman after WG Grace to score two triple-hundreds in first-class cricket but also to average 36.15 in Tests.

But it is for his Ashes-winning hundred that Brown should be

remembered. The 1894-95 series was when Test cricket took off in the public imagination. It was only the second series of five Tests and the first that was comprehensively covered via the telegraph. While the fifth Test was going on in Melbourne in front of almost 100,000 spectators over the five days (the Saturday crowd of 29,000 was the largest for a single day in Australia to that point), large crowds waited outside

Brown under: He drank, he smoked, he won the Ashes for England. Jack Brown's hundred at Melbourne stood out in a golden series

newspaper offices in Sydney to read reports of every over about 10 minutes after it had been bowled in the neighbouring colony.

Down in Melbourne the Australians had won a toss that was so important that, when the England captain Andrew Stoddart called heads, he and George Giffen "ran to the coin and Giffen, with a joyous shout and a dive down on to the coin, exclaimed 'it's tails!'" (*Sydney Morning Herald*). Both sides were desperate to bat first in case rain came and damaged the uncovered pitch.

In the Melbourne decider Australia began with 414, which was all right but nothing special, and England replied with 385. Brilliant pace bowling by Tom Richardson then kept Australia in check, just about, as they made 267 second time round. All England had to do now was accomplish by far the highest run-chase achieved so far in Tests (the previous most successful chase had been 199).

England, or Mr AE Stoddart's team as they were then called, reached 28 for 1 on the fourth evening, then made the worst possible start to the fifth morning. The game was due to resume at noon but prompt starts were rare in those days and it was 12.08 before the first ball was delivered. Those few belated minutes were well used by the two Australian spinners, the offspinner Giffen and legspinner Harry Trott, who bowled to each other on the outfield while Stoddart took guard. Then, when Trott "was satisfied that his arm was swinging all right", he began with something that was not his normal legbreak but a quicker, straight ball. Stoddart the previous evening had been happily playing back and working Trott's legbreaks to the on side. But this time he was lbw, first ball of the day, and "Stoddart's face as he passed in plainly indicated that he was seriously disturbed".

There the game and the Ashes stood in the balance, with England 28 for 2 in pursuit of 297, waiting for a match-winner. Everyone knew it too, as the Australians "were fielding for their lives". For bowling, Australia had Giffen and Trott and his younger brother Albert Trott, who bowled pace in those days; and they also had a bowler who sounds as though he was the first mystery spinner seen in Test cricket and not the last with a dodgy action. Tom McKibbin bowled offbreaks mostly, with an occasional legbreak "thrown in".

In the same over that Stoddart was out Brown got off the mark with a four through mid-off when the last ball of Trott's over was "a poor one". At the other end Giffen tried to tempt Brown "to hit one up", then he tried to york him on leg stump but the wind made the ball drift further down leg-side and Brown helped – swept? – it round for four more.

The *SMH* did not report on every ball and every over, so we do not know exactly how many balls Brown received for his fifty. But we are told that he reached 40 in 18 minutes and 51 in 23, although *Wisden* has enshrined the time of his 50 as 28 minutes. In reaching it Brown glanced and cut the younger, faster Trott for boundaries and snicked another four while his partner Albert Ward played the dogged opening batsman. "Bravo, Brown" was shouted as he reached the landmark more quickly than anyone before or since.

Under the pressure imposed by England's third-wicket pair McKibbin faltered. "He was either pitching the ball so far to the off that the batsmen were cutting his trundling to ribbons, or else he was dropping the ball right on to the line of the stumps and the break

carrying it away to leg enough for the batsmen to hook." In the century stand Brown made 64 to Ward's 36.

At lunch England were 146 for 2 (Brown 80, Ward 41), and "at the table and in the gossip after luncheon the general opinion seemed to be that the Englishmen would get the runs" especially when Jim Phillips, the umpire the English team had brought with them to stand in the Tests, said the wicket was as good as ever.

Brown kept attacking after lunch, so rattling the fielders that Syd Gregory fumbled at mid-off to concede a single "and the public was quite astonished". When 88 Brown gave his only chance, dropped by Giffen at slip off Harry Trott; it might have been his quicker ball again as it had "a lot of pace on". Brown's hundred is officially listed as taking 95 minutes and was the fastest to date, even though it had been interrupted by the lunch break.

He kept going at almost a run a minute until he was out for 140 in "not more than two hours and 28 minutes". His partnership of 210 with Ward was the highest in Test cricket to that point, making England 238 for 3 and leaving a simple task against deflated bowlers.

"The spectators rose in a body and cheered Brown again and again as he came in after his grand innings," the *SMH* recorded, while outside their Sydney office "a deafening cheer went up that showed a sportsmanlike recognition of the brilliant playing of the Englishmen".

Jack Blackham, now an Australian selector, remarked: "Brown and Ward batted so well that all the finest of our bowlers could do nothing against them." Praise indeed from the Australians, as we have come to expect from them. It would just be nice if his own compatriots had given Jack Brown more recognition. ∎

The Wisden Cricketer, May 2005

Scyld Berry is editor of *Wisden Cricketers' Almanack* and also cricket correspondent of the *Sunday Telegraph*

5th Test, Melbourne, March 1-6 1895
England won by 6 wickets

AUSTRALIA WON TOSS

GHS Trott		b Briggs	42		b Peel	42
W Bruce	c MacLaren	b Peel	22	c and	b Peel	11
G Giffen*		b Peel	57		b Richardson	51
FA Iredale		b Richardson	8		b Richardson	18
SE Gregory	c Philipson	b Richardson	70		b Richardson	30
J Darling	c Ford	b Peel	74		b Peel	50
JJ Lyons	c Philipson	b Lockwood	55		b Briggs	15
H Graham	c Philipson	b Richardson	6	lbw	b Richardson	10
AE Trott	c Lockwood	b Peel	10		b Richardson	0
AH Jarvis†		not out	34	not out		14
TR McKibbin	c Peel	b Briggs	23	c Philipson	b Richardson	13
Extras		b3 lb10	13		b5 lb6 nb2	13
Total		148.4 overs	414		123.2 overs	267

Fall of wickets 40 101 126 142 284   32 75 125 148 179
286 304 335 367   200 219 219 248

Bowling (1st) Richardson 42-7-138-3, Peel 48-13-114-4, Lockwood 27-7-72-1, Briggs 23.4-5-46-2, Brockwell 6-1-22-0, Ford 2-0-9-0
(2nd) Richardson 45.2-7-104-6, Peel 46-16-89-3, Lockwood 16-7-24-0, Briggs 16-3-37-1

ENGLAND

A Ward		b McKibbin	32		b GHS Trott	93
W Brockwell	st Jarvis	b GHS Trott	5	c and	b Giffen	5
AE Stoddart*	st Jarvis	b GHS Trott	68	lbw	b GHS Trott	11
JT Brown		b AE Trott	30	c Giffen	b McKibbin	140
AC MacLaren	hit wicket	b GHS Trott	120	not out		20
R Peel	c Gregory	b Giffen	73	not out		15
WH Lockwood	c GHS Trott	b Giffen	5			-
FGJ Ford	c AE Trott	b Giffen	11			-
J Briggs	c GHS Trott	b Giffen	0			-
H Philipson†		not out	10			-
T Richardson		lbw b GHS Trott	11			-
Extras		b8 lb8 w4	20		b6 lb5 w2 nb1	14
Total		133 overs	385		88.1 overs	298-4d

Fall of wickets 6 110 112 166 328   5 28 238 278
342 364 364 366

Bowling (1st) Giffen 45-13-130-4, GHS Trott 24-5-71-4, AE Trott 30-4-84-1, McKibbin 29-6-73-1, Bruce 5-1-7-0
(2nd) Giffen 31-4-106-1, GHS Trott 20.1-1-63-2, AE Trott 19-2-56-0, McKibbin 14-2-47-1, Bruce 3-1-10-0, Lyons 1-0-2-0

Umpires T Flynn and J Phillips   Test debuts TR McKibbin (Aus)

1897-98
1st Test Dec 13-17, Sydney †Eng 551 & 96-1; Aus 237 & 408. Eng won by 9 wkts.
2nd Test Jan 1-5, Mel †Aus 520; Eng 315 & 150. Aus won by an inns & 55 runs.
3rd Test Jan 14-19, Ade †Aus 573; Eng 278 & 282. Aus won by an inns & 13 runs.
4th Test Jan 29-Feb 2, Mel †Aus 323 & 115-2; Eng 174 & 263. Aus won by 8 wkts.
5th Test Feb-Mar 2, Syd †Eng 335 & 178; Aus 239 & 276-4. Aus won by 6 wkts.

1899
1st Test Jun 1-3, T Bridge †Aus 252 & 230-8 dec; Eng 193 & 155-7. Match drawn.
2nd Test Jun 15-17, Lord's †Eng 206 & 240; Aus 421 & 28-0. Aus won by 10 wkts.
3rd Test Jun 29-July 1, Head †Aus 172 & 224; Eng 220 & 19-0. Match drawn.
4th Test Jul 17-19, Old T †Eng 372 & 94-3; Aus 196 & 346-7 dec. Match drawn.
5th Test Aug 14-16, The Oval †Eng 576; Aus 352 & 254-5. Match drawn.

1901-02
1st Test Dec 13-16, Syd †Eng 464; Aus 168 & 172. Eng won by an inns & 124 runs.
2nd Test Jan 1-4, Melbourne Aus 112 & 353; †Eng 61 & 175. Aus won by 229 runs.
3rd Test Jan 17-23, Ade †Eng 388 & 247; Aus 321 & 315-6. Aus won by 4 wkts.
4th Test Feb 14-18, Syd †Eng 317 & 99; Aus 299 & 121-3. Aus won by 7 wkts.
5th Test Feb 28-Mar 4, Mel †Aus 144 & 255; Eng 189 & 178. Aus won by 32 runs.

1902
1st Test May 29-31, Edgbaston †Eng 376-9 dec; Aus 36 & 46-2. Match drawn.
2nd Test Jun 12-14, Lord's †Eng 102-2. Match drawn.
3rd Test Jul 3-5, Sheffield †Aus 194 & 289; Eng 145 & 195. Aus won by 143 runs.
4th Test Jul 24-26, Old Trafford †Aus 299 & 86; Eng 262 & 120. Aus won by 3 runs.
5th Test Aug 11-13, T Oval †Aus 324 & 121; Eng 183 & 263-9. Eng won by 1 wicket.

Golden memories

In 1902, at the height of cricket's Golden Age, England and Australia played out an epic Ashes contest with a legendary climax. One hundred years later, **Eric Midwinter** recalls one of the greatest series of all time

I t was in 1902 that the new century began to take its characteristic shape. Edward VII was crowned, although owing to the monarch's appendicitis the event was deferred from June 26 to August 9. There was also a new prime minister. In July Lord Salisbury, "the Victorian Titan", yielded office to AJ Balfour, a more subfuse and prudent figure, typical (with three or four vivid exceptions) of the more managerial, less theatrical premiers of the 20th century.

It was a Conservative government, also predestining an era in which the Tories would rule for three quarters of the century. Football was destined to be the sport of the age. In that rapidly developing arena Sheffield United, very much a form team of the time, beat Southampton 2-1 in the FA Cup final at Crystal Palace in a replay. The Blades' star was tireless "Nudger" Needham, tenacious in defence and adroit in attack, still to be reckoned among the pick of England's half-backs. As for Southampton, their right-back was once CB Fry – and Sheffield United were to play a minor role in the coming season's cricket.

Cricket had reached its apogee. If the establishment of the official County Championship in 1890 and the onset of war in 1914 marks out the parameters of cricket's Golden Age, then 1902 was its centrepoint. England fielded an XI that summer which many regard as their strongest ever.

The batting was formidable. In the first Test in May at Edgbaston (Birmingham's first) England fielded 11 players who had all scored first-class centuries, including the wicketkeeper AFA Lilley, who made over 15,000 first-class runs in his consistent career, and Gilbert Jessop, a frightening proposition at No.8. There was an admirable balance to the bowling while, in the likes of Archie MacLaren, Len Braund, Johnny Tyldesley and Jessop, England had specialist fieldsmen of choice competence.

The first two Tests – at Edgbaston and Lord's were rain-affected draws – with England in the ascendancy. By the beginning of July, when the teams repaired to Sheffield, the Australians had recovered something of their good form and at Bramall Lane, home of the FA Cup winners, the tourists inflicted what *Wisden* called a "severe disaster" on the confident England side. Australia batted soundly, but not convincingly, as Sydney Barnes, replacing Lockwood, took 6 for 49.

However, the Australian total of 194 was 49 more than England could manage in response, as Jack Saunders and Monty Noble took five wickets apiece. Clem Hill then made a hundred and Trumper a whirlwind 62 as the tourists set a daunting target of 339 and England lost by 143 runs, Noble bagging another six wickets. It was to be Sheffield's solitary Test match.

The last two fixtures in the five-match

rubber were dramatic enough to earn labels related to players, though for different reasons. At Old Trafford, "Tate's match" was won by the Australians by a mere three runs after a rain-affected game featuring "extraordinary fluctuations of fortune", according to *Wisden*. In the second innings, with the score on 16 for 3 after Australia had resumed 37 runs ahead, Fred Tate reprieved the Australian captain Joe Darling on the square-leg boundary; Darling went on to make 37, his side's top score, and the next wicket did not fall until 64. When England replied, needing 124 to win, Tate was bowled by Saunders with just four runs required in this, his only Test match.

The Oval Test became known as "Jessop's match" and was just as keenly contested, with England emerging victors by one wicket. Australia batted forcefully to make 324, against which England could muster only 183 and, despite a second-

England's XI: (back row, l-r) George Hirst, Arthur Lilley, Bill Lockwood, Len Braund, Wilfred Rhodes, Johnny Tyldesley; (front row, l-r) CB Fry, Stanley Jackson, Archie MacLaren, Ranji, Gilbert Jessop

innings collapse, England needed 263 with the wicket moist and torn. At 5 for 2 and then 48 for 5, a third Australian victory was the obvious outcome. But then Jessop played his legendary innings. After an awkward start he hit a staggeringly outrageous century in 75 minutes, then the fastest Test century and since surpassed in terms of minutes only by Jack Gregory, who took 70 minutes to reach his

66 England fielded an XI that summer which many regard as their strongest ever. The batting was formidable.99

hundred against South Africa at Johannesburg in 1921-22.

At the finale of the series Hirst, with a battling half-century, was joined in another historic alliance by his old ally, Rhodes. It is now usually claimed that the Yorkshiremen's supposed agreement that "we'll get 'em in singles" is apocryphal, but cricket's folklore happily remains as potent as its factual account. Whatever was said, the two prototypical professionals made the 15 necessary for a face-saving win.

Is it right to term a team which also on occasion included such talented men as Lionel Palairet, Tom Hayward and Bobby Abel as England's greatest ever when they could not reclaim the Ashes?

It is true that CB Fry had a poor series and Ranji was lost through injury for part of the rubber, and it is fair to add that the Ashes were regained in 1903-04 and retained in 1905. What must also be mentioned – and it is further ammunition to those who judge these the golden years – is that the 1902 Australians were arguably the strongest team to have visited these shores and some would not hesitate to compare them with the impressive Australian sides of the 1940s and 1990s onwards.

Given the relative weakness of the English opposition at those two other junctures, the 1902 summer, rain-hit although it was, found England and Australia at the highest point of conjoined skill the two countries have reached. ∎

The Cricketer, August 2002

Eric Midwinter is a cricket historian

The human catapult

Gilbert Jessop, whose quickfire century at The Oval turned the game for England, was much more than just a big hitter, says Christopher Pierpoint

England's victory over Australia by one wicket at The Oval in 1902 is often associated with the last-wicket stand of 15 between George Hirst and Wilfred Rhodes. A century ago there were no man-of-the-match awards but had there been one for this game it would have gone neither to Hirst nor Rhodes, but to the young Gloucestershire captain – Gilbert Jessop.

Jessop, known as "The Croucher" for his distinctive stance, had developed a reputation as a hard-hitting batsman long before that innings. He had played for Gloucestershire even before he went up to Cambridge in the autumn of 1895, while Hirst and Rhodes would already have been acutely aware of Jessop's prowess for in 1897 he had hit 101 out of 118 in 40 minutes for the university against Yorkshire at Harrogate. He hit the ball over the ropes 12 times and out of the ground another six, at a time when six runs were scored only for hits out of the ground.

When Jessop toured America with Plum Warner's side in 1897 a local poet, Ralph Paine, was inspired to describe him as "… the human catapult who wrecks the roofs of distant towns when set in his assault".

A favourite story about Jessop is one told by Neville Cardus. As a small boy one day at Old Trafford, when Lancashire were playing Gloucestershire, Cardus missed the last few minutes before lunch to buy his drink of lemonade for the interval. He was so short that his head barely came above the bar counter and he had just given his order when there was a tremendous noise and the glasses on the counter, together with other items of crockery, were sent crashing in all directions.

Young Cardus thought the end of the world had come but the barman had seen it all before and was able to reassure him. "Don't worry, son," he said. "It's only Mr Jessop just beginning his innings."

The Cricketer, August 2002

Mind the windows: Gilbert Jessop

1903-04
1st Test Dec 11-17, Syd †Aus 285 & 485; Eng 577 & 194-5. Eng won by 5 wkts.
2nd Test Jan 1-5, Mel †Eng 315 & 103; Aus 122 & 111. Eng won by 185 runs.
3rd Test Jan 15-20, Ade †Aus 388 & 351; Eng 245 & 278. Aus won by 216 runs.
4th Test Feb 26-Mar 3, Syd †Eng 249 & 210; Aus 131 & 171. Eng won by 157 runs.
5th Test Mar 5-8, Mel †Aus 247 & 133; Eng 61 & 101. Aus won by 218 runs.

1905
1st Test May 29-31, T Bridge Eng 196 & 426-5 dec; Aus 221 & 188. Eng won by 213 runs.
2nd Test Jun 15-17, Lord's †Eng 282 & 151-5; Aus 181. Match drawn.
3rd Test Jul 3-5, Head †Eng 301 & 295-5 dec; Aus 195 & 224-7. Match drawn.
4th Test Jul 24-26, Old T †Eng 446, Aus 197 & 169. Eng won by an inns & 80 runs.
5th Test Aug 14-16, T Oval †Eng 430 & 261-6 dec; Aus 363 & 124-4. Match drawn.

1907-08
1st Test Dec 13-19, Syd †Eng 273 & 300; Aus 300 & 275-8. Aus won by 2 wkts.
2nd Test Jan 1-7, Mel †Aus 266 & 397; Eng 382 & 282-9. Eng won by one wicket.
3rd Test Jan 10-16, Ade †Aus 285 & 506, Eng 363 & 183. Aus won by 245 runs.
4th Test Feb 7-11, Mel †Aus 214 & 385; Eng 105 & 186. Aus won by 308 runs.
5th Test Feb 21-27, Syd Aus 137 & 422; †Eng 281 & 229. Aus won by 49 runs.

1909
1st Test May 27-29, Edg †Aus 74 & 151; Eng 121 & 105-0. Eng won by 10 wkts.
2nd Test Jun 14-16, Lord's Eng 269 & 121; †Aus 350 & 41-1. Aus won by 9 wkts.
3rd Test Jul 1-3, Headingley †Aus 188 & 207; Eng 182 & 87. Aus won by 126 runs.
4th Test Jul 26-28, Old T †Aus 147 & 279-9 dec; Eng 119 & 108-3. Match drawn.
5th Test Aug 9-11, T Oval †Aus 325 & 339-5 dec; Eng 352 & 104-3. Match drawn.

1911-12
1st Test Dec 15-21, Syd †Aus 447 & 308; Eng 318 & 291. Aus won by 146 runs.
2nd Test Dec 30-Jan 3, Mel †Aus 184 & 299; Eng 265 & 219-2. Eng won by 8 wkts.
3rd Test Jan 12-17, Ade †Aus 133 & 476; Eng 501 & 112-3. Eng won by 7 wkts.
4th Test Feb 9-13, Mel †Aus 191 & 173; †Eng 589. Eng won by an inns & 225 runs.
5th Test Feb 23-Mar 1, Syd †Eng 324 & 214; Aus 176 & 292. Eng won by 70 runs.

1912
1st Test Jun 24-26, Lord's †Eng 310-7 dec; Aus 282-7. Match drawn.
2nd Test Jul 29-31, Old Trafford †Eng 203; Aus 14-0. Match drawn.
3rd Test Aug 19-22, The Oval †Eng 245 & 175; Aus 111 & 65. Eng won by 244 runs.

HERO No.1

Jack Hobbs

Tests

Batting

Matches	61
Runs	5410
Highest score	211
Average	56.94
Hundreds	15
Fifties	28

Bowling

Balls	376
Runs	165
Wickets	1
Average	165.00
Best bowling	1-19

First-class

Batting

Matches	834
Runs	61760
Highest score	316*
Average	50.70
Hundreds	197
Fifties	273

Bowling

Balls	5217
Runs	2704
Wickets	108
Average	25.03
Best bowling	7-56
5-for inns	3
10-for match	0

v Australia

Batting

Matches	41
Runs	3636
Highest score	187
Average	54.26
Hundreds	12
Fifties	15

The greatest and the kindest

RC Robertson-Glasgow writes his memories of Sir Jack Hobbs following The Master's death in December 1963

JACK HOBBS was my hero. He was the greatest batsman that I ever saw and, very occasionally, had the pleasure to bowl to. He was the kindest cricketer I have known, whether to other cricketers or to spectators whom he might never see again. He had a boyish leg-pulling humour, which stayed with him almost to the end of his life. He was religious in an undemonstrative manner. He was 'a very perfect gentle Knight'.

John Berry Hobbs came from Cambridge to Surrey and it was not long before he showed himself to be perfectly equipped by both art and temperament for any style of batting on any kind of pitch against any sort of bowling. He mastered spin and speed on grass or matting. When young, he conquered spin or 'cut' on the South African mat; when comparatively elderly, he would hook bumpers off his face on the grass of Australia or England. He was always in position. He always seemed to have the extra split second of time that makes the difference. And he did it all with a grace that cannot be transferred into words.

As to genius, there is nearly always argument about its peak or meridian. Were Dickens's earlier works his best? Did Beethoven never again approach his youthful splendour? So with Sir John Hobbs there are some who say that those who never saw his pre-First War brilliance never really saw Hobbs at all.

And yet, for most of us, regardless of our age, he reached and settled on the top of his mountain when he was around the age of 40, when his opening partner for England was Herbert Sutcliffe, for Surrey Andrew Sandham. Indeed, it is arguable that no greater pair of opening batsmen ever walked out from the pavilion for England than Hobbs and Sutcliffe. Twice during the mid-1920s, in a Test match against Australia, on a bowlers' pitch, they made the bowlers look small: at Melbourne and at The Oval. The second of these two performances, at The Oval, ended a period of Australian dominance that was beginning to seem incapable of ending.

But I hope the reader will exercise an understanding forgiveness if I say that for me there were two of Hobbs's 197 centuries which will always have more meaning than any that he scored in the fiercer and more famous fields of Test cricket.

These two centuries belong to a hot August weekend in 1925, at Taunton where the horizon facing the pavilion is made beautiful by the Quantock hills. At any time the crowd would come to see Hobbs, just as in later years they would come to see Stanley Matthews play soccer. But this August weekend at Taunton had its own particular excitement. For a month or so Hobbs had needed but one century, his 126th, to equal the first-class record of the Old Man, Dr WG Grace; and for a month or so Luck had shown herself an ill-natured lady.

And now here we were, the ground bursting at the seams and the roof of the little pavilion bending under the news-reel cinematograph men and their gear. Somerset batted first and, with a few exceptions, not well. Surrey had two hours' batting that Saturday. During that period Hobbs was not quite at his best. Not unnaturally he seemed at times anxious, especially against the slow left-arm bowling of the great JC White. He found more opportunity against JJ Bridges and RC Robertson-Glasgow. All in all, instinct took him to 91 not out at the drawing of stumps on that first evening.

It must have been, to Jack Hobbs, a very long Sunday. To some of us, of Somerset, Monday somehow seemed like break-up day at school: all was confusion and excitement. Jim Bridges and I were the bowlers. Early on I bowled a no-ball to Hobbs, which he diverted with a graceful inevitability to the leg boundary. Soon Hobbs scored a single to leg from Bridges.

So now WG Grace and JB Hobbs had each made 126 centuries. He made another hundred, beautifully, on the Tuesday, though there were comparatively few present at its making. This enabled Hobbs to go ahead of Grace at 127 hundreds. But it is not for me to say which of the two was the greater batsman. One constellation is no more glorious than another.

The record books tell us that Hobbs made 197 centuries in first-class cricket. Unlike some one might name, Hobbs was never greedy for runs. Look at those 197 centuries and see how many were between 100 and 130. "There are others," Hobbs would say to himself, "ready and able to take on the scoring. Let them have their turn." In the realms of greatness he was the artist, not the merchant. *The Cricketer*, March 1964

RC Robertson-Glasgow, or "Crusoe", played first-class cricket for Somerset and Oxford University and was one of the greatest of all cricket writers

> 66 He always seemed to have the extra split second that makes the difference. And he did it all with a special grace 99

1920-21

Australia handed out their first 5-0 thrashing in 1920-21 and on England's return **The Cricketer,** *edited by Plum Warner, launched. Warwick Armstrong's tough and aggressive cricket overcame a war-weary MCC (England toured as MCC until 1976-77). The new magazine began the dissection ... But the decade was not all gloom as a post-war euphoria produced some great series and great players – England finally winning back the Ashes in 1926 – to everyone's surprise*

The first whitewash

Never before until this tour has one side won a full five-Test series and the Australians are to be congratulated heartily on accomplishing a great feat. There are no excuses. In only one of the Test matches, the third at Adelaide, did we make a good fight and we must admit we have been fairly and squarely beaten by a superior side. Few people, here or in Australia, imagined that the Australians would be able to put such an excellent all-round combination into the field.

The MCC team have been disappointing. The loss of JW Hearne after the first Test was a heavy blow for he was, next to Hobbs, the best player on the side and an almost ideal man, with his cool head and superb defence, to go in first wicket down. He had been in splendid form up to the time of his illness and his straight bat and experience would assuredly have helped to wear down the Australian attack and to make the task of the subsequent batsmen considerably easier.

Before he was 21 Hearne scored a hundred in a Test match, a feat without parallel among English cricketers – Mr Clem Hill, probably the best left-handed batsman the world has seen, can lay claim to a similar feat among Australians –

and his breakdown in health was an irreparable blow. But making every allowance for the absence of Hearne, and for the minor injuries and accidents that are, apparently, inseparable from any touring side, we do not think that the team did itself justice and certainly, at this distance, it would appear that they were a collection of individuals and not a good working combination, essential in every class of cricket but especially in international cricket. They struck us as being, as one might say of a rowing eight, "ragged" and "not together".

Perhaps we overrated our batting strength, though the first six or seven names in the order inspired confidence; and it is certain that the War left its influence on our cricket, as it was naturally bound to do, slicing four years out of the lives of our players and depriving them of the practice and experience. The team, as a whole, was rather on the old side but at the time it was selected opinion was practically unanimous that, in the circumstances, it just about represented our cricketing strength.

We still believe in our batting strength but we had a long tail, especially in the first Test, and when Mr Douglas [captain JWHT Douglas]

England captains till 1921: r-l
Lord Harris,
J Lillywhite,
Hon Ivo Bligh,
AN Hornby,
AG Steel,
WG Grace,
AE Stoddart,
AC MacLaren,
Hon FS Jackson,
PF Warner,
AO Jones, CB Fry,
JWHT Douglas

found that he had no "stock" bowlers, like Mr FR Foster and Barnes on a previous tour, it might, conceivably, have been a wise policy to fill up his side with batsmen, leaving but, at the most, two men who could be regarded as a "tail". Everyone knew that there was no Barnes or Foster on the side and that Mr Douglas was not the bowler he was – indeed, we must reluctantly admit that there is no really great bowler in England – but there was plenty of bowling of various types and it was hoped that a fairly useful attack might be evolved.

Parkin took five wickets for 60 runs in Australia's first innings in the third Test, but his 16 wickets cost 41.87 each, and those critics who maintained that he tried too many tricks and that he did not realise sufficiently the value of length have been justified in their opinion. Mr Fender bowled well in the last two matches and we think his earlier inclusion in the side – he did not play in the first two Tests – would have been an advantage, especially as with his rapid, daring hitting he is quite likely to knock up 40 or 50 runs in double-quick time. Hitch was a failure. On the previous tour his fast bowling was expensive and ineffective and he is not now anything like the bowler he was then.

Frankly, our bowling was lacking in the highest class and nothing but that will get strong batting sides out on Australian wickets. Nor did the bowlers, as we have said, receive the assistance they might have expected from the fieldsmen and a high price was paid for dropped catches. There were exceptions to the general weakness of the fielding, Hobbs at cover point and Hendren anywhere but particularly in the long field being magnificent while Woolley brought off some fine catches in the slips. But too many fieldsmen had to be "hidden" and we must, in selecting England teams in the future, pay particular attention to the fielding and choose young men who can both run and throw.

Our failure to win even one Test match has naturally caused intense disappointment in this country but it will do us no harm, and on our own wickets and with a wide field of selection, we should be able to make the Australians fight hard to retain the "Ashes". We hope our selectors will "go for" the young men and they must endeavour somehow to find a match-winning bowler on hard wickets. The crowds beat all records and interest in cricket in Australia was never greater, so that, even if the MCC team have been defeated, they can say they have by their visit set cricket very firmly on its legs in the Antipodes; and every Englishman will rejoice at that. 🇬🇧

The Cricketer, May 7, 1921 (Volume 1, issue 1)

From 'a correspondent' (many pieces in early editions of *The Cricketer* had no credited writer)

Australia captains till 1921; l-r
DW Gregory,
WL Murdoch,
PS McDonnell,
HJH Scott,
JMcC Blackham,
G Giffen,
GHS Trott,
J Darling,
C Hill,
MA Noble,
SE Gregory,
WW Armstrong

1920-21

1st Test, Dec 17-22, Sydney †Aus 267 and 581 (WW Armstrong 158, HL Collins 104); Eng 190 and 281. **Aus won by 377 runs.**

2nd Test, Dec 31-Jan 4, Melbourne †Aus 499 (CE Pellew 116, JM Gregory 100); Eng 251 (JB Hobbs 122, Gregory 7-69) and 157. **Aus won by inns and 91r.**

3rd Test, Jan 14-20, Adelaide †Aus 354 (Collins 162; CH Parkin 5-60) and 582 (C Kelleway 147, Armstrong 121, Pellew 104); Eng 447 (AC Russell 135*; AA Mailey 5-160) and 370 (Hobbs 123; Mailey 5-142). **Aus won by 119r.**

4th Test, Feb 11-16, Melbourne †Eng 284 (JWH Makepeace 117; Mailey 4-115) and 315 (Mailey 9-121); Aus 389 (Armstrong 123*; PGH Fender 5 122) and 211-2. **Aus won by 8 wickets.**

5th Test, Feb 25-March 1, Sydney †Eng 204 and 280 (Mailey 5-119); Aus 392 (CG Macartney 170; Fender 5-90) and 93-1. **Aus won by 9 wickets.**

1921

1st Test, May 28-30, Trent Bridge †Eng 112 (JM Gregory 6-58) and 147 (EA McDonald 5-32); **Aus** 232 and 30-0. **Aus won by 10 wickets.**

2nd Test, June 11-14, Lord's †Eng 187 and 283; Aus 342 and 131-2. **Aus won by 8 wickets.**

3rd Test, July 2-5, Headingley †Aus 407 (CG Macartney 115) and 273-7 dec; Eng 259 and 202. **Aus won by 219 runs.**

4th Test, July 23-26, Old Trafford †Eng 362-4 dec (AC Russell 101) and 44-1; Aus 175 (CH Parkin 5-38). **Draw.**

5th Test, Aug 13-16, The Oval †Eng 403-8 dec (LP Mead 182*; McDonald 5-143) and 244-2 (Russell 102*); Aus 389. **Match drawn.**

1924-25

1st Test, Dec 19-27, Sydney †Aus 450 (HL Collins 114, WH Ponsford 110; MW Tate 6-130) and 452 (JM Taylor 108; Tate 5-98); Eng 298 (JB Hobbs 115; JM Gregory 5-111) and 411 (FF Woolley 123, H Sutcliffe 115). **Aus won by 193 runs.**

2nd Test, Jan 1-8, Melbourne †Aus 600 (VY Richardson 138, Ponsford 128) and 250 (Tate 6-99); Eng 479 (Sutcliffe 176, Hobbs 154) and 290 (Sutcliffe 127; AA Mailey 5-92). **Aus won by 81 runs.**

3rd Test, Jan 16-23, Adelaide †Aus 489 (J Ryder 201*) and 250; Eng 365 (Hobbs 119) and 363. **Aus won by 11r.**

4th Test, Feb 13-18, Melbourne †Eng 548 (Sutcliffe 143); Aus 269 and 250 (Tate 5-75). **Eng won by an inns and 29 runs.**

5th Test, Feb 27-Mar 4, Sydney †Aus 295 and 325 (Tate 5-115); Eng 167 (CV Grimmett 5-45) and 146 (Grimmett 6-37). **Aus won by 307 runs.**

1926

1st Test, June 12-15, Trent Bridge †Eng 32-0. **Draw.**

2nd Test, June 26-29, Lord's †Aus 383 (W Bardsley 193*) and 194-5 (CG Macartney 133*); Eng 475-3 dec (EH Hendren 127*, JB Hobbs 119). **Draw.**

3rd Test, July 10-13, Headingley Aus 494 (Macartney 151, WM Woodfull 141, AJ Richardson 100); †Eng 294 (CV Grimmett 5-88) and 254-3. **Match drawn.**

4th Test, July 24-27, Old Trafford †Aus 335 (WM Woodfull 117, CG Macartney 109); Eng 305-5. **Draw.**

5th Test, Aug 14-18, The Oval †Eng 280 (AA Mailey 6-138) and 436 (H Sutcliffe 161, JB Hobbs 100); Aus 302 and 125. **Eng won by 289 runs.**

Thumping re-match

In the return series Australia's Test run reached eight wins before England, led by the Hon Lionel Tennyson, drew one. *The Cricketer*'s patience with Armstrong wore thin and cartoons became ever larger. Editor **Plum Warner** offers a solution to England's woes: give the under-35s a chance

The cricket season of 1921 will be remembered, if for nothing else, for two reasons. First, the weather was perfectly glorious; and secondly for the triumphal progress of the Australian XI, who did not lose a single Test match and until late in the season were undefeated.

In the wonderful weather that prevailed the game attracted enormous attendances in every part of the country and, in spite of our failure to win a single Test match, it may with confidence be said that cricket was never so popular.

The selection committee have been blamed for the results which followed but, though no selection committee has ever been infallible in its judgement, or ever will be, I am of the opinion that our defeats were caused by one fact, and one fact only, namely that we met a better side. Our selectors were faced with a very difficult task. In any event it would have been difficult to pick an England XI, for we had not recovered from the long years of war, and the task of the selectors was made doubly hard by the fact that Hobbs, the best batsman in the world and a superb fieldsman at cover point, and JW Hearne, the second best batsman in England against the best bowling, were both *hors de combat* from illness and accidents. Hobbs did take the field in the third Test match at Leeds but, as all the world knows, he was seized with sudden illness and had to be operated upon immediately. It was a cruel fate that decreed that this magnificent cricketer should not play a single innings for England.

Hearne played in the third Test match at Leeds but his health was regarded by the selectors as not good enough to meet the strain of such strenuous games and this was his solitary appearance in the Test matches. The loss of these two great batsmen had not only a material but a moral effect.

Everyone knows our bowling today is nothing like up to the pre-war standard. There is no Richardson or Lockwood among the fast bowlers, nor is there a Barnes, a JT Hearne or an Attewell among the medium pace right-handed bowlers and, with our bowling at the low ebb it was, judged by the international standard, it became more than ever essential that the fielding should be excellent.

Many of our most successful batsmen

today are past the age when activity and throwing power can be expected of them in the field and the absence of Hobbs made an incalculable difference to the off-side fielding. A great cover-point makes mid-off look a good fielder and here Australia had an enormous advantage, their fielding on the off-side and in the country being as near perfection as possible.

I would further suggest that the general committee of the MCC should be strengthened by the inclusion of younger blood – men actually playing in first-class cricket today. I have heard it urged that the difficulty of putting men on the committee of the MCC who are actually playing in first-class cricket is that, unless they play for Middlesex, they are practically debarred from attending meetings during the summer months.

The cricket and selection committee of the MCC might also be improved by the inclusion of men who are admittedly fine judges of cricket and cricketers. I mention no names but it is a notorious fact that some of the greatest names in cricket do not figure on that selection committee.

We must also get rid of the idea that a Test match of necessity requires great experience. Everybody must make a beginning in Test matches, and I would go more for the young men who are naturally quicker and more active in the field and who, given the opportunity, would train on into England cricketers.

There are today a large number of young cricketers of very great promise, and I hope that in picking future elevens to tour in Australia and in South Africa and to represent England here, preference will be given to the men who are under 35 years of age, except in the case of geniuses like Hobbs and Barnes. The number of runs that the Australians saved by their beautiful fielding is incalculable, and the remark made by a well-known cricketer that they always started a hundred runs ahead of us is not very wide of the mark.

There is, however, no need to be despondent. Cricketers of great skill abound in this country and it needs but a little organisation, and we shall in the near future produce an England XI worthy to hold their own with those of the past.

The Cricketer, Winter Annual, 1921-22

A series of two captains

Tennyson's last-minute call-up for the Lord's Test in 1921. By Steve Pittard

The Hon Lionel Tennyson was spending a convivial night with his chums at the Embassy Club on Old Bond Street when, well past midnight, he received a message that he was required for the 1921 Ashes Test at Lord's, starting later that day. Tennyson's response was that, if he had heard the good news earlier, he would have "knocked off a cigar or two". He then confidently struck a £50 wager that he would crack a half-century. England lost but his swashbuckling undefeated 74 won him the bet and also the captaincy.
The Wisden Cricketer, May 2006

Johnny Douglas' fighting instincts affected his batting. By David Foot

Johnny Douglas was said to be the fittest cricketer of his day. The body was taut and muscular. Douglas looked more like a boxer than a Test allrounder. And that was what he was, of course … The boxer's pluck made up for a somewhat saturnine character and no natural or easy affinity with the players. They still knew he would battle for them, not wantonly prepared to give his wicket away or be needlessly generous to the other side … But his cricket, whatever the groans about his painfully limited batting repertoire, should not be disregarded. He played in 23 Tests and, with SF Barnes gobbling up the wickets, he led England to an Ashes triumph in 1911-12, having taken over the captaincy when Plum Warner was ill. The pundits of the day went off his Test captaincy after the 1914-18 war and the records appear to bear that out. John William Henry Tyler ("Johnny Won't Hit Today" to the Australian public) Douglas may not have been everyone's idea of a figure of shining or inspirational endearment. But his innate courage never deserted him. That was poignantly evident in 1930 when he was drowned at sea trying to save his father's life, after two vessels collided in the fog. *The Wisden Cricketer*, April 2004

Australian diagnosis

Former England captain AC MacLaren explains what went right for the tourists

With the exciting finish at Scarborough, which resulted in only their second defeat of the tour, our Australian friends brought their first-class fixture list to a close. Many were delighted that JWHT Douglas had pulled off a meritorious win after battling away from the commencement of last autumn to the present day without tasting the sweets of a victory.

Many cricket lovers have asked the question, "Is this the best team Australia has ever sent over?" The Australian skipper is of the opinion that it is 50 per cent below those sides captained by Joe Darling; but those sides, in my opinion, contained no finer bowler than Ted McDonald, whose headwork and ability to get everything out of a wicket have been the prime factors in their successes.

For the first time, too, the XI contained two fast bowlers and with Gregory as good a bowler as Jones, if not quite so fast, this pair made the bowling equal to the standard of excellence one looks for in Test cricket. Armstrong was more successful than previously with his slow legbreaks of perfect length and with that one which came through quicker with no break, which resulted in so many lbws. That Armstrong should have so routed our county sides when always nursing his bowlers for the next Test match is highly creditable to the skipper, who kept his star bowlers in form throughout, and who bowled so well on these big occasions that he never had to draw on his reserves.
The Cricketer, September 17, 1921

Warwick Armstrong

Tests

Batting

Matches	50
Runs	2863
Highest score	159*
Average	38.68
Hundreds	6
Fifties	8

Bowling

Balls	8022
Runs	2923
Wickets	87
Average	33.59
Best bowling	6-35
5-for inns	3

First-class

Batting

Matches	269
Runs	16158
Highest score	303*
Average	46.83
Hundreds	45
Fifties	57

Bowling

Balls	43297
Runs	16405
Wickets	832
Average	19.71
Best bowling	8-47
5-for inns	50
10-for match	5

v England

Batting

Matches	42
Runs	2172
Highest score	158
Average	35.03
Hundreds	4
Fifties	6

Bowling

Balls	6782
Runs	2288
Wickets	74
Average	30.91
Best bowling	6-35

The Big Ship

Warwick Armstrong was large in girth and character, an uncompromising captain of Australia who won the first eight Tests when the Ashes resumed after the Great War

Following the 1920-21 whitewash Armstrong arrived in England (on the same boat as MCC) to defend the Ashes. The Cricketer profiled the Australian captain. By Senior Nimshi
Mr WW Armstrong, the captain of the Australian XI, has been described as "Australia's greatest cricketer of today" and on his form in the recent Test matches he would be chosen to represent the World against Mars should the inhabitants of that distant and interesting planet ever think of challenging us at cricket.

Very tall and very strong, almost an Alfred Mynn* in frame, he is built for long hitting and in general style is most attractive to look at, being a fine square-cutter as well as an extraordinarily powerful driver on both sides of the wicket. He will be 41 in May but he is today as great a batsman as ever. He is also an extremely accurate bowler and it is really wonderful how over after over he can drop the ball on the right spot and, when it comes to a matter of keeping down runs, the greatest of batsmen are reduced to scoring an occasional single.

He has the type of head on which caps do not fit easily but is the last person in the world whom anyone would venture to describe as 'swollen-headed' for, like most great men, he is modesty itself. Quite apart from his own triumphant successes in the Test matches in Australia, he won the admiration of all the critics by his able captaincy. He is good nature personified and will be immensely popular as captain.

Naturally we hope that he will not be successful in winning the rubber in the Test matches** but we wish him personally the best of good fortune for "Warwick", as he is called from one end of Australia to the other, is a stout fellow in more senses than one.
The Cricketer, April 30, 1921

By the end of the 1921 summer the editor of The Cricketer was exasperated. Armstrong, the series won, was so bored by the rain-affected final Test as it headed for a draw that he took to reading a newspaper in the outfield. It did not go down well
THE SECOND innings of England in the Test match at The Oval amounted almost to a farce. Armstrong did not bowl a single ball during this innings but fielded at deep third man and long leg at the far corner of the Vauxhall end of the ground and was seemingly extremely bored with the whole proceedings. It is true he brought off a fine catch that dismissed Fender but his entire want of interest in the game was a bad example to the many young men and boys who were watching and altogether inconsistent with the great traditions of cricket and especially Test match cricket. The captain of an Australian XI is, in

his own sphere, an important personage and he should set a good example. The match, as everyone realised, was bound to end in a draw but cricket should be played keenly for its own sake. Armstrong has been a wonderfully successful leader, having captained Australia 10 times in the last eight months without knowing what it is to meet with defeat but his action at The Oval last week was a sad ending to his career as a captain.
The Cricketer, August 27, 1921

Matthew Engel's review of Gideon Haigh's biography of Warwick Armstrong (The Big Ship, Aurum Press 2002) paints a modern picture
ONE FIGURE stands out [from the 1920s], not merely like a colossus – he was a colossus. At his peak Warwick Armstrong's weight went up to 22 stone, making him almost twice the man Steve Waugh is. (Booze was the most likely explanation.) His boots, in one of Gideon Haigh's happiest phrases, were like "small canoes". He was a cricketing colossus too. In the first two Ashes series after the Great War Warwick Armstrong led Australia to eight successive victories and his own contributions were substantial.

Since he was past 40 at the time, most of his cricket was actually played in the Golden Age. But he was not really a Golden Age man. As a batsman, he was, as the *Sydney Morning Herald* put it "never a stylist ... essentially laboured ... artisan in type". He bowled legbreaks that were successful mainly because they failed to turn. He "played at keeps", as the saying had it. At Trent Bridge in 1905 he had bowling figures of 52-24-67-1, not an analysis that sounds very Edwardian.

He was also unEdwardian in his approach: a "confirmed growler", as one Australian paper put it. Even genial Jack Hobbs had a grudge against him. "Someone called him a cricketing Falstaff," wrote Cardus. "That simile will not do ... He is all vigilance, suspicion and determination. The bat in his hand is like a hammer in the grip of a Vulcan." He later became an unusually forceful newspaper commentator, trenchant rather than perceptive: (Bradman "will probably be a good player later but, I think, is not a Test player at present," he told *London Evening News* readers at the start of 1929). Above all he took no nonsense from cricket administrators.

On the other hand he was an immensely popular figure among spectators in both England and Australia and Haigh finds flashes of kindness, with children especially, that suggest depths of humanity beneath the forbidding exterior. *Wisden Cricket Monthly, May 2002*

* Alfred Mynn was a giant, a vast round-arm fast bowler of the 19th century
** Australia won the series 3-0

Well played, England!

... well, better. In 1924-25 Arthur Gilligan was captain, the defeat 4-1 and a post-war generosity pervaded these ritual beatings. *The Cricketer* published this extract from the *Melbourne Herald* written by '**RH**'

We Australians are very proud of the feat of our men in winning the rubber once again. It gratifies our national pride, for it is one of our little conceits that cricket is played just a little bit better here than anywhere else in the world.

And you Englishmen are opponents whom it is an honour to defeat. Since you landed in Perth early in October, you have impressed us all with your determination to check Australia's run of success and you have let nothing interfere with your pursuit of that aim.

You have shown, as perhaps no other visiting team has done, the real team spirit. You have been a happy family all through and this is a great testimony to the loyalty of you all, as well as to the tact and good fellowship of your leader. With six men left out of each Test team it would be almost natural that some of you should be disappointed. If any of you have felt that disappointment, you have not let it be seen.

But, though we are proud of beating you, we should have been more satisfied with our success had the favours of fortune been more evenly bestowed. To lose the toss is a great handicap, to lose it three times in succession might well dishearten any side. But you fellows merely shrugged your shoulders, remarked "It's all in the game" and took the field determined by a supreme effort to counterbalance your bad luck.

Your bad luck did not end with the toss of the coin for Fate played you a scurvy trick in the matter of accidents. Tate, your bowling mainstay, Gilligan, Woolley, Hearne and Strudwick, all among your indispensables, have suffered injuries and thus your chances of success were sadly prejudiced. But even these misfortunes did not daunt you.

Your valiant fight in the third Test won everyone's admiration and in Melbourne yesterday morning every good sportsman was urging you on to victory. You went down in glorious defeat. You are not taking "The Ashes" back to England with you but you will take a great reputation as brave fighters and fine sportsmen. *The Cricketer*, May 9, 1925

Special interview with the English captain

The Cricketer also had a scoop – an exclusive interview with the England captain on his return. There were none of the probing inquiries modern captains have to endure. Rather the (anonymous) writer suggests it is the taking part that counts

AER Gilligan, looking extraordinarily bronzed and fit, is back again in England without having accomplished his great ambition of bringing back "The Ashes" but having brought back everything else. No more popular captain ever visited Australia and, though victory did not come his way, both he and his men played the game in a spirit which has endeared them for all time to the Australian public. Their reception, both on and off the field, was extraordinarily cordial, even affectionate, and when they returned home they met with a reception at Victoria Station that equalled, if it did not surpass, anything which they experienced in Australia. Their welcome on this last occasion was an object-lesson, showing as it did that victory is not necessarily the main objective. It is sufficient for good cricketers to have done their best, even if they have failed. The English captain has given several interviews to the newspapers since his arrival but we feel that, although he has already said a good deal about the tour, many of the finer points of the actual play have not yet appeared in print and we, therefore, deem ourselves particularly fortunate to have had the privilege of a long talk with the English captain. There can be no doubt that Mr Gilligan is a personality. He radiates a happy atmosphere and his great love of the game and his fine appreciation towards it come out in every word of his conversation. The laurels of victory were not his but in every other respect he was a conqueror!

Royal correspondent: King George V

"Therefore I die happy"

After four draws in 1926, a product of three-day matches and poor weather, the final Test at The Oval was to be played to a finish. Wilfred Rhodes was recalled in his 49th year, a young Harold Larwood played his second Test and **Plum Warner** rejoices

At five minutes past six on the evening of Wednesday, August 18, at Kennington Oval, Geary bowled down Mailey's wicket and after many long years of waiting and disappointment English cricket came into its own again.

As soon as it was realised that England had won the vast crowd gave a yell of delight and swarmed in front of the pavilion, a huge mass which extended right back to the pitch itself. There they stayed for half an hour, shouting themselves hoarse.

First Chapman, the young English captain, who had led his side so ably to victory, came on to the balcony to be acclaimed like a very Caesar. Then Collins, the Australian captain, and Chapman appeared together, and later came Hobbs and Sutcliffe, *par nobile fratrum*, who laid the foundation of our victory, Strudwick – and what Surrey cricketer was ever more popular than he? – and finally the whole of the England Eleven appeared to the accompaniment of such cheering as I have never heard.

And the crowd unmistakably interpreted what all those who take an interest in English cricket and who are concerned for its welfare feel, and that is that the tide of misfortune has turned at last, and the turn of the tide is welcomed with fervent enthusiasm.

This victory means everything to English cricket. Had we been beaten, despondency would have crept over the land. As it is, our cricket will be fortified and refreshed by this great victory. And I should like to say here that the Australians, like the good sportsmen and fine cricketers they are, were the first to congratulate us in the happiest and most spontaneous manner. Generous winners, they are also generous losers, as befits cricketers who have earned an imperishable reputation as splendid fighters. But for once they did not fight with that doggedness and persistence which have inspired so wholesome a respect in the minds of their adversaries ever since they first came to this country.

Everything came off for England. Every change of bowling on the part of Chapman was successful and a tribute to his leadership; every catch was caught. The Australians lost the match on Tuesday, and Hobbs and Sutcliffe won it for us by their incomparable batting. That first-wicket stand of our famous pair of 172 made victory almost a certainty for us. Had either of them failed, we might well have been out for a total of 180 or 200.

That they did not fail us at a time of most desperate crisis was only in keeping with their reputation. Never has English

Larwood, 21, catches Ponsford off Rhodes, 48

Ashes dashes: spontaneous charge at The Oval

cricket known a more dauntless pair: the greater the task the greater their endeavour. A glance at the score-sheet will show what they accomplished.

And there came from Yorkshire, somewhat against his will, one who had made his reputation before three at least of the present England team were born, and he had a marked influence on the result.

There must have been many schoolboys at The Oval, and I hope they watched the great Rhodes carefully and noted his easy action, his length, his spin and, above all, his cleverness. Ulysses earned a world-wide reputation for his cunning and Rhodes is the Ulysses of modern cricket. His return to the English eleven was indeed a lucky stroke.

To Chapman all England will offer her warmest congratulations. He is the happy warrior of the cricket field and he led his side with spirit, with judgment and with imagination. The youngest member of the side, Larwood, of Notts, took six wickets in the match for 116 runs and fielded well. He should have a big future before him but he must guard against bowling just short of a length.

August 18, 1926, was a great day for English cricket – a landmark, I venture to think, in our cricket history, and if I may be allowed to say so, it brought joy to my heart. I believed in our men and my confidence in their ability to defeat a powerful and generous foe has never wavered. Therefore "I die happy". I had set my whole soul and heart on our beating the Australians this year and our success has been made 1,000 times more pleasant by the perfectly charming way in which our doughty opponents took their defeat. Maybe I have waxed sentimental but there can be no good cricket without sentiment, a quality which enriches life and refines it and gives it zest. ◼ *The Cricketer, August 28, 1926*

One man dominated Ashes battles for the next two decades. Sir Donald Bradman was a statistical freak, twice as good as any of his contemporaries, a batsman of such genius that it was headline news when he did not score runs. One England captain devised such controversial tactics to thwart him that Anglo-Australian diplomatic relations came under threat. He is unequivocally regarded as the best ever. His greatness over-shadowed the greatness of others – Hammond for England, Morris, McCabe, Woodfull for Australia – and his success shaped and adorned the Ashes before and after the Second World War

Slow off the mark

Bradman's Test debut was so modest he was dropped. He was soon back but England ruled and Hammond scored what became 'Bradmanesque' runs. 'Second Slip' reports

ON LEAVING England our side were proclaimed as the best batting side we had sent but by the end of the tour everyone was talking about the length of our tail. Chiefly through Hammond, Hendren, Jardine, Hobbs and Sutcliffe we have done well, and others have taken their part from time to time, but this team will be remembered for Hammond's batting. In Test matches he beat the record aggregate, held since 1911 by GA Faulkner, who, in his five matches, scored 732 runs. That young South African's performance was thought at that time to be phenomenal; indeed, it was but all records are made to be broken. This young Gloucestershire batsman has shown that, for the time being, he is the best in the world. *Vixere fortes ante Agamemnona** goes the saying. What Hammond is now others have been. WG Grace was in the same position at the age of 20; others, too, when under 25. Given good health there appears to be no reason why the present champion should not carry on for another 20 years. The veteran Hobbs and his old partner have fully carried their weight, particularly in the third Test, when the wicket was tricky. They did the same thing at The Oval, it will be remembered, in the famous match when Chapman won his first victory. Then they were on their own midden but in this case the performance stands out better, for not only the wicket but also the great heat was against them. Sutcliffe's 135, at Melbourne, and Hobbs's batting in the last Test found these two great players at their best. In Jardine the captain had to hand a clever, improved batsman with that temperament which is so necessary for these contests.

It was our better bowling, backed up by brilliant fielding and wicketkeeping, that

Best bat: Wally Hammond (905 runs, aged 25 to Bradman's 20) just had time to claim the label

won us our matches. When Staples broke down, the side was robbed of a length bowler but White has proved one of the most useful bowlers we have had. Larwood and Tate did their part well, the former being very deadly. At Brisbane, in the first Test, when two batsmen got set, on came White to hold the fort. His feats of endurance were extraordinary for a man of his age. His accuracy was abnormal; he was seldom, if ever, collared. Geary, the fourth bowler, was hampered by early mishaps but he was always very useful. Much praise should be given to these four bowlers, who did much to win the matches.

They were backed up in the field. Duckworth was declared by many eminent Australian critics to be the equal of any wicketkeeper. [Australia's] WA Oldfield has long been held to be the best in cricket; from the results of this tour he would seem to have a rival. A good wicketkeeper makes for much; a magnificent wicketkeeper is worth his weight in gold. Chapman, disappointing as a batsman, was a most admirable captain, "one of the best England has ever had," according to MA Noble**.

There was much slow play; about 220 runs a day seemed to be the average. Long-drawn-out matches of this nature will not be welcomed in England. It is known,

❝One has heard of so many, many second Trumpers that one may have become rather sceptical❞

of course, that the hours of play are shorter out there, but play was unduly cautious. There must have been a great amount of attack on the leg side. Our opponents have always desired to play the matches out but these seven-day games are not conductive to the gaiety of nations.

When the Australians come here in 1930 they should have a very fine batting side. It is natural that all will want to see the two youngsters, Bradman and Jackson. One has heard of so many, many second Trumpers that one may have become rather sceptical, yet the play of both these batsmen has been such as to show them well worth their places for the next tour. ▣ *The Cricketer, Spring Annual, 1929*

*Brave men lived before Agamemnon
**Australian allrounder of repute who played through the Golden Age

---

The greatest win

Bradman's first Test was famous for Patsy Hendren's batting and England's margin of victory (still the heaviest in runs between any countries). The Don-to-be gets no mention

The pitch was more heavily grassed than are the wickets at Sydney, Melbourne and Adelaide, and its surface had a green tinge unlike the dun-coloured wickets of the other States.

After the opening day's play, when England scored 272 for 5, Australia were outplayed and eventually suffered defeat by 675 runs . They were unfortunate in losing Gregory and Kelleway after the close of the second day but England had established an almost impregnable position before these two players were out of the game. Gregory strained his knee and Kelleway had an attack of ptomaine poisoning* ...

The feature of England's first innings was the superb batting of Hendren. Joining Chapman when England had lost five wickets for 217, Hendren batted confidently from the start. He gave no chance. He was always complete master of the bowling and hit 16 fours ...

Larwood bowled at a tremendous pace in Australia's first innings, both he and Tate being assisted by a slight breeze, which blew from short leg to the batsman. Woodfull was out to the fourth ball of Larwood's first over to a magnificent catch in the slips and Ponsford was yorked in his third. Australia never recovered ...

England scored slowly early in their second innings but the batting was consistent. Heavy overnight rain, then hot sunshine made the wicket extremely treacherous on the last day, when seven wickets fell for 49 runs, but England deserve every credit for taking full advantage of the conditions and White returned a remarkable analysis (6.3-2-7-4) ...

Chapman's captaincy earned high praise and his decision not to enforce the follow-on was the right one. This was the first time a declaration has been made in a play-to-a-finish Test and the first time a Test had been played at Brisbane. The attendance of 75,000 was disappointing.
The Cricketer, Spring Annual, 1929

*Food poisoning, erroneously believed to be the result of ptomaine (a bacteria) ingestion. Not in scientific use now.

1st Test, Brisbane, Nov 30-Dec 5 1928
England won by 675 runs

ENGLAND WON TOSS

JB Hobbs	run out		49	lbw	b Grimmett	11
H Sutcliffe	c Ponsford	b Gregory	38	c sub	b Ironmon'r	32
CP Mead	lbw	b Grimmett	8	lbw	b Grimmett	73
WR Hammond	c Woodfull	b Gregory	44	c sub	b Ironmon'r	28
DR Jardine	c Woodfull	b Ironmon'r	35	not out		65
EH Hendren	c Ponsford	b Ironmon'r	169	c Ponsford	b Grimmett	45
APF Chapman*	c Kelleway	b Gregory	50	c Oldfield	b Grimmett	27
MW Tate	c Ryder	b Grimmett	26	c Bradman	b Grimmett	20
H Larwood	lbw	b Hendry	70	c Ponsford	b Grimmett	37
JC White	lbw	b Grimmett	14			-
G Duckworth†	not out		5			-
Extras	lb10 nb3		13	lb3 nb1		4
Total	175.3 overs		521	135.1 overs		342-8d

Fall of wickets 85 95 108 161 217
291 319 443 495

25 69 117 165 228
263 285 342

Bowling (1st) **Gregory** 41-3-142-3, **Kelleway** 34-9-77-0, **Grimmett** 40-2-167-3, **Ironmonger** 44.3-18-79-2, **Ryder** 6-2-23-0, **Hendry** 10-1-20-1
(2nd) **Grimmett** 44.1-9-131-6, **Ironmonger** 50-20-85-2, **Ryder** 14-3-43-0, **Hendry** 27-6-79-0

AUSTRALIA

WM Woodfull	c Chapman	b Larwood	0	not out		30
WH Ponsford		b Larwood	2	c Duckworth	b Larwood	6
AF Kippax	c and	b Tate	16	c and	b Larwood	15
HSTL Hendry	lbw	b Larwood	30	c Larwood	b White	6
C Kelleway		b Larwood	8	absent hurt		-
J Ryder*	c Jardine	b Larwood	33 (5)	c Larwood	b Tate	1
DG Bradman	lbw	b Tate	18 (6)	c Chapman	b White	1
WAS Oldfield†	lbw	b Tate	2 (7)	c Larwood	b Tate	5
CV Grimmett	not out		7 (8)	c Chapman	b White	1
H Ironmonger		b Larwood	4 (9)	c Chapman	b White	0
JM Gregory	absent hurt		-	absent hurt		-
Extras	b1 lb1		2	nb1		1
Total	50.4 overs		122	25.3 overs		66

Fall of wickets 0 7 24 40 71
101 105 116 122

6 33 46 47 49
62 66 66

Bowling (1st) **Larwood** 14.4-4-32-6, **Tate** 21-6-50-3, **Hammond** 15-5-38-0
(2nd) **Larwood** 7-0-30-2, **Tate** 11-3-26-2, **Hammond** 1-0-2-0, **White** 6.3-2-7-4

England lead the five-Test series 1-0
Umpires DA Elder and GA Hele Test debuts DG Bradman, H Ironmonger (Aus)

Blazering a trail: England's tourists: (back row, l-r) Duckworth, Ames, Mead, Tate, Hendren, Geary; (middle) Leyland, Staples, Hammond, manager Sir Frederick Toone, Sutcliffe, Larwood, Freeman; (front) Tyldesley, White, Chapman, Jardine, Hobbs

Australia's way forward

After their 4-1 defeat the Australian selectors were advised to think young, starting with Bradman. The advice comes from '**Third Man**, our special correspondent in Australia'

To restore her fallen cricket fortunes Australia must invest in young players of the right type. Such an investment has proved to be a profitable business for England and the Ashes have been a handsome dividend. With the rubber lost on the third Test, Australia had a great opportunity to give promising youths experience in the Test atmosphere. Rarely do England or Australia have two successive Tests in their own territory with nothing "hanging to" the result ...

The outstanding couple are D Bradman and A Jackson. Some were inclined to smile when I named D Bradman in *The Cricketer* last year as a strong possibility for the Australian Eleven but this season he scored so well that he forced his way into the team. Strangely dropped from the second Test, he signalised his return to the third Test with 79 and 112. Although Bradman played in the country until 1926, there is no suspicion of a rural touch about his batting. Footwork, and plenty of it, is the basis of his style and he is what one might term a common-sense batsman. He is 20 years old, of short, strong build, and is developing into one of Australia's best outfields. He knows the value of getting his feet near his bat when making strokes and leaves his crease fearlessly to spoil the length of the bowling. Bradman shows no trace of nervousness at the beginning of his innings and bats on, unperturbed, when wickets are falling. [He scored] 1,000 runs in a season of first-class cricket in Australia – to do this and get into the Australian XI in his second year in first-class cricket is an astonishing performance ...

Another 20-year-old New South Welshman, whom I consider to be little, if any, inferior to Bradman, is A Jackson, who played for his State when only 17. Jackson's batting is effortless and stylish. No fault can be found with his footwork when he is shaping to play the ball but I think he is inclined to over-do the effortless business at times and should put more weight behind his bat. His leg glance takes the eye, because he makes it with his body erect and the ball flashes away as he flicks the bat with deft wristwork. Nearly all his big scores for New South Wales have been made in the second innings, when his side needed runs. When 19 he scored two centuries in one match against South Australia.

The Cricketer, Spring Annual, 1929

The other one: Archie Jackson, 164 on debut

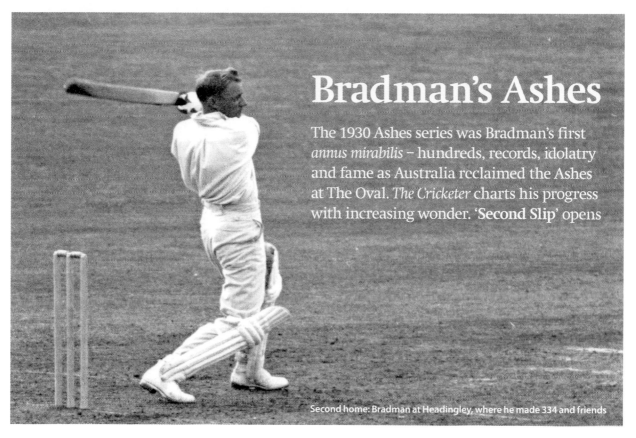

Bradman's Ashes

The 1930 Ashes series was Bradman's first *annus mirabilis* – hundreds, records, idolatry and fame as Australia reclaimed the Ashes at The Oval. *The Cricketer* charts his progress with increasing wonder. '**Second Slip**' opens

Second home: Bradman at Headingley, where he made 334 and friends

Together with all the English cricketing public I wish to extend a hearty welcome to the Australian side that has already begun its programme. I have seen various Australian teams since 1878 and played against several but never have I known such interest taken in their doings as is the case this year. "Have you seen them?" "What do you think of them?" are the questions with which one is assailed by all in train, tram or bus. It is the subject of the moment; it will endure for the summer; it will recur as long as these contests are in being. *The Cricketer*, May 3, 1930

Bradman makes history

On Saturday last, May 31, DG Bradman in the game with Hampshire at Southampton, completed a four-figure aggregate. Never before has an Australian reached so large a total so early in an English season. When Hampshire went in first, upon winning the toss, it seemed likely that he would not perform the feat but he just managed it off the last ball of the day in heavy rain. In order to give him a chance of thus making history, he had been sent in to open the innings. His large aggregate was made thus: v Worcestershire 236; v Leicestershire 185*; v Yorkshire 78; v Lancashire 9 and 48*; v MCC 66 and 4; v Derbyshire 44; v Surrey 252*; v Oxford University 32; v Hampshire 47*. *The Cricketer*, June 7, 1930

The first Test and despite Bradman's hundred England win – it was to be the host's high point of the season

1st Test June 13-17, Trent Bridge Eng 270 (JB Hobbs 78, APF Chapman 52, RWV Robins 50*; CV Grimmett 5-107) and **302** (Hobbs 74, EH Hendren 72; Grimmett 5-94); **Aus 144** (AF Kippax 64*; Robins 4-51) and **335** (DG Bradman 131, SJ McCabe 49). **Eng won by 93 runs.**

When Robins had Hornibrook caught at the wicket, Chapman had led England to victory over Australia for the sixth successive time. In a game in which so many did well it is almost invidious to mention individuals but no praise can be too high for the magnificent way Tate stuck to his work. What more can be said than that he bowled in his best form ... Hobbs's two great innings, Bradman's 100, Robins's successful debut, Kippax's beautiful 64 not out, Hendren's excellent 72, McCabe's confidence at a crisis, Richardson's gallant hitting and Hammond's slip catches were some of the chief features of this historic match ... Chapman could hardly have had a better game. He played two extremely valuable innings, in trying circumstances he kept up the spirits of his men, and managed his bowling with fine judgement. His fielding was as great as ever. *The Cricketer*, June 21, 1930 ▷

Forcing game: Bradman at Trent Bridge, where he introduced himself with a mere century

Lord's men: Maurice Tate and Percy Chapman

"Impossible to imagine greater batting"

It is short-lived joy at Trent Bridge as Australia's true talent comes bounding into view in an extraordinary run-glut at Lord's, which includes one of Bradman's greatest innings. And England scored 405 on the first day ...

2nd Test June 27-28, 30, July 1, Lord's **Eng 425** (KS Duleepsinhji 173, MW Tate 54; AG Fairfax 4-101) and **375** (Chapman 121, GOB Allen 57; Grimmett 6-167); **Aus 729-6 dec** (Bradman 254, WM Woodfull 155, Kippax 83, WH Ponsford 81) and **72-3. Aus won by 7 wkts.**

The [second] day's play was a complete triumph for Australia. White and Duckworth carried the England total to 425 and then from 11.35am till 6.30pm Australia scored 404 for the loss of only two wickets, in gloriously fine weather before a crowd of over 31,000.

Woodfull and Ponsford began with an opening partnership of 162, the latter falling to the first over when the game was resumed after both teams had been presented to the King, who was accompanied by Sir Kynaston Studd, the President of the MCC, in front of the pavilion. Ponsford played finely, hitting every ball in the middle of his bat, and so faultlessly did he and Woodfull play that only twice during their partnership was the ball hit in the air.

Bradman began in wonderful form and made his first 50 in an hour. Extraordinarily quick on his feet, he did what he liked with such an accurate bowler as White and never once lifted the ball. He made every possible stroke and at the end of the day had equalled Woodfull's score ...

Chapman's fielding was magnificent and he set an example which was keenly followed, but under difficult and trying circumstances many considered that the field might have been differently placed and that the bowlers should have been used more at different ends ...

On the [third day] in very hot weather and before another very large crowd Australia went further ahead. During the day two records were broken, Bradman carrying his score of 155 not out to 254, which is the largest individual score ever made in a Test match in this country, while the Australian total of 729 for 6 is the highest aggregate ever made in matches between England and Australia.

It was nearly 3pm before a magnificent catch at cover by Chapman, who held a hard hit at the extreme width of his right hand, got rid of Bradman. *It was the first time during his innings that the young New South Welshman had lifted the ball off the ground* during his stay of five hours and 20 minutes. He hit 25 fours. It would be impossible to over-praise Bradman's wonderful cricket. He is a player of genius and his astounding quickness of foot appears to enable him to dictate the length to the bowler. *The Cricketer, July 5, 1930*

The batting records did not last; Bradman begins his love-affair with Headingley, making the highest Test score and scoring a hundred in each session of the first day. Rain and pragmatism save England

3rd Test July 11-12, 14-15, Headingley **Aus 566** (Bradman 334, Kippax 77, Woodfull 50, Tate 5-124); **Eng 391** (WR Hammond 113, Chapman 45; Grimmett 5-135) and **95-3. Match drawn.**

With the breeze behind him Larwood bowled very fast and Tate and Geary were accurate, yet in 45 minutes Bradman, who had joined Woodfull, made 50 out of 61 by brilliant cricket and, when the hundred went up after 80 minutes, he had made 81 and Woodfull 17. A hit to square leg for four off Larwood gave Bradman a wonderful 100 amid great cheering, the score at lunch time being 136 for 1 – Bradman 105, Woodfull 29 ...

At 194 Woodfull was clean bowled in trying to force a good length ball past mid-on. After lunch Hammond and Geary had kept a good length and the rate of run-getting dropped but, with the new ball, Larwood and Tate came on again, and the batsmen made runs more freely. Leyland bowled at 254, but Bradman scored readily off his first over, which contained four full pitches. Shortly after he had passed his 200 Bradman made his first poor stroke, mis-hitting a ball from Tyldesley just out of Tate's reach at mid-on.

Hats on ... but a hero's welcome for Bradman returning to Headingley's pavilion after his 334

Bodyline in waiting: Douglas Jardine

Bradman continued to dominate the situation and at two minutes past six he beat R.E. Foster's record score of 287, made at Sydney in 1903. Foster's innings lasted seven hours and 20 minutes; Bradman's only five hours and a half. Bradman reached 300 and when stumps were drawn for the day the score stood at 458 for 3: Bradman 309*.

Bradman's magnificent innings came to an end on the second day, Duckworth making a splendid catch at the wicket. He

> 66 His timing was so perfect and his quickness of foot so supreme that he appeared to be able to force any ball 99

batted altogether for six hours and 20 minutes, gave but one chance – when 273 at the wicket off Geary – and hit 46 fours. It was an incomparable innings – he actually made 334 out of 506. His timing was so perfect and his quickness of foot so supreme that he appeared to be able to force any ball. He never seemed in any hurry, yet runs simply flowed from his bat, so perfect was his stroke play. It is impossible to imagine greater batting.

The Cricketer, July 19, 1930

Mainly Bradman
By mid-season Bradman's legend was assured – and he was not finished. *The Cricketer*'s 'Second Slip' knew history was being made

The season of 1930 may well be written down as the *annus mirabilis* of cricket, mainly due to Bradman. This astonishing player, not quite 22, has demonstrated again that records are made to be broken. Beginning at Worcester with 236 he followed with 185 not out. We then come to his 252 not out against Surrey and 191 against Hampshire, which took his aggregate past 1,000 runs in May, being the first Australian to do so. It had been hoped he might not do so well against the picked bowling of England but he has plainly shown us that the best we can produce is good enough for him – to score off.

Against us at Nottingham he took 131, and, of course, no one has forgotten his 254 at Lord's. Then comes his splendid performance at Leeds, where he showed us no mercy. In the first three matches alone he has beaten all previous records of his compatriots for the whole series. Probably the feature of his play is that he never hits the ball into the air when driving – the long hop may be occasionally hit off the ground but as often as not he keeps it on the floor. When one considers the circumstances, that he is a stranger to all the different surroundings of our many grounds, that he has never before played on our wickets, that he ran into such a May as may fitly be described as abominable, we cannot but the more wonder. He has given certainly an added interest to the game, for no self-respecting

follower of cricket will be satisfied until he has seen him at least once. *Vivat Bradman. The Cricketer*, July 19, 1930

The fourth Test was a rain-affected draw in Manchester – and Bradman gives the England bowlers some respite. But his form returns, almost inevitably, as Australia smash England at The Oval. The journey for this young Australian side that started in Brisbane 1928-29 with a 675-run defeat had ended with them gloriously claiming the Ashes in 1930 and Bradman hitting 974 runs at 139.14

4th Test July 25-29, **Old Trafford Aus 345** (Ponsford 83, Woodfull 54, Kippax 51, Grimmett 50); **Eng 251-8** (H Sutcliffe 74, Duleepsinhji 54; McCabe 4-41). **Match drawn.**

5th Test August 16-22, The Oval **Eng 405** (Sutcliffe 161, RES Wyatt 64, Duleepsinhji 50, Hobbs 47; Grimmett 4-135) and **251** (Hammond 60, Sutcliffe 54, Duleepsinhji 46; PM Hornibrook 7-92); **Aus 695** (Bradman 232, Ponsford 110, AA Jackson 73, Woodfull 54, McCabe 54, Fairfax 53*; IAR Peebles 6-204). **Aus won by an innings and 39 runs.**

As to the batting of Bradman and Jackson, it was magnificent. Jackson was far more himself than previously and one saw something of the style and grace that have caused him to be compared, in some measure in Australia, to Trumper. 🇦

The Bodyline Series

It was to become the most antagonistic series of all time and it still resonates today – Douglas Jardine, the public-school educated symbol of the old British Empire, devised brutal tactics to thwart Don Bradman's run-scoring. A battery of quicks led by Harold Larwood bowled very fast and at the body – Australia watched aghast – and lost the Ashes. '**Second Slip**' writes in ignorant anticipation of what was to follow

Bon voyage! Cricketers all over the world will, in a few weeks, be buying early editions of the different papers to see what is happening in Australia. Never before has interest been taken in a team to a greater extent than is the case with the side led by DR Jardine. During the whole of the past season the chances of the different players have been discussed – and there are few abodes in this country where the game has no followers – in every tram, railway carriage, bus or public house. During all this time the selectors have gone about their work, endeavouring to get the best team, advised by all and probably listening to none. The result is that their work has been almost universally applauded by those who understand the game. As we know, the team consists of five amateurs and 11 professionals. None of the amateurs from the great counties of Yorkshire, Lancashire and Nottinghamshire have gained a place ...

The work of the selectors was, in the first place, to choose a captain. They unanimously selected DR Jardine. The new leader has had a fine career as a batsman. He has played much for Surrey since his university days; has been always one of the first choices for the Gentlemen at Lord's and usually in the first half dozen of the end-of-season batting averages. He was captain of England last year in the matches against New Zealand and this year in the Test match against All-India, and he has had further experience in leading Surrey this season. No other man could have been chosen for what is the most important post in the English cricket world.

The Cricketer, September 17, 1932

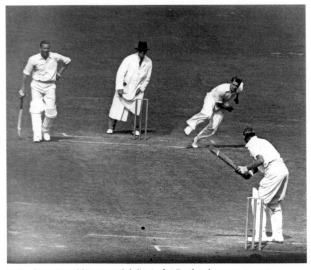
Firing line: Harold Larwood delivers for England

Gentleman first: Douglas Jardine leads out England at Melbourne

Tactics talk

Letter writers were in full voice about the team and tactics – some missing the mark.

Sir, Someone writing in the press said that WE Bowes had taken more of the first five batsmen than Larwood. The figures actually are:

Bowes 110 out of 190 – 57.89%
Larwood 95 out of 162 – 58.60%
In other words they are equal. The difference is of no statistical significance. Bowes will win the Ashes for us, his good-length balls will rear on the hard wickets which Larwood cannot manage owing to his height. Best wishes to your paper.
GWTH Fleming Medical Superintendent, County and City Mental Hospital, Burghill
The Cricketer Annual, 1932

Credit to Jardine
Has Jardine been given enough credit for the success of the MCC tour in Australia? I think he has been marvellous. Has anyone stressed the fact that the methods of Larwood and Voce were well known to the committee who selected them and that they were picked because of those successful methods. Was Jardine supposed to alter those methods, even if they are considered wrong, which is much open to question?
BH Hill
The Cricketer, May 6, 1933

A sensational opening Test: Bradman was not fit, Larwood terrified and Stan McCabe played an all-time great innings. But normal service is resumed on a slow, carefully prepared, Melbourne wicket. Bradman is out first ball to Bowes in the first innings but makes no mistake in the second

1st Test Dec 2-7, Sydney †**Aus 360** (SJ McCabe 187*, VY Richardson 49; H Larwood 5-96, W Voce 4-110) and **164** (Larwood 5-28); **Eng 524** (H Sutcliffe 194, WR Hammond 112, Nawab of Pataudi 102) and **1-0. Eng won by 10 wkts.**

Although Bradman had revealed dazzling form in an interstate match, his six innings against English bowling had been 3, 10, 36, 13, 18 and 23. It was obvious that, against the fast legside attack, he lacked his normal confidence. Bradman seemed jaded mentally – a condition to which a contributing factor was the stress of efforts to have his press contract sanctioned by the Board of Control. The result was that two doctors, who examined him on the eve of the Test, pronounced him not in a fit condition to play, although organically sound ...

Magnificent bowling by Larwood, who dominated the attack, put England on top early. Several Australian batsmen wore chest-pads as well as thigh-pads, and there was an outcry about leg tactics, although J Worrall, the former international, who is probably the soundest critic in Australia, wrote: "Larwood opened with an orthodox field and, although later this was changed and he bowled outside the leg stump, it was legitimate fast bowling. Voce's half-pitched slingers on the body-line provided about the poorest attempt at what should be Test bowling it is possible to conceive." ... McCabe by "death or glory" methods scored with delightful freedom and hit up 60 in less than an hour before the innings closed. Wall's share of the last-wicket stand of 55 was only 4 ... Australia's steady and persistent bowling contained nothing approaching the dynamic influence of a Larwood.

The Cricketer Spring Annual 1933

2nd Test, Dec 30-Jan 3, Melbourne **Aus 228** (JHW Fingleton 83) and **191** (DG Bradman 103*); **Eng 169** (Sutcliffe 52; WJ O'Reilly 5-63, TW Wall 4-52) and **139** (O'Reilly 5-66, H Ironmonger 4-26). **Aus won by 111 runs.**

The outstanding bowler was O'Reilly, who mingled legbreaks, "wrong-uns" and over-spinners. Varying his pace and making the ball come off at different heights, O'Reilly earned his wickets. In a batsman-like contribution Allen provided a contrast to the rest. Apart from him and Hammond, all the batsmen played almost entirely on the back foot. Those who had doubted whether Allen was quite up to Test standard were satisfied by his all-round cricket in this game in which he was the best of England's fast bowlers ... The England bowlers fought back splendidly on the third day and at the close of play appeared to have put their side in a favourable position. Australia's only consolation in a second innings of 191 was an impressive "comeback" by Bradman, who scored 103 not out in three hours while eight wickets fell at the other end. This was a different Bradman – not the dasher with audacious strokes but a batsman fighting grimly to save his side from collapse and to regain his own confidence and certainty. Viewed from every angle of batsmanship, this innings must be ranked for merit as probably the greatest Bradman has played. Frequently the best bowler does not have the best figures but Hammond's ability to spin the ball made him the most difficult of the English to attack ... England's sudden collapse came as a shock. Sending the ball into a good breeze, O'Reilly gained in flight and turn by slackening his pace ... The tenseness of the struggle throughout was a gruelling test of the captaincy of the two leaders. *The Cricketer* Spring Annual 1933 ▷

Free-scorer: McCabe

Dynamic: Larwood

Bowes arrow: Bradman is out first ball, his first Test duck, at Melbourne

On business: Bradman comes to stay

Bodyline comes to a head. The Australian public has their hero back and does not want to see the old enemy reclaim supremacy – especially not with what they view as unfair tactics. Adelaide, usually sedate, comes to the brink of riot as Jardine employs his leg-theory. Takings for the Tests break all records

Both sides made changes from the second Test match, Paynter and Verity replacing the Nawab of Pataudi and Bowes in the England XI, while Australia brought in Ponsford to the exclusion of O'Brien, who acted as 12th man.

The match began in perfect weather and, although there had been some rain the day before play started, the wicket appeared to be in perfect condition when England began batting, Jardine having beaten Woodfull in the toss, but it was quickly apparent that the ball was kicking. England could not have made a more disastrous start. With the total only 4, Jardine missed a well-pitched-up ball from Wall and had his leg stump hit. At 16 Hammond was well caught by Oldfield without settling down and then, after batting 45 minutes for 9, Sutcliffe was brilliantly caught by Wall at forward short leg. Ames played with the utmost caution but was beaten by Ironmonger's fast ball and lunch was taken with the score at 37 for 4 – a desperate position for England.

But Leyland, Paynter and Wyatt fight back to post a better-than-par 341

Larwood and Allen opened the England attack. The former had three slips, gully, short and long legs but no mid-off. Allen's field was orthodox. Off the Middlesex man's third ball Fingleton was caught and off the last ball of Larwood's second over Woodfull received a nasty blow over the heart

which set the crowd roaring at the bowler. Bradman began most confidently and then fell into the leg trap. McCabe, too, was caught on the leg side. Hammond might possibly have caught Ponsford off a very difficult chance when the batsman was 3 but the old partnership of Woodfull-Ponsford was not destined to produce a big stand, the Australian captain playing on at 51 to a ball from Allen which kept low. The score at the close of the second day was Australia 109 for 4.

On the third day Larwood and Allen began the bowling, the former having Allen at silly leg, Verity deep fine leg, Jardine short leg, Sutcliffe fine leg and Hammond out deep. Ponsford batted in his very best form and during a stay of just over three and a half hours hit eight boundaries. Grimmett fell to a magnificent catch by Voce in the slips and then, with the score at 217 for 7, Oldfield was hit by a ball from Larwood. The bowler could not be blamed for the accident but, when O'Reilly took Oldfield's place, the crowd booed every time Larwood bowled. O'Reilly made no show against the Nottingham fast bowler and, when Hammond bowled Wall, tea was taken as Oldfield could not resume his innings ...

England pile on the runs and Larwood and Allen run through Australia – only Bradman (66) and Woodfull, who carries his bat for 73, offering resistance. Oldfield did not bat in the second innings

In gaining such an easy win England accomplished a remarkable performance for at lunchtime on the first day they had four men out for 37 runs. Seldom, if ever, has a Test match been played under such unpleasant conditions. Two days before the match started the crowds, watching the Englishmen practising at the nets, made such a dead set at the players, especially

3rd Test, Adelaide, Jan 13-19 1933
England won by 338 runs

ENGLAND	WON TOSS						
H Sutcliffe	c Wall	b O'Reilly	9	c sub‡		b Wall	7
DR Jardine*		b Wall	3	lbw		b Ironmon'r	56
WR Hammond	c Oldfield	b Wall	2	(5)		b Bradman	85
LEG Ames†		b Ironmonger	3	(7)		b O'Reilly	69
M Leyland		b O'Reilly	83	(6)	c Wall	b Ironmon'r	42
RES Wyatt	c Richardson	b Grimmett	78	(3)	c Wall	b O'Reilly	49
E Paynter	c Fingleton	b Wall	77	(10)	not out		1
GOB Allen	lbw	b Grimmett	15	(4)	lbw		15
H Verity	c Richardson	b Wall	45	(8)	lbw	b O'Reilly	40
W Voce		b Wall	8	(11)		b O'Reilly	8
H Larwood	not out		3	(9)	c Bradman	b Ironmon'r	8
Extras	b1 lb7 nb7		15		b17 lb11 nb4		32
Total	146.1 overs		341		191.3 overs		412
					‡sub LPJ O'Brien		

Fall of wickets 4 16 16 30 186
196 228 324 336

7 91 123 154 245
296 394 395 403

Bowling (1st) Wall 34.1-10-72-5, O'Reilly 50-19-82-2, Ironmonger 20-6-50-1, Grimmett 28-6-94-2, McCabe 14-3-28-0

(2nd) Wall 29-6-75-1, O'Reilly 50.3-21-79-4, Ironmonger 57-21-87-3, Grimmett 35-9-74-1, McCabe 16-0-42-0, Bradman 4-0-23-1

AUSTRALIA							
JHW Fingleton	c Ames	b Allen	0			b Larwood	0
WM Woodfull*		b Allen	22	not out			73
DG Bradman	c Allen	b Larwood	8	(4)	c and	b Verity	66
SJ McCabe	c Jardine	b Larwood	8	(5)	c Leyland	b Allen	7
WH Ponsford		b Voce	85	(3)	c Jardine	b Larwood	3
VY Richardson		b Allen	28		c Allen	b Larwood	21
WAS Oldfield†	retired hurt		41	absent hurt			-
CV Grimmett	c Voce	b Allen	10	(7)		b Allen	6
TW Wall		b Hammond	6	(8)		b Allen	0
WJ O'Reilly		b Larwood	0	(9)		b Larwood	5
H Ironmonger	not out		0	(10)		b Allen	0
Extras	b2 lb11 nb1		14		b4 lb2 w1 nb5		12
Total	95.4 overs		222		69.2 overs		193

Fall of wickets 1 18 34 51 131
194 212 222* 222

3 12 100 116 171
183 183 192 193

Bowling (1st) Larwood 25-6-55-3, Allen 23-4-71-4, Hammond 17.4-4-30-1, Voce 14-5-21-1, Verity 16-7-31-0

(2nd) Larwood 19-3-71-4, Allen 17.2-5-50-4, Hammond 9-3-27-0, Voce 4-1-7-0, Verity 20-12-26-1

Series England lead the 5-match series 2-1 Umpires GE Borwick and GA Hele

Eight-wicket innocence: Gubby Allen

Jardine, that they had to be excluded from subsequent practice. There was a tremendous uproar when Woodfull was unfortunately struck over the heart, and the Australian captain's refusal to talk to [England manager] PF Warner*, who had gone to the dressing room to sympathise with him, on the grounds that the England team were not playing cricket in the proper spirit owing to the employment of the leg-theory, only added fuel to the fire. Subsequently PF Warner stated that the incident between himself and Woodfull had been amicably settled by Woodfull apologising to him. Woodfull, however, denied the apology but pointed out that it was not a personal affair with Warner but his disapproval of the methods of the English bowlers. Every time Larwood set his field for the leg-theory the crowd created a scene. There was a further uproar when Oldfield was struck by Larwood but the Australian wicketkeeper quickly let it be known that the bowler was in no way to blame. *The Cricketer*, Spring Annual, 1933

*PF Warner was also editor of *The Cricketer*

England maintain their tactics at Brisbane and reclaim the Ashes, Larwood taking another seven wickets in the match including Bradman twice

4th Test February 10 16 1933, Brisbane †Aus 340 (Richardson 83, Bradman 76, WM Woodfull 67, Larwood 4-101) and **175; Eng 356** (Sutcliffe 86, E Paynter 83, DR Jardine 46, O'Reilly 4-120) and **162-4** (M Leyland 86). **Eng won by 6 wickets.**

England made one change from the side successful at Adelaide, Mitchell taking the place of Voce. Australia had Love in place of Oldfield, who was forbidden to play by his medical advisers. For the third time in four matches Woodfull beat Jardine in the toss and the

Englishmen went out to field in sweltering heat. For the first time during the series Australia made a good start, the first wicket not falling until 133. The wicket appeared to be perfect when Larwood and Allen opened the bowling for England. Jardine made numerous bowling changes and continually altered his field. With Bradman in, he put Larwood on and set a leg field and the batsman was undoubtedly uncomfortable but he managed to survive. Bradman had found his form, some of his driving being magnificent, and when stumps were drawn his score stood at 71.

Bedrock: Eddie Paynter to the rescue

Strike bowler: Larwood steps up

England fought back in great style and on this day Australia lost much of their initial advantage. Larwood began with his leg-theory and by clean bowling Bradman and Ponsford in one over. Bradman, who hit 11 fours, was out trying to cut a ball on the leg stump, while Ponsford went too far over and made no attempt to play the ball that hit his leg stump ... The attendance of 29,572 was a record for Brisbane. The crowd behaved extremely well and paid generous tribute to Larwood's fine bowling.

The bowlers turn the game round, Paynter drags himself from his sick bed (tonsillitis, temperature 102) to rescue England from 216 for 6, Australia then set 160 for England to win and, despite losing an early wicket, the visitors make it. Amid some desperate news they had won the Ashes

On the final day the players all wore black armlets as a mark of respect for the late Archie Jackson ... Paynter came in and made the winning hit by hooking McCabe for six ... At the final reception to both teams PF Warner expressed the MCC's grief at the death of Jackson who, he said, would have been another Victor Trumper. Then Mr Warner proposed the Australians' health and the MCC players cheered. WM Woodfull, the Australian captain, congratulated the English team but hoped that in 1934 the Australians would repeat their 1930 performance, when they won the Ashes. "Our defeat will only spur us on to do a little better next time," he said. The Australian team drank the health of the MCC players in champagne and gave them three hearty cheers. DR Jardine said: "I am naturally delighted that we have regained the Ashes but hope I can say with Kipling that cricketers can meet triumph and disaster and treat the two imposters in just the same way." *The Cricketer*, Spring Annual, 1933 ▷

Double loss

On the day Australia conceded the Ashes Archie Jackson died, aged 23.

The death from consumption of AA Jackson at the tragically early age of 23 was received with the utmost regret by cricketers all over the world. Given good health and ordinary luck, he should have been one of Australia's batting mainstays for years. Born in Scotland on September 5, 1909, he was taken to Sydney when very young and was only 17 when he made his debut for New South Wales. After five seasons in first class cricket his health broke down at the end of 1930–31 and he migrated to Queensland.
As a stylist he perhaps more closely approached Victor Trumper than any of the younger generation and he was always a delight to watch as his main object appeared to be the making of his runs in the most graceful way possible. When only 19 he made 164 in his first Test at Adelaide (4th Test) in 1928–29. In England in 1930 he was far below his best, the sad reason for which is now well known. In the final game at The Oval his 73 made the recovery of the Ashes possible.
The Cricketer, Spring Annual, 1933

Voice of Australia: The Hill at the SCG, where the series ended with the Ashes already lost

Enduring the Ashes down under: To follow what was happening in away series England fans relied on radio bulletins and newspapers. As England inched over the line at Brisbane to win the series RC Robertson-Glasgow describes the pain and pleasure of coping with the matches at home

The deed is done, "determined, dared and done," as some bat-brained bard remarked of something or other some time; but, oh, my hat, the strain! Oh, my everlasting and anointed hat! They say that Mr Warner couldn't bear to watch what he could have seen. What about those who were only just daring to hear what they couldn't see? It is our own fault, of course. We needn't listen; we should sleep on and wake at 8 o'clock and then have three mental rounds to decide whether to shave in ignorance and

bathe in supine indifference or ... take the beastly [radio] into the bathroom and soap the frame and lean back and imbibe [the reports] at 8.15 ... or, as in this Test, at 8.50 or 9.50, or never! We should really pull ourselves together. After all, my dear fellow, it's only a game of cricket ... a game, do you hear? Ah! But is it? Isn't it, to some of us, part of ourselves, flowing in the veins, beating with the heart, hammering with the brain? I said to myself last summer, when in the midst of some abandoned orgy, masquerading under the name of cricket, I said to my soul, "This, you goof, is the thing; this is ripe fun; this is what they did at Hambledon, thus did Lumpy Stevens quaff his firkin ... I resolved at that profane moment that, when the Tests came round again, I would treat them as they deserve ... important, of course, great stuff, famous names, endless sieges, headlines but only

cricket. If we win, I said inly, I shall temper my hilarity with a modicum of restraint and decorum; if we lose, I shall meet the news with the iota of fortitude required ... like a passing toothache ... and turn to the things that matter, the routine of the day. Vain and futile resolve! Ludicrous self-deception! The insane bluebottle may rest his buzzing bestialities on the window-pane but the cricket lover is hopeless; he is without control, reprieve. There is no real chance of amelioration for him today. He should have lived in olden times, a pre-cable paradise. Some wandering rumour might have strayed across continents and oceans, much as, in the days of chivalry, news of Richard Cœur de Lion's imprisonment in Austria, or wherever they pouched him, percolated slowly through an unmechanical world, even then, neither wholly believed nor deeply appreciated. That is it. Today we must believe

1 The Australian cable of protest

"Bodyline bowling has assumed such proportions as to menace the best interests of the game, making protection of the body by the batsmen the main consideration. This is causing intensely bitter feeling between the players, as well as injury. In our opinion it is unsportsmanlike. Unless stopped at once, it is likely to upset the friendly relations existing between Australia and England."

3 The Australians' second cable

"We appreciate your difficulty in dealing with this matter without having seen the actual play. We unanimously regard "body-line" bowling, as adopted in some games in the present tour, as opposed to the spirit of cricket, and unnecessarily dangerous to the players. We are deeply concerned that the ideals of the game shall be preserved and we have therefore appointed a committee to report on the means necessary to eliminate such bowling from Australian cricket, beginning with the 1933-34 season. We do not consider it necessary to cancel the remainder of the programme."

5 The Australians' final cable

"We do not regard the sportsmanship of your team as being in question. It is the particular class of bowling referred to therein which we consider not in the best interests of cricket ... We join heartily with you in hoping the remaining Tests will be played with the traditional good feelings." *The Cricketer* Spring Annual 1933

2 The MCC's first reply

"We, Marylebone Cricket Club, deplore your cable. We deprecate your opinion that there has been unsportsmanlike play. We have fullest confidence in captain, team and managers and are convinced that they would do nothing to infringe either the Laws of cricket or the spirit of the game. We have no evidence that our confidence has been misplaced. Much as we regret accidents to Woodfull and Oldfield, we understand that in neither case was the bowler to blame. If the Australian Board of Control wish to propose a new law or rule, it shall receive our careful consideration in due course. We hope the situation is not now as serious as your cable would seem to indicate but, if it is such as to jeopardise the good relations between English and Australian cricketers, and you consider it desirable to cancel remainder of programme, we would consent, but with great reluctance."

4 The MCC's second reply

"We, the committee of the Marylebone Cricket Club, note with pleasure that you do not consider it necessary to cancel the remainder of programme and that you are postponing the whole issue until after the present tour is completed. May we accept this as a clear indication that the good sportsmanship of our team is not in question? We are sure you will appreciate how impossible it would be to play any Test match in the spirit we all desire unless both sides were satisfied there was no reflection upon their sportsmanship."

and, unless we are made of mud or stone, we cannot but appreciate. The news hits us a tremendous blow; we reel and stagger; and, senses recovered, dance a roundelay of delight or send to the tailor for the deepest mourning.

But oh, wicket! Fall, fall. Curse and d—n these boundaries! Where are the fielders? Are we playing with only five men? Stop bowling half-volleys, you wretched man! "He's out! Bradman is out; he tried to ... " Oh, never mind what he tried ... he's OUT! OUT!! Oh, Larwood, incomparable thunder-king! Work? A fig for work! A public holiday for me.

And, if you want to pile up your agony, have no radio of your own; sleep next door to one who has; with a thin wall between.

But I cannot do it again and live. Friday, Australia 251 for 3. Saturday, Australia 340; England 99 for 0. Sunday [rest day], with Hammond popping his head out of bunkers on the golf course, O'Reilly bowling ghostly googlies in the shorter rough. Monday, England 271 for 8. Black Monday; Tuesday, England, 356. Miracle Tuesday, Paynter Tuesday. Australia, 106 for 4. O my anointed, my everlasting hat! Wednesday, Australia 175. England 107 for 2. Speech is useless. Surely it must be; surely. Thursday – it is. Jardine, you are the happiest man in the world tonight! Gentlemen, two toasts. England and Australia.

The Bodyline cables

The tactics caused a string of correspondence between the Australian Cricket Board and MCC, threatening a cancellation of the tour. The most talked about and lucrative series in Ashes history was never going to be cancelled – MCC called Australia's bluff. *The Cricketer* publishes the telegrams in full. 🔃

In the manager's words

On the team's return, following a bonus victory at Sydney, the England manager and editor of *The Cricketer*, Plum Warner, puts pen to paper

During a very trying period for everyone concerned the team kept on an even keel, being cool, calm and sensible and never losing their sense of humour. In a word they were splendid. DR Jardine is one of the best captains on the field England has had. An acute observer and thinker, his management of the bowling and placing of the field were admirable and he demanded and obtained a high standard of fitness and discipline. Brave and tenacious, he would never ask anyone to do anything which he would not attempt himself. He was unswerving in his attitude and he bore the "barracking" of the crowd and the criticisms of the papers with calmness and dignity.

H Larwood may well claim comparison with any fast bowler of any age, his run-up to the crease, action, delivery and follow-through being models of rhythm and swing. Though much below the height usually associated with fast bowlers, Larwood has very long arms and is powerfully built about the back and shoulders. I cannot recall a more accurate fast bowler. When bowling "leg-theory in full blast," he had only two men on the off-side – a deep third man and a silly point. His bowling was undoubtedly the chief factor in the recovery of the Ashes. He owed much of his success to his captain, who managed him most ably, seldom bowling him for more than four or five overs at a time. Always the spearhead of the attack, he rose to great heights in the terrific heat at Brisbane.
The Cricketer, May 20, 1933

Speed trap: Bradman is caught by Allen off Larwood for 8 in the third Test at Adelaide

5th Test February 23-28, Sydney †Aus 435 (LS Darling 85, McCabe 73; Larwood 4-98) **and 182** (Bradman 71, Woodfull 67; H Verity 5-33); **Eng 454** (Hammond 101, Larwood 98; PK Lee 4-111) **and 168-2** (Hammond 75*, RES Wyatt 61*). **Eng won by 8 wickets.**

HERO No.3

Douglas Jardine

Test

Batting

Matches	22
Runs	1296
Highest score	127
Average	48.00
Hundreds	1
Fifties	10

First-class

Batting

Matches	262
Runs	14848
Highest score	214
Average	46.83
Hundreds	35
Fifties	72

Bowling

Balls	2582
Runs	1493
Wickets	48
Average	31.10
Best bowling	6-28
5-for inns	1
10-for match	0

v Australia

Batting

Matches	10
Runs	540
Highest score	98
Average	31.76
Hundreds	0
Fifties	4

An irresistible force

Douglas Jardine's desire to win back the Ashes at all costs brought him the urn and vilification in England and Australia. Which is why **Christopher Douglas** loves him

I T IS A PERVERSE choice, I know, because DRJ was not exactly a crowd pleaser – dour, defensive batting style, an awkward, stiff-legged way of moving around the field and a firm belief that any noise coming from the stands should be punished by an immediate 30-minute suspension of play. He captained England only 15 times (won 9, lost 1, drew 5) but, as time goes by, his stature seems to grow; and that is because in 1932-33 he took a side to Australia and regained the Ashes. Ray Illingworth and Pelham Warner are the only other England captains to have achieved this.

Douglas Jardine is the name more than any other that stands for the legendary British qualities of cool-headed determination, implacable resolve, patrician disdain for crowds and critics alike – if you are English that is. To Australians the name is synonymous with the legendary British qualities of snobbishness, cynicism and downright Pommie arrogance.

I certainly do not spend time re-reading accounts of matches that Douglas Jardine played in or watching old film of him, nor do I have his photo on my bedroom wall. But, since writing a biography of him over 20 years ago, I have always had an affection for him, not just as a fearless, single minded, scary, hook nosed sort of toff which I suppose part of me would quite like to be but because he was partly responsible for my education.

I left school at 15 and the two years I spent in my early twenties researching DRJ's life and trying to express it in coherent form was the nearest I got to going to college. There was not much money in it, so I had to subsidise the writing with scraps of TV acting work and doing the horses (I dedicated the book to my five biggest winners). It is safe to say I would have been the very last person DRJ would have chosen for the job.

I was deeply conscious of my unsuitability as I interviewed those who knew him: Percy Fender, Gubby Allen, Jack Fingleton, Bob Wyatt and so on. But having to get to grips with the single most important episode in DRJ's life – Bodyline – with very little prior knowledge, still less opinion, was probably an advantage.

The defenders of bodyline bowling have all died off and everyone is now agreed that it had to end. But the more interesting thing about it to me is that it had to start. It is true that Jardine was the first

to implement the strategy of fast short-pitched bowling with a packed legside field but it was a stage in the game's evolution rather than a dastardly one-off plan and it was always going to happen sooner or later. The lbw law, the pitches, the height of the stumps, even the size of the ball were all in the batsman's favour at the time and something had to give. Even Don Bradman, bodyline's chief target, admitted as much in a letter to MCC shortly before the tour.

There was nothing illegal about bodyline. DRJ had such a profound respect for the laws that he would never have countenanced it otherwise. It was not by any means guaranteed to work but he was prepared to risk everything on its success – death or glory. He called his account of the tour *In Quest of the Ashes* (splendidly reissued by Methuen with a brilliant foreword on bodyline by Mike Brearley) and he saw the campaign as something noble and knightly. "Fear and be slain" he would quote to his children in later life, and on the bodyline tour his bowlers would be reminded, as they enjoyed a final fag before taking the field, that "an hour of glorious life is worth an age without a name".

> **❝**Bodyline was a stage in the game's evolution rather than a dastardly one-off plan. It was going to happen sometime**❞**

He was not a villain but decades of Australian resentment have lent him a kind of villainous glamour that I find irresistible. Likewise his sense of humour: when Herbert Sutcliffe had a benefit match coming up DRJ sent him an umbrella for luck.

Until recently his portrait hung in the Long Room at Lord's, appropriately enough underneath Bradman's, DRJ's cool gaze staring directly into the faces of visiting teams as they clattered through the hushed interior on their way out on to the field. He has been moved to the bar now, as has Bradman, which I think is a pity because it always seemed gloriously ironic that the two great adversaries – the master strategist and the game's pre-eminent genius – should occupy the same patch of wall space. But Douglas Jardine has survived many attempts to airbrush him out of history and now his status as a sporting icon seems more secure than ever. ◪ *The Wisden Cricketer, October 2005*

Christopher Douglas is an actor and writer who created the fictional cricket characters Dave Podmore and Vic Tripe. He also wrote a biography of Jardine called *Spartan Cricketer*

The Bodyline hangover

Australia were hungry for revenge, England without Jardine (retired) and Larwood (unavailable). Bradman did little until his usual Headingley triple. The series was played out to MCC politicking. **RC Robertson-Glasgow** sums up

The first Test, though England lost it, was the most enjoyable. The second, at Lord's, was mainly Verity and sawdust. Manchester was all heat, huge scoring and for several in the press box, partial lack of visibility. It was hard to believe that the architect of the box had had a sense of angles. Five fielders and an umpire are not in themselves a game of cricket.

Leeds produced the magnificent stand between Bradman and Ponsford, also the most excitable and appreciative crowd of the five Tests. They swayed and murmured and barracked each other. Once the game was almost interrupted when a pickpocket so far forgot sense as to ply his art in a Yorkshire crowd. Heavy running constables rescued him. He left the ground in their company without a collar (perhaps as he entered it), and suffering from what is called rough handling.

Oval. Australia win the toss and the Ashes. Never looked like doing anything else. Again Grimmett, at his own round-armed best, and O'Reilly. Another noble act by Leyland. Huge advertisements of alcohol round the ground. Ames' injury to crown discomfiture. Woolley laughing as he kept wicket. The sudden end, wicket-grabbing, rush of feet, speeches, furious writing and telephoning, and so goodbye. England inferior in every way except opening bowling, an art Australia did not require. At this distance the absence of certain England players has become a matter of merely academic interest. ◪

The Cricketer Annual, 1934

Smile of the tiger: Bill O'Reilly, the Australian spinner

Pipe of peace: commentator Jardine outside The Oval

The Great Choke

Another series down under and after the first two Tests England were 2-0 up. They contrived to fail to regain the Ashes and to lose the series 3-2. The **Hon Mr Justice HV Evatt** reports for *The Cricketer*

Although the result of the Test series must have been disappointing to England, that result was reached only by the narrowest possible margin, not only in numbers but in actual cricket superiority.

Early in the season England's batsmen displayed considerable weakness against slow, legspin bowling, being greatly troubled in turn by Ward of South Australia, Frederick of Victoria and Mudge of New South Wales. The form was too bad to be true but the first Test at Brisbane saw the start of a mastery

> **66** It looked as though Australia would never recover in time to retain the Ashes **99**

over Ward that did not stop during his three Tests. Australia was surprised. By the end of the second Test Ward was "under control", McCormick did not seem to be able to maintain his length or pace and Bradman, though seemingly full of runs, had met with only moderate success. It looked as though Australia would never recover in sufficient time to retain the Ashes.

During the first two Tests the morale of England's team seemed to be at a maximum point. Allen had brought them to their highest pitch at precisely the right time. But even at Sydney there was an omen. Whilst Hammond was still batting, appearing to have assumed his old role of permanent occupant of the crease, the scoring board suddenly announced that Fleetwood-Smith, whose finger had kept him out of the

earlier matches of the season, had annihilated the Queensland batsmen. The crowd's gloom changed to cheering, and, as it turned out, Fleetwood-Smith played in the remaining three Tests and was largely instrumental in Australia's winning the fourth at Adelaide.

At Melbourne a new spirit seemed to inspire the side. Bradman clearly out-manoeuvred Allen on the second day by closing his innings at five minutes to three, thus securing the benefit of the tea interval break at 4pm. It was a great stroke of luck that the rain gave Bradman the opportunity of employing his tactics but it was also great skill to seize the opportunity so effectively.

In the fourth and fifth Tests Bradman's captaincy was faultless and I think he will become Australia's greatest captain since Noble. He has all the necessary gifts and they are bound together in a character which can steel itself against adversity. The Australian selectors did their work most efficiently. They did not hesitate to alter a winning team, nor were they ever "bustled" into drastically altering a losing team. The result was that, by the time of the fifth Test, they had built a very fine side.

Australia's batting naturally centred around Bradman and McCabe. The latter was extremely brilliant and his scoring was very consistent. The only fault that could be imputed to him was a tendency to hit a trifle indiscriminately after he reached the 60s or 70s, a tendency of which Allen took advantage. Bradman's three great innings in the last three Tests were decisive. Even

his list of records fails to show what a match-winner he has been; he has begun to move away from all the great Australian batsmen of the past. It is impossible to describe his amazing combination of safety and brilliance in his fifth Test innings. Although he never took a risk of any kind, he passed the century in 125 minutes! After the second Test many critics were inclined to assail him, asserting that his captaincy would destroy his batsmanship. Subsequently they were silenced in several languages. **◪**

The Cricketer, May 1, 1937

Run machines: Bradman and McCabe

1934

1st Test June 8-12, T Bdge †**Aus 374** (AG Chipperfield 99; K Farnes 5-102) and **273-8 dec** (Farnes 5-77); **Eng 268** (CV Grimmett 5-81) and **141** (WJ O'Reilly 7-54). **Aus won by 238 runs.**

2nd Test June 22-25, Lord's †**Eng 440** (LEG Ames 120, M Leyland 109); **Aus 284** (WA Brown 105; H Verity 7-61) and **118** (Verity 8-43). **Eng won by an inns and 38 runs.**

3rd Test July 6-10, Old Trafford †**Eng 627-9 dec** (Leyland 153, EH Hendren 132; O'Reilly 7-189) and **123-0 dec** (H Sutcliffe 69*); **Aus 491** (McCabe 137) and **66-1. Match drawn.**

4th Test July 20-24, Headingley †**Eng 200** and **229-6** (Leyland 49*); **Aus 584** (DG Bradman 304, WH Ponsford 181; WE Bowes 6-142). **Match drawn.**

5th Test August 18-22, T Oval †**Aus 701** (Ponsford 266, Bradman 244) and **327** (Bowes 5-55); **Eng 321** (Leyland 110) and **145** (Grimmett 5-64). **Aus won by 562 runs.**

1936-37

1st Test Dec 4-9, Bris †**Eng 358** (M Leyland 126) and **256** (GOB Allen 68); **Aus 234** (JHW Fingleton 100; W Voce 6-41) and **58** (Allen 5-36). **Eng won by 322 runs.**

2nd Test Dec 18-22, Syd †**Eng 426-6 dec** (WR Hammond 231*); **Aus 80** and **324. Eng won an by inns and 22 runs.**

3rd Test Jan 1-7, Mel †**Aus 200-9 dec** and **564** (DG Bradman 270, Fingleton 136); **Eng 76-9 dec** and **323** (Leyland 111*). **Aus won by 365 runs.**

4th Test Jan 29-Feb 4, Adelaide †**Aus 288** and **433** (Bradman 212; Hammond 2-57); **Eng 330** (CJ Barnett 129 and **243. Aus won by 148 runs.**

5th Test February 26-March 3, Mel †**Aus 604** (Bradman 169, CL Badcock 118, SJ McCabe 112); **Eng 239** (WJ O'Reilly 5-51) and **165. Aus won by an inns and 200 runs.**

The Ashes defence

A strong side led by Bradman dominated a rain-affected series in 1938 (not a ball was bowled in the fourth Test) – Stan McCabe and Bill O'Reilly added teeth to Bradman's tireless excellence – until a record-breaking final Test

Bradman's numbers stagger *The Cricketer*'s new resident statistician, EL Roberts, and that was before he started his 1938 run-fest

Dictionary makers of the future will be faced with the task of finding a definition for a new word – Bradmanism – and perhaps an adequate solution of this verbal problem would be: "an infinite capacity for unlimited run-getting" ... Bradman is Australia's most useful "12th man" because statistically he is the equivalent of two good batsmen. Fortunately for England's bowlers he does not have to be dismissed twice in each innings. *The Cricketer*, Spring Annual, 1938

At least the editor Plum Warner adds a patriotic note of optimism

When the names of the 16 players were announced, a wave of pessimism appeared to envelop the British Isles and there was much talk about "the invincibility" of our visitors. We see no reason whatsoever to despair of England's chances of regaining the Ashes this year.
The Cricketer, Spring Annual, 1938

Bradman kicks off his tour in familiar style

In each of his English tours Bradman has scored a double century in the first match v Worcestershire – 236 in 1930, 206 in 1934 and 258 in 1938.
The Cricketer, July 30, 1938

Sir Home Gordon watches Bradman (278) and Australia (502) play MCC at Lord's in May

*Aut Bradman aut nihil** was how a learned barrister described the Australian cricket at Lord's on the first day v MCC. [But the Australian batsmen] suggested a team of robots at the wicket, a combined mechanism for amassing vast aggregates: teutonic in disciplined scoring; titanic in implacable determination.
The Cricketer, May 21, 1938. *Either Bradman or nothing

As for the Test matches ...
Following Bradman's usual Headingley hundred and O'Reilly's 10 wickets the Ashes are safe

We have exhausted our vocabulary of praise in favour of Bradman. There never has been such a batsman. He wins matches for his side and he saves them as he did at Trent Bridge and at Lord's. And we hold that people are sometimes apt to forget in the glory of his stroke-play that he has an exceedingly strong defence. This was his third century in Tests this season (out of five innings), and his 15th against England, and he is not yet 30. *The Cricketer*, July 30, 1938

There is revenge at The Oval and Hutton's record-breaking innings

A large crowd was present in beautiful weather when Hutton and Hardstaff continued the England innings. The chief interest, naturally, centred on Hutton. At the start of the day runs came slowly and the Australians made the batsmen fight every inch of the way. Gradually Hutton approached Bradman's record of 334 and a beautiful cut off Fleetwood-Smith gave him the record. The crowd roared their

approval and Bradman raced to shake hands with the young Yorkshireman. The Australians toasted him and the spectators sang "For he's a jolly good fellow" and cheered again and again ... there was an air of unreality about the match, Hammond finally declaring at the tea interval with the score reading fantastically – 903 for 7.
The Cricketer, August 27, 1938

Bradman and Fingleton could not bat through injuries and England win. Major RT Stanyforth writes

We must sympathise with Australia in the injuries to Bradman and Fingleton which robbed us of satisfaction and made a great game a farce ... But even Bradman cannot hope to win a match in the face of 903 for 7. ◪ *The Cricketer*, September 3, 1938

Watching brief: boys at The Oval strain for a view

The war takes its toll

A war-weakened England went to Australia and endured a tough time. But Denis Compton and Alec Bedser emerged, as did an Australian great, Keith Miller. *The Cricketer*'s 'Australian Correspondent', **Ray Robinson**, reports

Keep in mind that the Tests of 1946-47 in Australia differed from pre-war rubbers between evenly matched sides. Sent a year earlier than MCC intended – because of the plea by the Attorney-General that the Australian people would otherwise be disappointed – the English team was not properly equipped for the opposition encountered. Forgetfulness (or worse, heedlessness) of this had much to do, I think, with bear-baiting criticism of Hammond as captain, irritation with the umpiring and other pinpricks which failed to mar the pleasure given the crowds ...

The bowling was so inadequate that usually it looked as if two men, Wright and Bedser, would have to turn on something almost superhuman to keep Australia's scoring within bounds. The average age of the Australian team was 29, four years less than the Englishmen's. The side had so many suitable bowlers that wherever Bradman looked in the field he would meet the eager eyes of someone worthy of a turn.

In the early matches Hutton, Hammond and Compton dealt with the bowling in a manner that promised tall totals. They were soon known as The Big Three. When they simultaneously lost Test form, England's innings became as irregular as a peace treaty session with Messrs Bevin, Byrnes and Molotov* sitting tongue-tied.

As if the disparity in bowling, age and range of batting did not weigh the scales enough, the luck of the toss and two thunderstorms denied the Englishmen a chance in the first Test. More exasperating

was the luck of the umpiring. Usually debatable decisions work out fairly evenly over a Test rubber but weight of evidence suggests that the umpires were [making mistakes against England]. No good was done by those who, up hill and down dale, insisted on making a fuss about such decisions and left the inference that English batsmen had more to fear than Australians.

Criticism which would make Hammond the scapegoat is unjust. Like others before him (including Bradman in 1938) he found that captaincy of a touring team in an Anglo-Australian Test rubber brought a heap of problems and side-issues to his door, and his leadership fell below the impressive standard he had set in England against the Australians.

Criticisms of Hammond's handling of his team in the field were holes of a kind that could be picked in any captain of a losing side and

overlooked in a victorious skipper. To Australian eyes the chief defect in his captaincy was that away from the grounds he did not mingle among his men more. A motor firm's provision of a car for his use meant that he often travelled apart from the main body of the team.

Bradman, who was fighting off ill-health when the season opened, captained Australia with long-sighted efficiency. His choice of bowlers for each situation was almost unerring. After the first Test put Australia one up the position suited his cleverness in placing run-tight fields. Happenings in the fourth Test prompted HL Collins, former Australian captain, to write that cricket as a game had disappeared and that the policy of the Australian side was that it must not lose ...

Wright's loping run brought laughs until the crowds got used to it. The batsmen did not join in; they were preoccupied with more uneasy lunges and snicks than any other legspin bowler from England has caused since World War 1 ...

From the moment Compton found true form his batting deeply impressed Australians. He often found himself batting amid a crisis, so had to deny himself most of the liberties he enjoys taking. Compton passed fifty in eight of his last 10 innings (including four consecutive centuries) and was the greatest outfield favourite with the crowds since Patsy Hendren ... Australians farewelled the Englishmen with gratitude for re-establishing big cricket in Australia. ◪ *The Cricketer*, Spring Annual, 1947

*British, American and Russian politicians (respectively) involved in post-war foreign policy

Favourites: Compton (l) and Hendren

The Invincibles

In 1948 possibly the greatest Australian side to tour England arrived, led by Don Bradman who announced he would retire from first-class cricket at the end of the series. The side did not lose a game and won the Test series 4-0. Before the summer **Ray Robinson** picks out the key players

A t 39 **Bradman** looks more like his pre-war self than he did when the Englishmen were in Australia two seasons ago. The transformation from the wan, mistiming batsman who struggled grimly for runs in October and November, 1946, is enough to make an agnostic believe in faith healing. Besides regaining nearly all his matchless footwork he has re-discovered a youthful spirit in his approach to his play. Against India, once he sighted the bowling to his satisfaction, there was usually more dash in his batting than in the period just before the war. Yet he is liable to cramp in the legs and he tore a muscle in the left side below the ribs while batting in the last Test. Bradman has the shrewdest brain in cricket today and his players are glad it is working for, not against, them. English onlookers are fortunate that his farewell season in Test cricket will be on their grounds. **KR Miller**, 28 (New South Wales). This grand cricketer has been bowling too much. Usually it

would hardly be a matter for complaint if a player's usefulness as a bowler subtracted something from his run-getting. But Miller is a batsman of such peerless quality that to risk dimming his brilliance is a disservice to cricket. The gifted six-footer has livened the imagination of Australia's cricketing youth, and the hoisting of his name on the scoreboard is a signal for a chorus of delight. **RR Lindwall**, 26 (New South Wales). The world's fastest bowler is a fair, athletic man. His approach is a model of smooth acceleration and his balance at speed is reflected in his control of direction and length. **RN Harvey**, 19 (Victoria). Fifth of a family of six cricketing brothers. When the team begins play Neil Harvey will be 19 – the youngest Australian on a Test tour of England since the famous left-hander, Clem Hill, in 1896. Harvey is a left-hand batsman and brilliant fieldsman, too. With a natural sense of timing he goes for his strokes spiritedly. His feet are on the path to greatness. ◼ *The Cricketer*, Spring Annual, 1948

Picture of perfection: The Australians at Trent Bridge during the 1948 tour

EL Roberts continues barely to believe Bradman's statistics

Since December 22 1945 Bradman has batted in 29 first-class matches and in 27 has scored a hundred or an innings over 50, or both. During this period he has scored 3,566 runs (average 99.08), 18 hundreds and 10 other innings over 50, and averaged 122.96 runs per match. And of the above Niagara of runs 1,533, including seven hundreds, were scored in 11 Tests v England and India, his average being 117.92. It is amusing to remember that in 1946 there was much speculation as to whether the poor old man would try to "come back" or would unobtrusively retire to the nearest shelf. *The Cricketer*, June 26, 1948

That 721

'The Invincibles' (as they were becoming known) scored 721 *in a day* against Essex. Harry Gee sees them do it

I saw nearly every stroke of that record day's play at Southend but I feel sure that the impressions of the Essex wicketkeeper, Rist, will be of greater interest than my views. Rist enjoyed his unenviable, and unique, experience. Bradman fascinated him by his perfection of timing and accuracy of placing while scoring 187 in little more than two hours. "He left his strokes so late," said Rist, "that quite often I found the ball struck almost out of my hands. Now and again he seemed to be worried by a ball spinning away to the slips but before you could say 'Jack Robinson' he'd be outside the off stump and pulling the ball past mid-on." … Rist did not remind me that he conceded only seven byes in the huge total. *The Cricketer*, May 29, 1948

Captain marvel: Bradman after Headingley

Hip, hip ... : England cheer the Don at The Oval

... Hooray! Bradman is bowled for a duck

The series is a wonderful valedictory tour of success for Bradman yet it has a twist. Bradman, needing only four to have a Test average over 100, is bowled for a duck in his last innings

1st Test June 10-15, Trent Bridge †Eng 165 (JC Laker 63; WA Johnston 5-36) and **441** (DCS Compton 184; KR Miller 4-125); **Aus 509** (DG Bradman 138, AL Hassett 137; Laker 4-138) and **98-2** (SG Barnes 64*). **Aus won by 8 wkts.**

Bradman is still a very great batsman and, if he does not "murder" the bowlers as of yore, he still "wounds" them grievously. His defence seems impregnable and he was only once beaten, by Yardley. Hassett is a great and most attractive player and, if at one time on the second day he and his captain gave the impression of allowing the bowlers to dictate to them, it must be borne in mind that the bowling was extremely accurate and the field well placed.

The bumpers occasionally bowled by Miller led to booing by a section of the crowd. A fast bowler has every right to send down a short-pitched "flier" but his manner before delivering such a ball – with a toss of his mane and, as The Times put it, a "petulant" mien – was apt to give the impression that intimidation was, at least, part of his object. *The Cricketer, June 26, 1948*

2nd Test June 24-29, Lord's †Aus 350 (AR Morris 105) and **460-7dec** (Barnes 141); **Eng 215** (Compton 53; RR Lindwall 5-70) and **186** (ERH Toshack 5-40). **Aus won by 409 runs.**

It may be unpleasant to have to admit it but it is no good shutting our eyes to facts that are patent to all – we are being taught a lesson which should do us no end of good in

the future. It remains only for us to congratulate Bradman and his splendid team. Their treatment of us has been drastic, but the patient will recover. Meanwhile they are doing us a power of good. *The Cricketer, July 10, 1948*

Again, 2-0 down after two, England battle against the weather at Old Trafford before dominating at Headingley. Until Bradman remembered that this is his favourite ground and leads an astonishing run chase

3rd Test July 8-13, Old Trafford †Eng 363 (Compton 145*) and **174-3dec** (C Washbrook 85*); **Aus 221** (Morris 51; AV Bedser 4-81) and **92-1** (Morris 54*). **Match drawn.**

4th Test July 22-27, Headingley †Eng 496 (Washbrook 143, WJ Edrich 111) and **365-8dec** (Compton 66); **Aus 458** (RN Harvey 112) and **404-3** (Morris 182, Bradman 173*). **Aus won by 7 wkts.**

Harvey made all sorts of beautiful strokes on the off side. No cricketer in the whole series can have scored a finer century on his first appearance. We can only remember two balls which he played at and missed. He opened with remarkable confidence for a boy of 19. Possibly a slow or medium-paced bowler bowling at his leg stump with six men on the on-side might keep him quiet ...

Tuesday, July 27, 1948, was probably the most disappointing day from an English point of view, in all the long history of matches between England and Australia, and the great crowd at Leeds which previously had so keenly and impartially applauded both sides, were so stunned and disappointed that there was only some perfunctory clapping as Bradman and

Harvey returned to the pavilion at 6.18 pm. It was not that they did not appreciate that Australia had won a great victory with only 12 minutes to spare but that one and all felt that the match had been thrown away by indifferent leadership [Yorkshire's own Yardley] and bad fielding. *The Cricketer, August 7, 1948*

Bradman has only one chance to say good-bye as Australia win by an innings again after Lindwall routs England on a wet wicket for 52 (of which Hutton made a staggering 30)

5th Test August 14-18, The Oval †Eng 52 (Lindwall 6-20) and **188** (L Hutton 64; Johnston 4-40); **Aus 389** (Morris 196; WE Hollies 5-131). **Aus won by an inns and 149 runs.**

Then came Bradman to be enthusiastically applauded by the large crowd and the English team, led by Yardley, gathering round him and taking off their caps. It was a stirring scene and worthy of a glorious cricketer and a fine captain. Whether the great Australian was overcome by this tremendous outburst of appreciation we know not but he was clean bowled second ball by a very good length googly from Hollies and returned amidst as great cheering as had greeted his appearance at the wicket. Rarely, indeed, does a cricketer receive such an ovation. Grace, Hobbs, MacLaren and Hammond have been the recipients of such appreciation from the cricket-loving public but they seldom come more than once or twice in a generation. Bradman has played his last Test. It would be superfluous to praise his greatness as a batsman. Clearly his name will live in cricket history. No name will be greater than his. ◼ *The Cricketer, August 21, 1948*

Don Bradman

Tests

Batting

Matches	52
Runs	6996
Highest score	334
Average	99.94
Hundreds	29
Fifties	13

First-class career

Batting

Matches	234
Runs	28067
Highest score	452*
Average	95.14
Hundreds	117
Fifties	69

v England

Batting

Matches	37
Runs	5028
Highest score	334
Average	89.78
Hundreds	19
Fifties	12

Other records

Highest Test averages*

DG Bradman	99.94
RG Pollock	60.97

*Min 20 innings

Highest first-class averages*

DG Bradman	95.14
VM Merchant	71.64

*Min 80 innings

Most Test double-centuries

DG Bradman	12
WR Hammond	7

Most first-class scores over 300

DG Bradman	6
WR Hammond	4
WH Ponsford	4

Does anyone compare?

Cold, hard facts dictate that no sportsman in history is a match for Bradman, writes **Frank Keating**

I have a confession to make. At the turn of the millennium I joined in the game of naming the century's best sportsman. I took unparalleled achievement and peerless mastery for granted but also announced charm, chivalry and a glistening in-born spirit for fair play as crucial yardsticks. My starring shortlist of six, announced in reverse order, was: Bradman, Pele, Evonne Goolagong, Jack Nicklaus, Lew Hoad and, my Sportsman of the Century, Sir Garfield Sobers.

The mighty Don, for all his off-the-scale records, was only sixth by my standards ... Most pundits nominated prizefighter Muhammad Ali (formerly Cassius Clay) as Sportsman of the Century – a judgement which he would certainly go along with. I was there in Deer Lake, Pennsylvania, when he mused: "I guess I'm the only man in the whole history of the universe who has become world-famous under two different names." Ali transcended his sport and his fame infiltrated a host of different corners – political, social and cultural. And he was a scintillating boxer in his heyday, sure. But by no means was Ali invincible – a number of them bested him. Who, unless the rules are radically changed, will ever come along and treat Bradman's records as so much chicken-feed?

Bradman's batting records will never be broken. You might say the game has changed. Sure, Bradman changed it irrevocably. "Incredible and indelible," as Matthew Engel wrote, and the more you pore over Bradman's figures, the more you need to pour yourself a stiff drink in astonished wonder – then another, I suppose, in stupefied celebration.

There is one man who might yet, in my lifetime even, seriously challenge Bradman's all-sports' pre-eminence. The golfer Tiger Woods looks as if he could have it in him. [When] Woods had become only the second golfer to win three major titles in a single year, an epic piece in *The Independent* by James Lawton pronounced: "As natural as Pele ... As tough as Bradman ... As pretty as Ali ... As clean as Carl Lewis ... As prolific as Sampras ... at 24, Tiger Woods is already well on the way to proving himself the greatest sportsman that ever lived."

There is a statistical way of making this judgement. Charles Davis, a mathematician from Melbourne, published *The Best of the Best*, a book in which he contrived with logarithms and computer slide-rules a statistical system for measuring the tops in a variety of sports. Having fed in no end of data, Davis's method came up with his premier league table – Pele was top on 3.7, golfer Jack Nicklaus second with 3.5, basketball's Michael Jordan logged 3.2 and Bjorn Borg 3.15. But when the barmy boffin fed in Bradman's stats they as good as exploded Davis's Richter scale. Bradman's

"score" reached 4.4 and rising, and Davis pronounced that – mathematically speaking – the batsman's career should simply not have existed. To reach a comparable level a footballer would have to score a goal a game in 100 internationals, a tennis player take more than 15 singles titles at Wimbledon, a golfer win more than 25 majors. Bradman, in other words, was a superman beyond the confines of the medium which measured talent. Bradman ... had made his game unplayable. Up to a point.

When John Woodcock selected his 100 best cricketers in 1997, he placed WG Grace first and Bradman second, which surprised some. Grace was the out-and-out prophet. He "invented" and exported the very sport which Bradman moulded to his own ruthless genius; he was the founding father of the banquet which Bradman was able to feast off. I agree with Woodcock that Grace remains "the most magnificent figure in the game's history". As Jack Hobbs once said: "The Don was too good. He spoiled the game. He got too many runs. He was too mechanical ... We don't want to see another like him. Not that I ever think we shall."

> **Mathematically speaking, Bradman's career should not have existed ... He made his game unplayable**

For sport should be above mathematics. Sport lives off life and shade and colour and personality. GK Chesterton understood when he wrote: "There is a great man who makes every man feel small. But the really great man is the man who makes every man feel great." Did Bradman make those who watched him feel great? Or awestruck? As the grand Australian columnist, Les Carlyon, once put it: "You might wish your son might bat like Bradman, but you don't necessarily want him to take on Bradman's persona. Such a kid would be fussy and finicky and wouldn't be much fun."

On the other hand, I have always enjoyed the Australian author Thomas Keneally's recollections of a lower-class Sydney upbringing in the 1930s: "At school the only history was European history. If we spoke of literary figures, we spoke of Englishmen. Cricket was the great way out of cultural ignominy for, while no Australian had written *Paradise Lost*, our Don Bradman had made 100 before lunch at Lord's."

My own candidate for sportsman of the 20th century would have understood this better than I did when I picked him. When Brian Lara overtook his Test-record 365, Sir Garry said: "The word 'great' is used far too often. You can't call Don Bradman great, and Brian Lara great, or even David Gower great as well. If Lara and Gower were great, then you simply have to invent a different word for Bradman." *Wisden Cricket Monthly*, April 2001

Frank Keating is a sports columnist for *The Guardian*

Friendly fire: The England captain Freddie Brown, who lost the 1950-51 series but won Australian friends

48

England stop the drift

Another heavy series defeat but a stirring victory in the last Test pointed towards better days ahead for England. The Australian public loved the spirit shown by the visiting captain, 40-year-old Freddie Brown, and felt their own team lacked the flair of previous years. **Ray Robinson**, 'Our Australian Correspondent', writes

History slipped one cog in repeating itself when England's victory at Melbourne in February ended the illusion of Australian invincibility. It took 15 post-war Test matches to bring the great day, one more than the number required after World War One, though the losses in each period were the same (11).

By determination and deeds for a losing side Brown soon established himself as the hero of the season, ranking with those fine pre-war captains and popular men, Chapman and Allen, in the estimation of the Australian cricket followers. On top of that, the crowd's admiration for the way he uplifted his side and for his resolute play was heightened by their sympathy with the under-dog, England. A significant tribute was paid him by a vegetable barrowman at the Quay, Sydney, who called: "Fine lettuce ... nine-pence ... hearts like Freddie Brown."

The acclamation at the end of the final Test was the most enthusiastic ever given a captain from England. Australian crowds always like a man who gets runs when others can't, especially one who does so by spirited batting. In the second and third Tests Brown proved that the ball could be hit hard to the boundary by front-of-the-wicket strokes with a frequency and reasonable safety we had almost forgotten. His drives seemed to be full of red corpuscles, like the ruddy face above the kerchief knotted at his neck.

In his common-sense captaincy Brown was ever self-sufficient; he often consulted Hutton and Evans in addition to his vice-captain, Compton. He repeatedly set run-saving fields for accurate bowling a shade short of a length, and his bowlers made free use of the plugging leg-stump attack, backed by a so-called leg slip. These tactics put the onus on the Australian batsmen to take risks if they wished to score quickly. As leader of a side often struggling after batting breakdowns Brown was entitled to resort to these stratagems to retrieve the situation. The joke of it was that the crowds and many critics blamed the batsmen.

In his captaincy throughout the season Hassett seemed to weigh every move with the knowledge that a dozen pens were raised to tell the world Bradman would have done this or wouldn't have done that. After Hassett's men won the rubber, 3-0, several critics roasted him and his batsmen for failure to produce sparkling cricket. People not closely concerned about degrees of docility of wickets and artifices of field-placing lost patience with the batsmen. Not quite 21,000 crossed the road to see the final match of the one-sided rubber begin – the smallest Melbourne crowd within memory on the opening day of a Test. The day Australia lost eight wickets on a holding Melbourne pitch and Hassett saved his side with 92 at the rate of 26 an hour, one critic wrote that Australia's batsmen had slipped because they had lost Bradman's offensive spirit.

Alec Bedser's accurate and lively bowling meant more than any other single factor. The Surrey giant was the man who kept giving England a chance, only to see most of the batsmen fail in their part. Morris, the great left-hander (who had set a post-war record of 696 runs in the 1948 rubber), fell to Bedser in five of his nine innings, recalling Sir Donald Bradman's difficulties in his last season against the big medium-pace bowler. Hutton's play won him the rare distinction of being acknowledged by both sides as the greatest batsman in the world.

Haunted by knee trouble that put him out of the second Test, Compton suffered a series of failures in the Test matches. Some sought to explain this by mean gossip of a kind I never expected to hear about the man who has kept England's flag flying so often in post-war struggles. A sufficient answer to such whispering should have been Compton's [runs] in his other eight first-class matches.

The Cricketer, Spring Annual, 1951

The English reaction to the defeat is equally optimistic. The editor Plum Warner explains that bad luck led to the large margin of defeat and has high hopes for the future

One does not like to talk about luck at cricket but it is a fact that we did experience ill fortune in the recent Test series, with regard to illness, injuries and accidents. None was more ready to admit it than the Australians themselves. In the first Test the winning of the toss meant the winning of the match. In the second it must always be remembered that Compton could not play owing to his knee

trouble. In the next Test the fates were really too much. At last Brown won the toss and there was a fair score on the board when Bailey received a blow on his right thumb which put him out of action for the rest of the game, so we lost not only his batting but his bowling. Wright was injured and he, too, retired from the game without delivering a single ball. Without two of our leading bowlers the handicap was insuperable. Easily beaten in the fourth Test match at Adelaide there were, nevertheless, encouraging periods in the game for England, and Hutton's superb innings will never be forgotten.

The first four Test matches had shown that the gap between England and Australia that had appeared so large in the post-war period was gradually but surely closing and in the final Test the England XI at last achieved their goal. For Brown's inspiring leadership and admirable bowling this memorable victory was a just reward. Nobody could have done more to deserve success – both on and off the field. In spite of the series result we feel that we are building up a good England side and Australian opinion seems to support us. There have admittedly been disappointments but those players will surely profit by the experience gained in the hard school of Australian cricket. *The Cricketer, Spring Annual, 1951*

The Cricketer reviews John Kay's 1950-51 tour book *Ashes to Hassett*

Mr Kay, who begins with the assertion that "Cricket's tide is turning", supplies much information beyond the ordinary run of comment on an English tour. He tells us that FR Brown had no illusions about the probable outcome of the matches. He then disillusions English readers on various matters relating to Australian cricket: for instance, there are no more all-night queues for places to watch a Test match, young and promising Australians are not presenting themselves in large numbers – in fact, cricket is being neglected by Australians, who are far more interested in the Melbourne Cup*; the ball does swing, very considerably, in the Australian atmosphere, the "Hill" at Sydney is not the resort of witty and well-informed critics and the Australians are not overwhelmingly hospitable ...

In dealing with the matches he refrains from long and detailed reports. Depression and exhilaration may be derived in almost equal measure from *Ashes to Hassett*, with its vivid photographs. I have only one regret – which is that Mr Kay has allowed himself to be drawn into the now too prevalent habit of questioning an umpire's decision. True, he does it a great deal less offensively than some of his colleagues, confesses that the press box was at square leg and merely records general dissatisfaction expressed in dressing rooms and elsewhere. Still, it is a regrettable tendency and, among commentators no less than cricketers, it should be regarded as constituting contempt of court. *The Cricketer, May 12, 1951*
*A major horse race

1950-51

1st Test December 1-2, 4-5, Brisbane †**Aus 228** (RN Harvey 74; AV Bedser 4-45) and **32-7 dec** (TE Bailey 4-22); **Eng 68-7 dec** (WA Johnston 5-35) and **122** (L Hutton 62*; JB Iverson 4-43). **Aus won by 70 runs.**

2nd Test December 22-23, 26-27, Melbourne †**Aus 194** (AL Hassett 52; Bedser 4-37, Bailey 4-40) and **181** (KA Archer 46; FR Brown 4-26); **Eng 197** (Brown 62; Iverson 4-37) and **150** (Hutton 40; Johnston 4-26). **Aus won by 28 runs.**

3rd Test January 5-6, 8-9, Sydney †**Eng 290** (Brown 79; KR Miller 4-37) and **123** (Iverson 6-27); **Aus 426** (KR Miller 145*; Bedser 4-107, Brown 4-153). **Aus won by inns and 13 runs.**

4th Test February 2-3, 5-8, Adelaide †**Aus 371** (AR Morris 206; DVP Wright 4-99) and **403-8 dec** (JW Burke 101*); **Eng 272** (Hutton 156*) and **228** (RT Simpson 61; Johnston 4-73). **Aus won by 274 runs.**

5th Test February 23-24, 26-28, Melbourne †**Aus 217** (Hassett 92; Bedser 5-46, Brown 5-49) and **197** (GB Hole 63; Bedser 5-59); **Eng 320** (Simpson 156*; Miller 4-76) and **95-2** (Hutton 60*). **Eng won by 8 wkts.**

First blood: Australians scramble for the stumps after winning the first Test at Brisbane

"We want Len"

It took over 20 years but England reclaimed the Ashes in a summer of dreadful weather, draws and drama. Australia dominated, England led by Len Hutton hung on and nicked one of the great series in the final match. *Cricketer* editor, **Plum Warner**, previews

England have a far stronger side today than in 1948 when we were fairly and squarely beaten by as great a team as has ever represented Australia, under the mighty Sir Donald Bradman, but Australian supporters, while admitting that the absence of Sir Donald is bound to be severely felt, hold the view that their present side, under AL Hassett, will prove itself good

enough to retain the Ashes. They stress their fielding and wicketkeeping will be as good as ours and they pin their faith in Miller and Lindwall as an opening pair of fast bowlers with Johnston as good a first change as any captain could desire. *The Cricketer, May 2, 1953*

Bill Bowes, the Yorkshire quick bowler turned journalist, writes the Test reports

for *The Cricketer*. The first game was rain wrecked – but Alec Bedser made the most of the conditions with 14 for 99

1st Test June 11-13, 15-16, Trent Bridge †Aus **249** (AL Hassett 115; AV Bedser 7-55) and **123** (AR Morris 60; Bedser 7-44); **Eng 144** (L Hutton 43; RR Lindwall 5-57) and **120-1** (Hutton 60*). **Match drawn.**

Season's stars: above Alec Bedser, the Trent Bridge destroyer; left Hutton answers the call "We want Len" on the balcony of The Oval's pavilion; below Trevor Bailey, in a break from type, hits out as he saves the Lord's Test

A wet Trent Bridge pitch can be the easiest pitch in the world for batsmen and [in the final innings] the Australian attack, without a finger-spin bowler of the Wardle-Tattersall variety, could do nothing. Hill, who is perhaps the nearest approach to a finger spinner, performed like most Australian bowlers under these conditions. He bowled on the short side and never gave the batsmen the ball ... Jogging along, quietly and comfortably as could be, England reached 100 off a Davidson no-ball. Hutton with a push for two from Davidson reached his own 50 and even the Australians joined in the applause ... And so England finished only 109 runs behind with nine wickets in hand and one was left with the thought of what might have been had the rain not come.

The Cricketer, June 27, 1953

The second game is a thrilling draw with Keith Miller throwing everything at England's finest, with both bat and ball, and, famously, Trevor Bailey batting forever with Willie Watson

2nd Test June 25-27, 29-30, Lord's †**Aus 346** (Hassett 104; Bedser 5-105, JH Wardle 4-77) and **368** (KR Miller 109; FR Brown 4-82); **Eng 372** (Hutton 145; Lindwall 5-66) and **282-7** (W Watson 109, TE Bailey 71). **Match drawn.**

Match drawn. That bare announcement gives no idea of the many thrilling changes in the run of play. How first Australia, then England, and Australia again had a stranglehold loosened. It cannot convey any idea of the magnificent fast bowling and team-work of Australia on the third morning of the match, or the defensive play of England's batsmen on the final day which brought a draw as glorious as any victory ... To single out any one player in this thrilling opening to the third day's play would be wrong. Lindwall, Miller, Hutton, Compton, all four were superb. There were 45 minutes of the best cricket I have seen in years. Vintage stuff! Every ball a thrill.

England start the final day 20 for 3 needing a notional 343 for victory on a turning pitch. They did not expect to last – maybe that's why they do

Perhaps in the very impossibility of things there was a mental ease for the batsmen. They were without responsibility ... An amazing match, full of surprising changes, had ended honourably. There had been a great crowd and record gate receipts, and for 11,000 spectators on the last day a memory to last a lifetime. *The Cricketer, July 11, 1953*

The next game, at Old Trafford, is destroyed by the weather, much to the chagrin of readers. One writes

Surely it is time to review the position of Manchester as a venue for Test matches. I would suggest the following courses: (a) Instead of fixing the match time after time around the second week in July, try a different period (b) Abandon Test matches at Old Trafford altogether and stage them at Edgbaston (c) Allot a minimum of a fortnight

for each five-day Test scheduled to take place at Manchester. **GA Savage**, Paignton, Devon. *The Cricketer, August 8, 1953*

3rd Test July 9-11, 13-14, Old Trafford †**Aus 318** (RN Harvey 122; Bedser 5-115) and **35-8** (Wardle 4-7); **Eng 276** (Hutton 66, DCS Compton 45, TG Evans 44*). **Match drawn.**

At Headingley comes the fourth draw in succession – but no dull game – again England dig into their defensive reserves and survive a thrilling Australian dart for victory

4th Test July 23-25, 27-28, Headingley **Eng 167** (TW Graveney 55; Lindwall 5-54) and **275** (WJ Edrich 64; Miller 4-63); †**Aus 266** (Harvey 71, GB Hole 53, Bedser 6-95) and **147-4. Drawn.**

By some magnificent defensive cricket against some of the most antagonistic fast bowling seen since 1948 England fought yet another drawn game. When the last ball of the fourth Test was bowled Australia needed only 30 runs to win and they had six wickets in hand. They held an initiative since the second ball of the game when Hutton was bowled by Lindwall and England never shook off the grip taken or eased the pressure exerted. *The Cricketer, August 8, 1953*

And so it all comes down to The Oval ...

5th Test Aug 15, 17-19, The Oval †**Aus 275** (Lindwall 62) and **162** (RG Archer 49; GAR Lock 5-45); **Eng 306** (Hutton 82; Lindwall 4-70) and **132-2** (Edrich 55*). **Eng won by 8 wkts.**

England won the fifth and final Test match against Australia at The Oval by eight wickets. After four drawn games it meant that England had won the rubber. It was a victory due to the fact that England had by far the better balanced side with bowlers suitable for any type of pitch ... Compton finally took four to square leg to bring England the victory. What a yell went up. England had won the Ashes for the first time in 20 years. Thousands of spectators flocked across the pitch to take up position outside the dressing rooms and there they chanted: "We want Len." ... Satisfaction in the result must not blind us to the need to build strongly. *The Cricketer, September 5, 1953*

When the wind blows ...

England headed to Australia with one seriously quick bowler in Frank 'Typhoon' Tyson in a strong, balanced attack that also included Brian Statham. After embarrassing defeat in the first Test they brought the Ashes safely home. **CB Fry** – the great allrounder from the Golden Age – writes in anticipation

We may well await events likely to accrue from Tyson's speed which on his form last season was poignantly impressive. Then, too, Statham is fast enough for anything, with a valuable record of consistent accuracy. With Mr Bailey already a proved value this is a powerful broadside. The difficulty will be how to bring it to bear in a salvo. So we must hope that our Mr Hutton has the Nelson touch. Even a half-Nelson would do. Hence it is that, fortified by distance, I prospectively accord our XI ex-18 a pleasant victory. Let us hope that our Great Expectations do not end in a Bleak House. That would be the very Dickens. *The Cricketer Annual, 1954*

The Cricketer's 'Special Representative in Australia' Ray Robinson reviews the tour in the Spring Annual

Farewelling Hutton and his team in Melbourne, Arnold Seitz, president of the Victorian Cricket Association, said: "The better team has won – much as we regret having to say it." The old Rhodes Scholar was voicing the opinion of most Australians that the Englishmen had retained the Ashes on their merits. By the third Test match it became clear that Australia had no counter to the high-speed bowling of Tyson and Statham. Tyson, with his purposeful stride and obvious shoulder power, and Statham with his rhythmic run and flexible arm, made an unforgettable sight which never failed to stir me. They desolated Australia's batting in a way not seen since Larwood and his fellow-bowlers ravaged it in the Bodyline Tests 22 years earlier. As far as memory can be trusted over such a span, I believe that Tyson is as fast as Larwood was then. As a pair he and Statham are the swiftest I have ever seen in

action for England. In the rubber they took 46 wickets of the 80 wickets shared by nine English bowlers.

So Hutton carried the day with fast bowling. He managed it without the friction that marred Jardine's similar triumph in 1932–33. His fast bowlers kept bouncers within reasonable limits and did not use them in combination with a packed leg field. The support given the fast bowlers by Appleyard and the allrounder TE Bailey was of much more than a fill-in nature. Both had an influence on victory by taking good wickets at important times. Besides proving a master-strategist in evolving and directing a match-winning pattern of attack, Hutton successfully handled the lesser rôle of speechmaker in easy, conversational manner ...

England is envied for possession of two such batsmen as the vice-captain PBH May and MC Cowdrey, whom Hutton rightly classed as the two best batsmen in the world under 25. After the innings defeat in the first Test England's hopes were faint on the third day of the second Test when the third wicket in the second innings fell with the side still 19 runs behind. The 116 partnership by May and Cowdrey was the turning point of the whole series. May was

Assembling for Oz : Appleyard, Wilson and Hutton, the Yorkshire contingent minus Wardle

the first of the team to score a Test century. He is the noblest straight driver in international cricket, equally punishing off front foot or back. Cowdrey's batting, as solid as his build, is remarkably mature for an undergraduate of 22. The Oxford captain's chin never strays far from his shirt collar and I have never seen anyone else play so close to his front leg, the stanchion of his defence and his powerful driving, patient and well-placed. He often spared half-volleys but wickets were always precious when he came in. In the Melbourne Test innings in which Cowdrey scored 102 the other batsmen managed only 80.

Australia had the opening bowling combination of Lindwall and Miller in only two of the four Tests that decided the rubber. Miller missed the second Test because of a swollen knee and Lindwall the fourth because of a calf injury. It is impossible to calculate the difference this made. At 35, Miller is still unrivalled as an allrounder for a big occasion but the amount of bowling he does will have to be tapered off if he is to do himself anything like justice as a batsman. In looking past this inspiring cricketer for captain, the Australian Board of Control did not give their team the best chance of wresting the Ashes from England. The board's invidious decision placed Ian Johnson in an unenviable position. His task was not eased by repeated published reminders that a number of leading Australian and English critics thought the wrong man was leading Australia. Though he lacked Miller's flair, I thought Johnson did fairly well. On the main count he could not be held to blame for his batsmen's failure to cope with high-speed bowling, which he himself faced resourcefully and resolutely.

The Cricketer, Spring Annual, 1955

After the first Test Tyson has warmed up, cut down his run and is working up an unmatchable pace. Ray Robinson records Typhoon's match-by-match destruction, starting with the second Test at Sydney

There was an air of expectancy around the ground when Harvey and Burke went out to continue Australia's innings, needing 151 runs for victory. The first hour or even the first few overs when the English fast bowlers would be fresh might well determine the closeness of the struggle, and so it turned out. In Tyson's second over he clean bowled Burke and Hole, both of whom were beaten by sheer pace, and for a long time the atmosphere was unbelievably tense ... When Johnston, Australia's last line of defence, came to the crease 78 were still wanted; and this was the signal for Harvey to attack. Monopolising the strike – and in this he was helped by the slowness of the fielders – he unleashed a succession of superb strokes and, with Johnston co-operating at the other end, the runs ticked up. After 40 minutes the stand was worth 39, when Johnston flashed once too often on the leg-side and England were home by a bare 38 runs. Statham's stamina and accuracy in the face of a strong wind had been the perfect complement to the sustained and shattering speed of Tyson.

Tyson does it again at Melbourne, blazing his way through a flimsy and terrified Australian line-up

Between noon and twenty past one Australia lost their last eight second-innings wickets for 36 runs in one of the most sensational collapses of all time, Tyson taking six of them for 16 runs in 6.3 overs and Statham two. From this moment nothing could stop Tyson and Statham and it is sufficient testimony to Tyson's incredible performance that his analysis has never been bettered by a fast bowler in the history of Test matches between England and Australia.

The old nemesis Keith Miller puts up a fight at Adelaide as England chase down an awkward final-innings total – it was not enough and the Ashes were safe

Miller in a superb opening spell saw to it that the Ashes would not easily be retained. He sent back Edrich, Hutton and Cowdrey in three overs and England's hitherto straightforward task assumed formidable proportions. May, not in the least perturbed, was batting with fine assurance when he slightly mis-timed an off-drive and Miller fielding at extra-cover flung himself to his left and brought off an amazing catch. Another wicket and England would have been seriously in trouble, but Compton showed no less skill than May, while Bailey proved the ideal partner at the other end. Miller, returning for a last desperate assault, was hit for 10 in one over, and England were almost safe when with four to win Bailey was lbw. Evans arrived to knock the last nail in the Australian coffin and England, as well as retaining the Ashes, had won her first series in Australia since 1933.

For once the readers of _The Cricketer_ seem in whole-hearted support of selectors, team and even management following the Ashes win. One letter writer says

In all the joy of retaining the Ashes two important people are being overlooked – the selectors and the manager [Geoffrey Howard]. Never, perhaps, have the selectors been more vindicated than they have been for this MCC tour. When the tour party was announced there were great rumblings in the North. It was said that some of the best players were being left at home in favour of the "old school tie brigade". Has the result not shown that the selectors may know rather more about the team selection than the man in the street – or more than even some newspaper correspondents? And in all the congratulations showered on captains and teams do we forget the work of managers? I have a feeling that a manager has an important hand in the success of a touring side. Anyone who has been on nothing more pretentious than a week's tour in this country will know what I mean. I feel that Mr Howard deserves to share the plaudits with Mr Hutton. Yours, etc, **HGB Wilson**, Dewsbury, Yorks.

The Cricketer, Spring Annual, 1955

Typhoon brewing: Frank Tyson

1954-55

1st Test Nov 26-27, 29-30, Dec 1, Brisbane **Aus 601-8 dec** (RN Harvey 162, AR Morris 153); **†Eng 190** (TE Bailey 88) and **257** (WJ Edrich 88). **Aus won by an inns and 154 runs.**

2nd Test Dec 17-18, 20-22, Sydney **Eng 154** and **296** (PBH May 104); **†Aus 228** (RG Archer 49; FH Tyson 4-45, Bailey 4-59) and **184** (Harvey 92*; Tyson 6-85). **Eng won by 38 runs.**

3rd Test Dec 31-Jan 1, Jan 3-5, Melbourne **†Eng 191** (MC Cowdrey 102; Archer 4-33) and **279** (May 91; WA Johnston 5-25); **Aus 231** (JB Statham 5-60) and **111** (Tyson 7-27). **Eng won by 128 runs.**

4th Test Jan 28-29, 31, Feb 1-2, Adelaide **†Aus 323** (LV Maddocks 69) and **111**; **Eng 341** (L Hutton 80; R Benaud 4-120) and **97-5. Eng won by 5 wkts.**

5th Test Feb 25-26, 28, Mar 1-3, Sydney **†Eng 371-7 dec** (TW Graveney 111); **Aus 221** (CC McDonald 72; JH Wardle 5-79) and **118-6. Match drawn.**

Not out: mid-pitch chaos in the first Test between Richardson and Cowdrey, who both survived

The turn of spin

The series was dominated by one man – and one match – more than any since Bradman in 1930. Jim Laker, the understated Yorkshireman who played for Surrey, took 19 wickets at Old Trafford which turned out to win the series. Australia still had stars in Miller, Lindwall and Harvey but England had the greater expectations. **Alan Ross**, poet, editor and *The Observer*'s cricket correspondent, writes

I t will, I suspect, be different this summer. I fear, unless Miller re-emerges as a batsman, be far less enjoyable to watch. Burke, Mackay, Burge, McDonald and Rutherford are not, nor ever will be, great or graceful players. Technically, a score of English county players are their superiors. But by their simple limitations, by their patience, they may prove able to extend the Australian innings long enough for the cement to harden, on which Harvey and Miller can trace the enigmatic variations of their genius ...

As yet, these five are untried against bowling of swing in English conditions: but one of the strange facts about English and Australian cricket at the moment is that it is the Australian bowlers who are best equipped to make use of our climate, the English bowlers to exploit theirs. I would prefer Lindwall and Miller as a pair to Statham and Tyson over here, just as the latter proved the more destructive in Australia. Always it was with the old ball that Tyson made his breakthrough, and though the raised seam of the new ball gives

Statham an added kick, his flight is almost as straight in his first over as in his 20th ...

The Australians in England – how much magic, infused by so many great players, so many tours – is there in that phrase. It will not be long now: and it is a dull fellow whose blood does not stir to the fact.
The Cricketer, Spring Annual, 1956

The first Test ends in a draw – rain taking too much time out of the game – but Bill Bowes finds his early-season stride describing a near run-out on the opening day

Cowdrey pushed a delivery from Miller towards the covers and set off for what, with any other fieldsman in the world except Davidson chasing after it, would have been an easy two runs. As Richardson turned for the second run he realised the danger, shouted "No" and tried to turn to scramble back himself, but instead he lost his balance and his bat and went sprawling. In the meantime Cowdrey was chasing down wicket as hard as he could go. Wicketkeeper Langley catching the throw from Davidson and doubtful about a run-out at his end lobbed the ball up wicket to Miller, and in the meantime Richardson scrambled to his feet and set off, minus bat, for the bowler's end. Miller fumbled, finally gathered and then lurched to the stumps falling and flattening all three as Richardson flashed home ... not out. *The Cricketer*, June 23, 1956

The second Test is at Lord's, Australia's – and Keith Miller's – happiest of hunting grounds ... and it does not disappoint. A ferocious display from Australia's talisman gives Australia an unexpected lead in the series. Bill Bowes again

... All in all it was a friendly opening until May drove Miller majestically to the sightscreen at the Nursery end. It was such a good stroke that Miller applauded but straight away he discarded his second sweater and came roaring into attack. He bowled a couple of deliveries which spat from the pitch to whizz chest high past the batsman. May tried hard but unsuccessfully to get an edge to the first.

Still smarting under the memory of May's four, Miller bowled the first ball of the third over chest high past Watson. Then he made one straighten on the Lord's slope to find the edge of the bat, hit Watson on the pads and lob for a catch to Benaud in the gully. With high over-arm actions, holding the seam upright in the fingers and hitting the ball into the ground, both Miller and Archer made the ball deviate.

Miller ends with 10 for 152 in the match as England crumble in the fourth innings

Miller had filled the breach in the Australian bowling caused by the injury to Crawford, bowled 34 overs and, for a man who was to be used for "shock stuff", had been a magnificent "stock" man ...

Since that first opening stand by McDonald and Burke Australia had held the initiative. Trueman's bowling on the Saturday evening almost put England back into the game again. But, without detracting from Miller's great efforts, it has to be said that England's batting failed badly. It is easy to put the finger on the painful spot but where to turn for a cure is a problem for the selectors. *The Cricketer, July 7, 1956*

In the third Test Laker starts to get his teeth into the Australians – although 11 wickets at Headingley is a paltry return in comparison with what is to come. England win by an innings following a May hundred

May, in magnificent form, went to his fourth half-century of the series by hitting Benaud through the covers for four and celebrated by hitting yet another boundary to long-on ...

A 23,000 crowd had loved it all. It had been "needle" cricket of the highest order. And of May and Washbrook what is it necessary to say? They had joined in a fourth-wicket stand adding 187 runs. May had the glory of a century and Washbrook, giving the perfect answer to his critics and joy to his supporters, was ready to carry on [the next day] with a score of 90 not out [he made 98] ...

England had won by an innings and 42 runs and the crowd surged across the field to give Laker his due. The offspin bowler had followed his first innings figures of 5 for 58 runs with an even better second innings performance. He had bowled 41.3 overs, 21

maidens, 55 runs, 6 wickets, and today had taken 5 for 24 runs. Lock had three wickets for 40 runs in this innings to give him a match return of 7 for 81 – the whole match a triumph for the Surrey spin "twins".

All square and two to play in the series means that interest will now be maintained until the very last game. England were worthy winners and without the weekend rain might have done even better. They had one great slice of luck in that they won the toss! *The Cricketer, July 21, 1956*

And then comes Laker's Match at Old Trafford – the greatest bowling achievement of all time [dealt with overleaf]. In the final Test at The Oval, with the Ashes safely retained, Laker manages to dominate again, nearly causing an upset and certainly causing fright as the series draws to a close

The 1956 Test series ended with England winning two, Australia one and two matches being drawn. Laker, the dominant factor in the England successes, had taken 46 wickets in the series, including seven of 15 that fell in this final game.

The Cricketer, September 1, 1956 ▷

Dashing: star allrounder Keith Miller hits out

Top table: captains Peter May and Ian Johnson

For the first time since the turn of the century England have won three Test series in a row against Australia. The 1956 Australian team failed deplorably against the offspin of Laker. Their record against counties, if included in the Championship table, would not have put them in the top six. One of the wettest seasons on record cannot excuse their very ordinariness. They lost the Test series 2-1, they won only seven first-class fixtures and a festival game, and their failure against the turning ball, or inability to spin it themselves, produced a harsh but general judgement that they were the worst balanced touring side for over 50 years ... To understand the Australian failures, go back to the Hutton tour of Australia when Tyson and Statham carried all before it. It called for a changed approach by the Australian selectors. Whereas the emphasis had been put on players who could hit the ball about in the manner of Bradman and score fast and entertaining runs there were no players who had the Bradman technique. With the weaknesses exposed by speed the pendulum swung the other way. The Australian selectors looked for players who would stand up to the ball. Tyson and Statham had to be negatived.

So we had a side with fundamental weakness against offspin and they found pitches which, when dry, enabled Laker to turn the ball. The Australian method of playing [spin] is to go down the wicket. Laker, as a finger-spin bowler, could foil that method by bowling quicker and with a lower trajectory. A consummate artist, too, with every trick of the trade at his command, he wreaked havoc. It was Laker who dominated the Test series.

The Cricketer Annual, 1956

Sad indeed is the decline (temporarily only I hope) of Australian cricket, for it is much better to defeat a strong opponent than a very weak one, and it is only too apparent that the present Australian team is the weakest which has visited these shores for many a long day. Their record against the counties proves this without any doubt. While cricket has never been the No.1 sport in Australia, it appears that it is much less so now than ever and therein lies the trouble. Tennis seems to have taken a big grip and, until youngsters can be lured back to the willow by some means or other, Australian cricket looks likely to take a back seat for a long time to come. Yours faithfully, **T McAdam**, Dumbarton, Scotland.
The Cricketer, August 18, 1956

The King: Jim Laker of Surrey and England at The Oval in 1956

And so to Old Trafford and a pitch that is so perfect – following the rain – for Jim Laker that Australians still moan about it more than 50 years later. He had taken nine wickets in the first innings, bowling Australia out for 85, and they had followed on. Laker had already taken all 10 in an innings against the tourists for Surrey in May. Now, on the final day, as Bill Bowes describes, this happens

The last shower of rain fell at Old Trafford just after 5am and the ground staff, working from 6am, had the pitch and outfield ready for play within 10 minutes of the scheduled time for the start. At 11.40am Bailey and Laker began the bowling but it was soon obvious that the rain-soaked pitch had little to offer the bowlers. There was still a lot of cloud about and little to dry the pitch …

Good defensive batsmanship could save the day for Australia. McDonald did well, and so did Craig at the other end – 30, 60, 90 minutes went by and still these two batsmen defended to splendid purpose. No matter how May rang his bowling changes they had the reply. They positioned well, they saw the new ball off and at lunchtime had taken the score to 112 for 2. Australia needed to occupy the crease for four more hours.

Unfortunately for them the sun came out during the break and, after Bailey had bowled one more over so Lock and Laker could change ends, it seemed obvious that there was now a little help for the spinners. Twice in Lock's first over to Craig he beat the bat with deliveries which turned and lifted slightly. Twice in Laker's first over to McDonald he also beat the bat. And in his third over of the afternoon Laker began to strike. He had Craig, who had batted almost four and a half hours for 38, lbw.

Lightning strike: Laker after taking all 10 Australian wickets for Surrey at The Oval

4th Test, Old Trafford, July 26-31 1956
England won by an innings and 170 runs

ENGLAND WON TOSS

PE Richardson	c Maddocks	b Benaud	104
MC Cowdrey	c Maddocks	b Lindwall	80
Rev DS Sheppard		b Archer	113
PBH May*	c Archer	b Benaud	43
TE Bailey		b Johnson	20
C Washbrook	lbw	b Johnson	6
ASM Oakman	c Archer	b Johnson	10
TG Evans†	st Maddocks	b Johnson	47
JC Laker	run out		3
GAR Lock	not out		25
JB Statham	c Maddocks	b Lindwall	0
Extras	b2 lb5 w1		8
Total	158.3 overs		459

Fall of wickets 174 195 288 321 327
339 401 417 458

Bowling (1st) Lindwall 21.3-6-63-2, Miller 21-6-41-0, Archer 22-6-73-1, Johnson 47-10-151-4, Benaud 47-17-123-2

AUSTRALIA 1st innings

CC McDonald	c Lock	b Laker	32		c Oakman	b Laker	89
JW Burke	c Cowdrey	b Lock	22		c Lock	b Laker	33
RN Harvey		b Laker	0		c Cowdrey	b Laker	0
ID Craig	lbw	b Laker	8		lbw	b Laker	38
KR Miller	c Oakman	b Laker	6	(6)		b Laker	0
KD Mackay	c Oakman	b Laker	0	(5)	c Oakman	b Laker	0
RG Archer	st Evans	b Laker	6		c Oakman	b Laker	0
R Benaud	c Statham	b Laker	0			b Laker	18
RR Lindwall	not out		6		c Lock	b Laker	8
LV Maddocks†		b Laker	4	(11)	lbw	b Laker	2
IWG Johnson*		b Laker	0	(10)	not out		1
Extras			0		b12 lb4		16
Total	40.4 overs		84		150.2 overs		205

Fall of wickets 48 48 62 62 62
73 73 78 84

28 55 114 124 130
130 181 198 203

Bowling (1st) Statham 6-3-6-0, Bailey 4-3-4-0, Laker 16.4-4-37-9, Lock 14-3-37-1
(2nd) Statham 16-10-15-0, Bailey 20-8-31-0, Laker 51.2-23-53-10, Lock 55-30-69-0, Oakman 8-3-21-0

Umpires: DE Davies and FS Lee   England lead the 5-Test series 2-1

McDonald went to his 50 by hitting Lock, who still tended to pitch short, for two fours and a two in one over. But in Laker's next over at the other end Mackay obligingly repeated his stroke of the first innings and edged a ball to slip where Oakman made the catch.

Miller defended grimly for 15 minutes before, drawn forward by Laker, he missed and was, like Mackay, out for a "duck". The next batsman, Archer, was out to the second ball he received for the third "duck" in succession. Benaud and

> **66** How strangely weak the Australians are against offspinners! Laker deserved every cheer **99**

the magnificently subdued McDonald put a temporary end to England jubilation. They defended until teatime when Australia, still with a chance of saving the day, were 181 for 6.

Laker, however, with a tea interval rest for his spinning fingers, came into the fray refreshed. Once again he began to strike life out of the pitch and he ended McDonald's 337 minutes' defiance by making him edge a catch to Oakman in the leg trap. A

few minutes later he bowled the defiant Benaud – and Australia with only two wickets to fall had 90 minutes of play ahead of them.

For 20 minutes Lindwall and Johnson defended, but then came Laker's ninth victim with Lindwall also caught in the leg trap. Laker had now got 18 wickets in the match, a truly great performance, and if he could claim the last wicket he would be the first bowler ever to take 10 wickets in a Test-match innings.

With almost bated breath the crowd watched Lock bowl his succeeding over, and Oh, what cheering broke out when Laker got Maddocks lbw! For the second time this season he had got all 10 against Australia. Magnificent. It had been Laker's match.

His final figures were 51.2 overs, 23 maidens, 53 runs, 10 wickets. It meant that England, one match to the good and only one Test to play, had retained the Ashes. Australia lost by one hour, and one could have wished that their first-innings defiance had been similar to that of today. How strangely weak they are against offspinners! The crowd flocked to the pavilion and shouted enthusiastically for Laker to appear. He deserved every cheer. ◪

The Cricketer, August 4, 1956

Blessed release: Laker in action

1956

1st Test June 7-12, T Bdge
†**Eng** 217-8 dec
(PE Richardson 81) and
188-3 dec (MC Cowdrey 81);
Aus 148 (RN Harvey 64; JC Laker 4-58) and **120-3** (JW Burke 58*). **Match drawn.**

2nd Test June 21-26, Lord's †**Aus** 285 (CC McDonald 78) and **257** (R Benaud 97; FS Trueman 5-90); **Eng** 171 (KR Miller 5-72) and **186** (Miller 5-80). **Aus won by 185 runs.**

3rd Test July 12-17, Head †**Eng** 325 (PBH May 101, C Washbrook 98), **Aus** 143 (Laker 5-58) and **140** (Laker 6-55). **Eng won by inns and 42 runs.**

5th Test Aug 23-28, T Oval †**Eng** 247 (DCS Compton 94; RG Archer 5-53) and **182-3 dec** (DS Sheppard 62); **Aus** 202 (Miller 61; Laker 4-80) and **27-5. Match drawn.**

Dominance threatened

By the end of the 1950s England led the way in world cricket. But there was a creeping complacency, as the ever astute **Bill Bowes** notes in *The Cricketer* Spring Annual 1958 – and by the time England headed down under that winter, it had become an unstoppable growth

England are world cricket champions. In days when it seems to be the accepted rule that we should belittle our performances this fact should be noted. England, since FR Brown's team won the last Test match of the 1950–51 series at Melbourne – and so ended Australia's run of 26 post-war Tests without defeat – have successfully beaten and held, either at home or abroad, every other cricket-playing country. Slowly but surely, first under Sir Leonard Hutton and then, in more recent series, under Mr Peter May, England have built a pretty formidable cricket team. A four-pronged England attack, with spin and speed in equal measure, has successfully disposed of all opposition ...

Under present-day conditions I believe the England team could beat a world side. But this is not a justification for complacency. There are signs that conditions are going to change. Can they hold the title on faster, truer, pitches? Don't you think they will have been to look at the Bulli and Merri Creeks, from where they draw the silt? Do you think there will be any reason to water the pitch at Melbourne as it was alleged in 1954–55? Will they want to give our bowlers still more sporting pitches? I think we will need to work, and work hard, for our successes next winter. It is not a time for complacency.

The Cricketer, Spring Annual, 1958

An Australian opinion

To the editor

The consensus of opinion of the critics abroad is that England will retain the Ashes. Probably they may be right but on the other hand they may be in for a surprise. Added to the five fast bowlers will be Laker, Lock and Wardle, a wonderful trio on English wickets but will they obtain the same spin on our wickets? The English side will be strong in batting up to No.7 but then a tail commences. Richardson has to open the innings with Watson, aged 38. It is granted that the English captain – May – is the best batsman in the world today, and a fighting captain, but it has occurred to me that his uncanny luck in tossing may desert him on this tour and everyone knows what winning the toss means to a side over a five-day Test. I suggest to England not to be too complacent.

Yours faithfully,
Keith B Docker,
Strathfield,
New South Wales,
Australia

Action man: fast bowler Gordon Rorke

Hell bent: Meckiff's action was queried

Destroyed down under. Bill Bowes witnesses an arrogance then panic that leads to humiliating defeat for the 'world champions' in an ill-tempered tour marred by the no-balling of Australian Ian Meckiff for throwing ('jerking')

With a team little changed from that which earned the title of being world champions, England, during an inglorious tour of Australia, were defeated by four games to nil. It was the worst tour of Australia since 1921 when England, rebuilding after the war, lost all five Tests. It was a tour marked by poor performances and marred by injuries and incidents. The impression gleaned from the victors was one of uneasy virtue rather than triumph. There was not a victory in the series which had the crowd cheering at the dressing room and calling for speeches. There had been doubtful umpiring decisions, and much more than that, the Australian selectors had condoned a type of bowling which every spectator knew was not justified by law. The peal of victory had a hollow ring ... If there was one regrettable tendency on the part of the players as a whole it was towards complacency – in the early part of the tour. Seven years of success on the cricket field had not brought team spirit so much as a belief that, when needed, everything would come right.

After a season of cricket in England it is understandable that cricketers on the journey to Australia should have a complete rest. There is no complaint that players did not have early morning PT and, apart from fielding practice late on the trip, took the opportunity for a laze.

Such was the complacency of the England party, so certain were they that things would come right, that serious practice at the start of the tour was never entertained. A cursory examination of the nets would decide them unfit for practice; there would be danger if Trueman or Tyson bowled really fast. The fresh air and gentle exercise of a golf course was much to be preferred. It was not unusual to see Trueman bowling left-hand, Loader trying legbreaks and Tyson offspinners. Not once did I see someone in authority standing behind the net and bringing a player to task. On one occasion after the England team had decided the nets were unfit to use for their morning practice the Australian team, watched by the selectors, with fast bowlers going flat out, had two hours' practice in the afternoon ...

[After the first game] Australia were happy to be one Test match up but it was generally agreed that England had been most unlucky. They had a comfortable win over South Australia and they went into the second Test at Melbourne without a worry.

Again May won the toss, again came that lively first morning pitch, the first three wickets were lost with only seven runs scored, but even so Bailey, May and Cowdrey helped to take England's final score to 259 and splendid bowling by Statham (7 for 57) limited Australia's first innings advantage to only 49 runs. Everything was still all right.

All right, that is, for only a matter of minutes! May, manager Brown, every member of the England party, press and supporters, were soon painfully aware everything was wrong. Meckiff came good. He began to hurl the ball down straight and true. He took six wickets for 38 runs, England were skittled out on a beautiful true, fast, pitch for only 87 and Australia went to victory in the second Test by eight wickets. Too late it became obvious that everything had not come right with the England batting. Complacency went in the instant. May ordered intensive practice to begin immediately.

He might just as well have ordered the moon. The huge

Melbourne stadium, so vastly altered for the recent Olympic Games, could offer no facilities for intensive practice. The groundsman had all his work cut out to make the playing area fit for Tests.

Shaken from complacency, with May and Cowdrey once again the mainstay of the batting, England managed to make a drawn game of the third Test. It left Australia two up and only two matches to play. To hold the series May had to take a gamble. He put Australia in to bat on a lovely pitch at Adelaide and at the end of the first day's play, with Australia 200 for 1, it was obvious that all hopes of England staging a late rally had gone. Australia, with McDonald scoring 170, totalled 476 in their first innings and a rather disconsolate England team, especially against fast bowler Rorke, lost by 10 wickets.

This defeat meant Australia had regained the Ashes and by playing a fast-bowling battery of Davidson, Lindwall, Meckiff and Rorke in the final Test they won the series 4-0 ...

So far as "jerking or throwing" is concerned I need only say that on one occasion I was walking on the beach and passed some youngsters playing cricket. I heard one say: "I'm Jimmy Burke." He ran up to the bowling mark and deliberately threw to the other end. I chuckled rather sadly. There was a fear for the future of cricket besides humour in my mind. Apart from Queensland every state side in Australia has a fast bowler of doubtful action. When I greeted Ray Lindwall on his selection for the fourth Test and congratulated him he said, with a grin: "Yes, I'm the last of the straight-arm bowlers."

I shall never believe Sir Donald Bradman and his co-selectors had no doubts about the action of Meckiff, Rorke, Slater or Burke. I do not believe they were right to hide behind the fact that "no umpire had ever no-balled them". Time will prove whether the best interests of cricket were served. ◪

The Cricketer, Spring Annual, 1959

Too dull, too dull

Gordon Ross, editor of *Playfair*, delivers his tour verdict – which hinted of the difficulties to come in the 1960s

I derived no enjoyment from my Test cricket in 1958, it was far too lop-sided and, frankly, if Test cricket is going to develop into a little matter of under 200 runs a day, then I shall look elsewhere for my cricketing pleasures as, I fear, all too many people are already doing. I hope we might throw some attacking players into the hum-drum of Test cricket and, when we get them there, allow them to play a natural game. I hope that Dexter is not told: "No hooking before lunch and no square cutting before tea!" If we are going to sink as we did in Australia, irrevocably and irretrievably, then I would much rather the ship go down with all guns blazing than by having nine players bowled out going back on their stumps.

The Cricketer, Spring Annual, 1959

England's Test failures

The England team's performance was miserable. The team were, simply, no match for Australia. In the match at Brisbane it took nearly five days to score 665 runs, Bailey taking 7½ hours to score 68 runs, and on the third day of the match 106 runs were scored in five hours on an easy paced wicket. Modern cricket is being ruined by a lack of proper footwork by batsmen and a negative and defensive attitude by batsmen and bowlers. Yours, **WP Toone**, Cepians, Eire

The Cricketer, April 25, 1959

1958-59

1st Test Dec 5-6, 8-10, Brisbane †**Eng 134** and **198** (TE Bailey 68; R Benaud 4-66); **Aus 186** (CC McDonald 42; PJ Loader 4-56) and **147-2** (NC O'Neill 71*). **Aus won by 8 wkts.**

2nd Test Dec 31, Jan 1-2, 4-5, Melbourne †**Eng 259** (PBH May 113; AK Davidson 6-64) and **87** (I Meckiff 6-38); **Aus 308** (RN Harvey 167; JB Statham 7-57) and **42-2. Aus won by 8 wkts.**

3rd Test Jan 9-10, 12-15, Sydney †**Eng 219** (Benaud 5-83) and **287-7 dec** (MC Cowdrey 100*; Benaud 4-94); **Aus 357** (O'Neill 77; JC Laker 5-107) and **54-2. Match drawn.**

4th Test Jan 30-31, Feb 2-5, Adelaide **Aus 476** (McDonald 170; FS Trueman 4-90) and **36-0**; †**Eng 240** (Cowdrey 84; Benaud 5-91) and **270** (May 59; Benaud 4-82). **Aus won by 10 wkts.**

5th Test Feb 13-15, 17-18, Melbourne **Eng 205** (PE Richardson 68; Benaud 4-43) and **214** (Graveney 54); †**Aus 351** (McDonald 133; Trueman 4-92) and **69-1** (McDonald 51*). **Aus won by 9 wkts.**

Chucked out: Colin Cowdrey is caught behind off Ian Meckiff as England lose the second Test at Melbourne by eight wickets. Meckiff took 9 for 107 in the match.

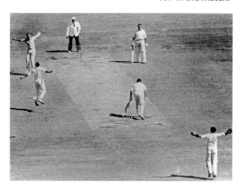

Keith Miller

Test matches

Batting

Matches	55
Innings	87
Runs	2958
Highest score	147
Average	36.97
Hundreds	7
Fifties	13

Bowling

Balls	10461
Runs	3906
Wickets	170
Average	22.97
Best bowling	7-60
5-for inns	7
10-for match	1

First-class career

Batting

Matches	226
Innings	326
Runs	14183
Highest score	281*
Average	48.91
Hundreds	41
Fifties	63

Bowling

Balls	28070
Runs	11087
Wickets	497
Average	22.30
Best bowling	7-12
5-for inns	16
10-for match	1

v England

Batting

Matches	29
Runs	1511
Average	33.57

Bowling

Wickets	87
Average	22.40

The all-round Invincible

He was never part of the establishment, says **David Frith**,
but for talent and charisma Keith Miller was out on his own

THERE HAS never been a more glamorous cricketer than Keith Miller: not even Imran Khan. Miller's entry into the field generated every kind of crowd excitement. His stride was that of the catwalk. His sleek hair anticipated Elvis. And his flashing smile showed admirers and adversaries alike that he was delighted to be there, privileged to be enjoying himself in the cause of entertainment. He was looking forward to swinging his bat, banging down a bouncer or plucking a catch out of nowhere.

Miller was a cricketer of moods, ever responsive to a challenge but bored by stalemate, chivalrous in both victory and adversity. He was one of those players whom it would be wrong to judge by statistics, impressive though those are.

He was strikingly Australian in physique and in his friendly openness; insouciant, modest, never forgetting a name (unless – sometimes – when addressing one of his four sons). But as Len Hutton, one of his greatest adversaries, cautioned, it was not wise to hit Keith for four: better to run him away for singles. Hutton was forever bewitched by Miller's unpredictability. In one over there might be a wicked bouncer off three paces, an innocuous half-volley and then a googly. He never bothered measuring out a run-up.

England claimed him too. Miller served with 169 Squadron during the Second World War, stationed in Norfolk, flying Beaufighter and Mosquito fighter-bombers. From his raw experiences of war he subscribed passionately to the conviction that cricket should always be essentially for recreation.

There was just time before the War for Miller to make his first-class debut. In February 1938, when he was only 18, he hit 181 for Victoria against Tasmania at the MCG. His outstanding potential was emphasised with a further century against Don Bradman's South Australia (with the cunning old spinner Clarrie Grimmett bowling), also at the MCG, in the New Year 1940 Sheffield Shield match. When he joined the air force he had bowled 56 balls in first-class cricket.

It was not until he burst on to the scene at Lord's in the matches played by the Australian Services XI towards the end of the war and in the 'Victory Tests' of 1945 that his power with the bat and potential for rattling batsmen with raw pace and sharp bounce off a short run-up were fully revealed. "What does this chap bowl?" England's Denis Compton inquired of the Australian Services wicketkeeper Stan Sismey. Miller's first ball, released after a short gallop, a shimmy of the shoulder and a fast sweep of the arm, whistled past Compton's head.

Miller stroked the first of his seven Test centuries in the 1946-47 Adelaide Ashes Test and after a moderate series against India he took a prominent part in the never-to-be-forgotten 1948 tour of England. And that series is remembered as much as anything for the fiery Lindwall-Miller opening attack, energised as it was by the nonsensical regulation that allowed a new ball after 55 overs. Miller's cascade of bumpers at Trent Bridge in the first Test worked the spectators into a frenzy. It was probably the only time in his life that the popular Miller was booed and jeered. He merely laughed, rolled his sleeve up and bucked into his next delivery. In terrible light his bosom friend Compton fell into his stumps, having scored 184, and walked off without his familiar smile, ignoring Miller's congratulations, though they were soon sharing a drink.

Miller's damaged back prevented him from bowling in the Lord's Test and he took only 13 wickets in that series while Lindwall and Bill Johnston claimed 27 apiece. But Miller's animated presence always placed him centre stage. Only Bradman attracted more people through the turnstiles. Keith Miller's relationship with Bradman was unusual. He was one of those close to The Don who were irritated by aspects of his nature. The 1948ers were mainly new boys who demonstrated an almost humble respect for their 39-year-old skipper. Not Miller. He tossed the ball back to his captain, saying he thought he had already made it clear that his back was too painful and he was not able to bowl.

> **66** He diverted his aircraft after a bombing raid so that he could get an aerial view of Beethoven's birthplace **99**

A bone of contention among his legions of disciples was that he was never entrusted with the captaincy of Australia. The Australian board has always preferred the 'safe' captain, the establishment man. Only when Ian Johnson was forced from the field in the West Indies in 1955 was Miller permitted to act as Test captain. And in that short span he brought a dynamism to proceedings that spotlighted what Australia might have forsaken.

The 1956 venture, his final tour, was one that Australia has ever since wished to forget. But at Lord's he had done his favourite ground proud with five wickets in each innings to put Australia one up. It was the tourists' only victory but the Australian hero, object of as much female as male adulation, stamped that match flamboyantly as his own. As the players left the field he lifted the bails from the umpire's pocket and, considerate to the last, tossed them as souvenirs into the crowd to the side of the pavilion.

There was a rebellious yet contrary streak about Miller's psyche, even allowing that his extroversion often blanketed a sentimental nature. This was the man who diverted his aircraft many miles off course after a bombing raid so that he could get an aerial view of Beethoven's birthplace; the man who would terrify one batsman after another through the afternoon, only to spend the evening humming classics in the company of the delicate and sensitive Neville Cardus. *The Wisden Cricketer, December 2004*

While the rest of the world swung to an exciting new groove cricket languished – no revolution, no creative explosion, just plenty of draws. In the Ashes only 10 of 25 games forced a result. The Cricketer recognised this – and defended it – but a desperate air of gloom runs through the articles. And it did not help that the Ashes were stuck down under

Begone, dull care

Australia had played a thrilling series against West Indies, that included the first tied Test. More of the same was called for – by Lord's command. **Ray Robinson** previews

The upsurge of interest caused whenever an Australian team is chosen to tour England is swelling higher this year. People's expectations have been enlivened by the stimulant of exciting cricket in Australia's Tests against West Indies. The essence of it all lay in the approach to the game by both captains and players. It was never lost, even though runs did not always flow quickly. The former Test captain AER Gilligan was moved to say: "The cricket is probably the best I have ever seen. What a wonderful experience England will have if this cricket standard can be retained for the tour, eliminating dull, boring Tests!"

The Cricketer, Spring Annual, 1961

If that series was not inspiration enough, the governing bodies issue directives to entertain. Would Colin Cowdrey listen?

Test and county cricket will be more attractive from this summer. No longer will these be just pious words, for included in a memorandum issued by the newly formed Committee of Inquiry is the statement. "County Selectors should be drastic in dealing with players they consider are not co-operating sufficiently in the new approach." It was explained at Lord's that this "drastic treatment" means that dull players should be dropped from a side until they mend their ways. *The Cricketer, Spring Annual, 1961*

And did it work? First Test, run glut, draw. But England are bowled out cheaply first time and need to dig out the result. Bill Bowes reports from all the Tests

1st Test, June 8-10, 12-13, Edgbaston †**Eng 195** (R Subba Row 59; KD Mackay 4-57) and **401-4** (ER Dexter 180, Subba Row 112); **Aus 516** (RN Harvey 114, NC O'Neill 82). **Match drawn.**

Harvey and Lawry looked as if they could bat for a week ... O'Neill joined Harvey, who was now pushing the ball about with easy precision, and for a man who was supposed to have a knee injury he ran singles in a manner which caused one critic to comment, "I wish I had two knees like his bad one."

The inspirational captain Richie Benaud does try to force a result

Benaud bowled. He tried over the wicket. He tried round the wicket and pitching into the bowler's rough outside the offstump of the left-handers. The batsmen were equal to every subterfuge. The arrears were wiped off and left far behind as the Dexter-Barrington partnership flourished. *The Cricketer, June 24, 1961*

Ready for action: Cowdrey and his England team for the first Test at Edgbaston in 1961

Australia's traditional dominance at Lord's continues – a venue coming under increasing criticism for poor wickets

2nd Test June 22-24, 26, Lord's †Eng 206 (Subba Row 48; AK Davidson 5-42) and **202** (KF Barrington 66; GD McKenzie 5-37); **Aus 340** (WM Lawry 130) and **71-5. Aus won by 5 wkts.**

For many years now Lord's has been the most unreliable of grounds. The ball lifts unexpectedly to grind knuckles to the bat handle and it is a matter of luck whether the ball then flies for a catch or falls safely to earth. It strikes me as not being a good cricket wicket if a batsman through no fault of his, and no excellence on the part of the bowler, can be out. *The Cricketer, July 8, 1961*

May replaces Cowdrey as captain and Fiery Fred at his aggressive best on his home ground levels the series

3rd Test July 6-8, Headingley †Aus 237 (Harvey 73; FS Trueman 5-58) and **120** (Harvey 53; Trueman 6-30); **Eng 299** (MC Cowdrey 93; Davidson 5-63) and **62-2. Eng won by 8 wkts.**

Although the fast bowler [Fred Trueman] was operating off his shortened run I declare he bowled even faster. Ball after ball, with unerring precision, he dropped into the dusting bare patches. Bringing the ball back like a fast offspinner he moved in to shatter the stumps of Simpson and so claim three wickets in 15 balls at a cost of only one run. Benaud was his next victim, bowled out for a duck, thus the first Australian captain since 1902 to be out for a pair ... The third Test had been a bowler's match. Unlike Lord's there had been no physical danger. There had been tremendous incident but the joy of seeing some of the finest stroke players in the world demonstrate their skill had been denied. *The Cricketer, July 22, 1961*

Benaud turns the fourth Test on the final afternoon and Australia retain the Ashes. Bowes senses an ill-wind blowing

4th Test July 27-29, 31, August 1, Old Trafford †Aus 190 (Lawry 74; JB Statham 5-53) and **432** (Lawry 102; DA Allen 4-58); **Eng 367** (PBH May 95; RB Simpson 4-23) and **201** (ER Dexter 76; R Benaud 6-70). **Aus won by 54 runs.**

Anything was possible on this last day but only 12,000 came to watch. England, if they wanted to win, had to score 256 in 230 minutes ... Dexter came in – and Dexter took charge. He produced a range of strokes putting to shame what had gone before. He drove, late cut and pulled with powerful effect. A huge six brought the 150 on the board in just over two hours but then came a change in fortunes. Dexter, having made 76, hitting 14 fours and one six, tried a late cut at Benaud and nicked a catch to Grout. May came in and was bowled round his legs for a duck. Close gave a most undistinguished display, edging over slips for two, swinging and missing four times, hitting one six and then hitting a catch to square leg. Subba Row was bowled by Benaud after making 49. Murray edged a catch to Simpson at slip. Barrington stood in front of a straight ball from Mackay ... With Australia cock-a-hoop, the game went into 10 minutes of extra time. Then Davidson, coming on for Benaud, bowled Statham ... Australia had gone to a splendid victory by 54 runs and Benaud in a magnificent spell had sent down 32 overs and taken six wickets for 70 runs. *The Cricketer, August 5, 1961*

England drop Trueman – "the most antagonistic fast bowler in the world" (Bowes again) – for Tony Lock, May win the toss and bats on a pitch perfect for Fred. England have to save the game again

5th Test August 17-19, 21-22, The Oval †Eng 256 (May 71; Davidson 4-83) and **370-8** (Subba Row 137; Mackay 5 121); **Aus 494** (PJP Burge 181, O'Neill 117). **Match drawn.**

When they are fighting a rearguard action, England cricketers always seem to be at

Nicked: Benaud gets Dexter – the end begins

their best. With six wickets still to fall and only 83 runs in arrears there was still hope that England would salvage something from the wreck of the Test series. They could not, by any stretch of the imagination, win the game. A pitch so good that England might force a drawn game could not also produce conditions to win ... At the close England were 370 for 8, Allen not out 42 and the match was saved. *The Cricketer, September 2, 1961*

No rearguard excitement can paper over the slow scoring by England, as cricket writer Leslie Smith explains

Even in the match which England won at Headingley, Australia still scored the faster. When it is considered that England have such stroke-players in their side as May, Cowdrey and Dexter the slow rate is difficult to understand. For far too many years now England have played cricket the "safe" way. It has brought a fair measure of success, even though it has been mostly dull to watch. Now not even success can be given as an excuse. With the Australia-West Indies series fresh in their minds and the knowledge that the public can be brought back to the game if it is played in the right way, surely England could have made a greater effort. They might still have lost but it would have been better to fail when playing positive cricket. *The Cricketer, September 2, 1961*

Bill Bowes backs this view

Enthusiasm, a greater love of playing cricket, a determination to get on with the game: these were the main factors in Australia's successful defence of the Ashes in England last summer ... England never "give it a go". Although the best batsmen in England are amateurs, the general approach to the job of scoring runs is coldly professional and [this] tends to the eradication of mistakes than a spirit of adventure ... Our England batsmen are frightened of getting out ... Never, at any time, in Tests or otherwise, did Benaud and his men play cricket of a type likely to turn the spectator away. If a game is to be worth watching, it has to be so obviously worth the playing. I wonder if almost all our trouble and disappointment in England are because the players do not find much fun? *The Cricketer Annual, 1961*

Rare drama: Fred Titmus loses his middle stump to Alan Davidson in the third Test at Sydney

Nothing ventured ...

England headed to Australia in high hopes but returned empty-handed with Test cricket's reputation for entertainment threatened. '**Topspinner**' writes monthly 'Cables from Australia' and it starts ... with a draw

In six days the series changed its complexion. We began the first Test on the last day of November with two defeats behind us, one, from New South Wales, the worst ever suffered at the hands of a State side. In the days before Brisbane there were too many loose ends lying about to make the prospect encouraging. Australia were justifiably confident, more so after they had recovered in their first innings from 140 for 5 to 404 all out. England, however, survived the match and gathered their thoughts ...

The Test at Melbourne marked a notable centenary. It is 100 years since the first English side played there and the bunting was out ... The result has "made" the series. Whatever happens from now on every match will have a bearing on the rubber. If Australia had won, it would have been hard to see England catching them. Success, however, should close the ranks of Dexter's side. Failure has revealed cracks in the Australian façade. Benaud, their captain, and Sir Donald Bradman, chairman of selectors, will revel in the battles ahead. So will Dexter. And so, I am sure, will you, by whatever medium and in whatever temperature it may be ...

It was, in the event, a thrilling match and from England's point of view a memorable one. Incredible though it was, Australia were outbatted, outbowled and eventually outfielded. Whereas at Brisbane England had always occupied the "outside lane", they were now on the "inside" all the way.

They scored faster and more handsomely, with Dexter holding the torch. Cowdrey, having returned to form with a gargantuan innings against South Australia, had a classical hundred and shared a vital partnership with Dexter ...

At 5.15pm on the fourth day England, tired but not dissatisfied, took the last Australian wicket. Their bowlers had been heroic and Trueman, reserved for the second

Child's play: a premature invasion of the SCG anticipating the end of the third Test

Leading spinner: Richie Benaud

Leading lights: Statham and Dexter, left

new ball, had finally broken the back of Australia's resistance.

The Cricketer, February 1963

Australia level at Sydney, then draw at Adelaide as Statham becomes the top Test wicket taker

What more could one ask? With one Test left the rubber between England and Australia is level, a state of affairs that has existed only once in Australia since 1894–95. This was on GO Allen's tour 26 years ago when Australia lost the first two Tests before winning the last three. Dexter's side lost at Sydney after winning at Melbourne and at Adelaide the fourth Test, like the first, was drawn. The Ashes are therefore in the balance and this, so late in the tour, is more than we had

hoped for. In Australia the interest is high, although in terms of brisk adventurous play it has been a disappointing series. The fear of failure has prevailed over the urge to take a chance. *The Cricketer, March 1963*

It was not with a bang but a whimper that the Test series ended at Sydney. The rubber was shared and the Ashes remain in Australia's keeping for another year ... The last Test went as it did partly because neither side was good enough, by Anglo-Australian standards, to dictate terms ... The failure at the last was one of courage and, when stumps were drawn for the last time, there were none of the scenes that normally mark the end of a series. The loving cup was not called for. Instead the people went glumly home. ◪ *The Cricketer, April 1963*

"Root out slow play"

The commentators were not convinced by the dreary pace. Ray Robinson points the finger from an Australian perspective, EW Swanton defends from an English one

Ray Robinson accuses: If good really can come out of evil, Test cricket could benefit from the stalemate series which ended here with half the paying customers hooting the last two batsmen off the field. One [letter sent to the papers] written the day the MCC team left ended: *"It is a sad blow to cricket that Harvey and Davidson are quitting the game but they shouldn't be lonely, as they are retiring at the same time as 100,000 spectators."* When two such captains as Richie Benaud and Ted Dexter – protagonists of lively cricket – find it beyond them to make a Test match look like a cricket match it is high time that the game's controllers rooted out the causes of tactics that led to the slow-clapping and booing of two of the world's best teams. The only constructive suggestion I can make is that the authorities take as starting-points Dexter's opinion that the Ashes are a dampener on good cricket and the Duke of Norfolk's farewell comment: *"I would like to forget that each match is part of a series and say this is the Sydney Test, this is the Melbourne Test, this is the Lord's Test ..."* Instead of wooing the Australian cricket public from the feeling that they would rather watch West Indians than Englishmen playing Australia, the recent Tests have strengthened that trend.

EW Swanton defends: It was a great pity that in the decider England acquiesced so mildly in accepting the difficulties of the Sydney wicket and the appalling slowness of the whole field and so surrendering the early initiative to the Australians who, when their second innings came along, considered themselves justified in going strictly on to the defensive. For generally speaking, over the series, England within the limitations imposed by their fielding and sometimes by the captain's irregular field placings, had shown fully as much thrust as Australia. The scoring rate of the two sides had been almost identical at around 44 an hour ... Incidentally, in view of the horrible wailing noises made in some quarters at the end of the tour, it is worthwhile comparing the 1962–63 scoring rates with the overall rates in England-Australia Tests since the war. Assuming 108 balls an hour they are as follows: England 39, Australia 46. Without going further into analysis and figures let me give a personal opinion for what it is worth that, *considering what they had*, Dexter's side acquitted themselves pretty well. *The Cricketer, April 1963*

1962-63

1st Test Nov 30, Dec 1, 3-5, Brisbane †**Aus 404** (BC Booth 112, KD Mackay 86*) and **362-4 dec** (WM Lawry 98, RB Simpson 71); **Eng 389** (PH Parfitt 80, KF Barrington 78; R Benaud 6 115) and **278-6** (ER Dexter 99, G Pullar 56). **Match drawn.**

2nd Test Dec 29, 31, Jan 1-3, Melbourne †**Aus 316** (Lawry 52, Mackay 49; FJ Titmus 4-43) and **248** (Booth 103, Lawry 57; FS Trueman 5-62); **Eng 331** (MC Cowdrey 113, Dexter 93; AK Davidson 6-75) and **237-3** (DS Sheppard 113, Cowdrey 58*). **Eng won by 7 wkts.**

3rd Test Jan 11-12, 14-15, Sydney †**Eng 279** (Cowdrey 85; Simpson 5-57, Davidson 4-54) and **104** (Davidson 5-25); **Aus 319** (Simpson 91, BK Shepherd 71*; Titmus 7-79) and **67-2. Aus won by 8 wkts.**

4th Test Jan 25-26, 28-30, Adelaide †**Aus 393** (RN Harvey 154, NC O'Neill 100) and **293** (Booth 77, Simpson 71; Trueman 4-60); **Eng 331** (Barrington 63, Dexter 61, Titmus 59*; GD McKenzie 5-89) and **223-4** (Barrington 132*). **Match drawn.**

5th Test Feb 15-16, 18-20, Sydney †**Eng 321** (Barrington 101) and **268-8 dec** (Barrington 94, Sheppard 68); **Aus 349** (PJP Burge 103, O'Neill 73; Titmus 5-103) and **152-4** (Burge 52*, Lawry 45*). **Match drawn.**

"The murderer of cricket"

The 1964 series took the Ashes to a new low. When, in five sunny days at Old Trafford, the match barely made it into a third innings, the press sharpened their knives. But **Richie Benaud**, now writing for *The Cricketer*, sums it up differently

They have been labelled as the worst side since 1912 and the worst bowling side in the last 20 years. It is said of this attack that there are no Lindwalls, Millers and Davidsons – too true. Nor are there any O'Reillys, McCabes or Bradmans, and certainly England haven't got Compton and Hammond, or Bedser and Doug Wright. The names in this Australian attack are virtually unknown with the exception of McKenzie, but they certainly shouldn't be underrated during the next six months. *The Cricketer, May 22, 1964*

John Woodcock charts the dismal series in his match reports. The first Test at Trent Bridge was hit by bad weather, as is the second

When the Lord's Test match is half destroyed by rain, it is a sad business. That was its fate; and there is a long time to wait before Australia play there again. Before the match wicket and weather seemed set fair.
The Cricketer, July 3, 1964

Into the third game and there is cricket and a result at last in what Woodcock calls 'Burge's Match'

A magnificent innings by Burge, who reached his century in the last over of the day, turned the match in its tracks. If Australia win the Ashes, as seems likely, they will look back on Burge's innings as having been decisive. Titmus opened the bowling with Trueman. In 27 overs he took 2 for 25. Australia batted as if Titmus had some hidden power, though the ball turned only slowly. This will be known as 'Burge's Match'. Again it showed how

the stature of an Australian tends to grow in the atmosphere of a Test match, and of an Englishman to decline. *The Cricketer, July 17, 1964*

The fourth Test, at Old Trafford, is magnificent in its futility – a two-day triple hundred from captain Bob Simpson (Bradman took half the time) and the bore draw to end bore draws. Woodcock writes:

[Bob Simpson's] defensive technique could scarcely be faulted. There was much to admire about his everlasting innings. It was a remarkable achievement to bat for two days with hardly an error. As entertainment it ranked with chess by post ... It was unfertile in the end; it was dour always; but it was never quite devoid of meaning. *The Cricketer, August 14, 1964*

In a new column called 'The Cricket Press' John Reason charts the media reaction

"The murderer of cricket," wrote JL Manning, in the *Daily Mail*, of Bobby Simpson's 311. "A spiritless, senseless bore," said Peter Wilson, in the *Daily Mirror*. "It killed spectators' interest stone dead," said Crawford White, in the *Daily Express*. "A pointless formality," said Ian Wooldridge, in the *Mail*, of the fourth Test match generally. "One long, boring farce," said Crawford White's colleague, Keith Miller ... Six senior members of the press were asleep.
The Cricketer, August 14, 1964

> **❝It was unfertile in the end; it was dour always❞**

Batting forever: Australia captain Bob Simpson pads up ... again

In the final game at The Oval, another draw, Woodcock celebrates a landmark bowling achievement and a young star in the making, even if he is a product of his time

Australia's last five wickets added 135, four of them falling to Trueman, who thus became the first bowler ever to take 300 wickets in Test cricket ... At close of play Boycott was still there, having batted almost faultlessly for 74 not out. To say that he has something of Sutcliffe's phlegmatic temperament is to pay him a high compliment. His batting does not give aesthetic pleasure so much as practical satisfaction. Boycott reached his first Test hundred in four hours. He has been a real find in the series. *The Cricketer, August 28, 1964*

Five Tests decided by one hundred at Headingley in the middle of the series ... Richie Benaud in his valedictory column suggests it was not as bad as the press would have you think

A dull year – poor cricket – no interest in the county games and the Test matches even worse – this is the sort of thing I have been hearing from people following the conclusion of the final Test at The Oval. I began to think perhaps I had been watching cricket in a different country for most of the cricket I saw during the season was interesting and even at times wonderfully exciting. ◪
The Cricketer, September 11, 1964

Batsman gain, bowler pain

The trip to Australia in 1965-66 did not exactly set the pulses racing either. Pitches were slow and England won a Test, then lost the next to batting failure. **John Woodcock** finds enough to enjoy in mission unaccomplished

A glance at the final averages for the Australian tour will always give an accurate idea of the chief problem facing Mike Smith's side. Whereas nine of his batsmen averaged over 45, the most successful bowler took only 36 wickets at 30 runs apiece. On their last four outings in the field MCC conceded totals of 273 for 1, 516, 488 and 545 for 8 declared, which means that each wicket they took between January 25 and February 16 cost them 63 runs.

In the end the weakness of their attack, on pitches that were invariably true and too often slow, caught up with them. But before that happened they had taken a lead in the series, as ER Dexter's team did in 1962-63 and now, as then, it was their batting which let them down in the critical match. This was the irony of the tour. They were on top of the world when they went to Adelaide for the fourth Test match, and yet they were bowled out for 241 and 266 ...

With the series level the final Test at Melbourne was awaited with the utmost interest. MCC preceded it with one of their best batting displays, making 449 runs in a day against New South Wales at Sydney after being forced to follow on. The captains promised that they would be "out to win". They vowed that the tour wouldn't fizzle out like the last one. But come the time, this is exactly what it did.

After a splendid day's cricket to start with, on which England recovered from 41 for 2 to 312 for 5, thanks to a brilliant innings by Barrington, the two sides forgot their resolutions. England began it all by adding only 66 in 90 minutes after lunch on the second day, instead of declaring or forcing the pace. After this Simpson saw no reason for heroics and Australia batted until there was only 70 minutes left at the end of the match. The third day was much the worst and mercifully the whole of the fourth day was lost to rain, so that we were left on the Wednesday to see whether Cowper, who had come in on Saturday afternoon, could beat Garry Sobers' record Test score of 365 not out.

Sir Donald Bradman, with a twinkle in his eye, said to me once: "If I had my time again there's one record Len wouldn't hold – that's his 364." The Don was pleased, I expect, that his 334 remained intact from Cowper's challenge as the highest Australian Test innings. The curator at Melbourne was partly responsible for this disappointing match.

But there were more than enough good things about the tour to outweigh the mediocre and the unenterprising. For a side that left England with such limited prospects it was a grand effort to come so near to recapturing the Ashes. In almost every match there was some splendid batting to please the crowds.

The bowlers were opposed to a very strong batting side. Except in the Test match at Sydney even two of the best offspinners in the world, Titmus and Allen, got few balls past the bat. The most encouraging improvement was shown by Jones, who took only one wicket fewer than McKenzie in the same number of Test matches and bowled four fewer overs.

What, I wonder, is Smith's future? If the idea is to go round the world not losing Test matches he has a very successful record, having led England 15 times over the last three winters, in India, South Africa and Australia, and been beaten only once. But he has won only twice. Smith is inclined to use the automatic pilot. He is more a foreman than captain ...

Not often does such a golden chance of winning the Ashes come England's way as came to them now, with Australia one match down and their ranks open. Under Simpson's efficient captaincy – he was, of course, absent at Sydney – they soon pulled themselves together. Australia's bowling is not so good and they would help themselves, as well as the game in general, if all curators from Perth to Brisbane were told, in no uncertain terms, to make their pitches faster. That should be the next stage in restoring the popularity of the game, a process to which Smith's side made a laudable contribution. ∎

Hard work: Trueman bowls down under

The Cricketer, March 1966

1964

1st Test June 4-6, 8-9, T Bridge **†Eng 216-8 dec** (G Boycott 48) and **193-9 dec** (ER Dexter 68; GD McKenzie 5-53); **Aus 168** and **40-2. Match drawn.**

2nd Test June 18-20, 22-23, Lord's **Aus 176** (TR Veivers 54; FS Trueman 5-48) and **168-4**; **†Eng 246** (JH Edrich 120). **Match drawn.**

3rd Test July 2-4, 6, Head'y **†Eng 268** (JM Parks 68; NJN Hawke 5-75) and **229** (KF Barrington 85); **Aus 389** (PJP Burge 160; FJ Titmus 4-69) and **111-3** (IR Redpath 58*). **Aus won by 7 wkts.**

4th Test July 23-25, 27-28, Old Trafford **†Aus 656-8 dec** (RB Simpson 311) and **4-0**; **Eng 611** (Barrington 256, Dexter 174; McKenzie 7-153). **Match drawn.**

5th Test August 13-18, The Oval **†Eng 182** (Hawke 6-47) and **381-4** (Boycott 113); **Aus 379** (WM Lawry 94; Trueman 4-87). **Match drawn.**

1965-66

1st Test December 10-11, 13-15, Brisbane **†Aus 443-6 dec** (WM Lawry 166, KD Walters 155); **Eng 280** (FJ Titmus 60; PI Philpott 5-90) and **186-3** (G Boycott 63*). **Match drawn.**

2nd Test December 30-January 1, 3-4, Melbourne **†Aus 358** (RM Cowper 99; BR Knight 4-84) and **426** (PJP Burge 120, Walters 115); **Eng 558** (JH Edrich 109, MC Cowdrey 104; GD McKenzie 5-134) and **5-0. Match drawn.**

3rd Test January 7-8, 10-11, Sydney **†Eng 488** (RW Barber 185, Edrich 103; NJN Hawke 7-105); **Aus 221** (Cowper 60; DJ Brown 5-63) and **174** (Titmus 4-40, DA Allen 4-47). **Eng won by an inns and 93 runs.**

4th Test January 28-29, 31- February 1, Adelaide **†Eng 241** (Barrington 60; McKenzie 6-48) and **266** (Barrington 102; Hawke 5-54); **Aus 516** (RB Simpson 225, Lawry 119; IJ Jones 6-118). **Aus won by an inns and 9 runs.**

5th Test February 11-12, 14-16, Melbourne **†Eng 485-9 dec** (Barrington 115, Walters 4-53) and **69-3; Aus 543-8 dec** (Cowper 307, Lawry 108). **Match drawn.**

Rain, runs and politics

Richie Benaud and **Sir Neville Cardus** – now writing for
The Cricket – anticipate the anticipation

"Great Hope": Paul Sheahan at Old Trafford

Benaud writes: Nothing is more calculated to stir the blood of an English cricket follower than the arrival of an Australian team. Paul Sheahan and Doug Walters arrived with a reputation that will take some living up to; I believe that by the end of this tour they will have confirmed their rating as two of Australia's finest young players to travel overseas since the end of the war.

The Cricketer, May 3, 1968

Sir Neville Cardus, *The Guardian*'s illustrious cricket correspondent, writes Whenever an Australian team comes to England, or, for that matter, whenever an England team goes overseas, my ironic appetite is always stimulated by the thought, nay, the certainty, that at least one reputation will suffer eclipse, at least one individual Great Hope will be blighted. Perhaps the most astonishing of all such "flops" was that of Surrey's "Bill" Lockwood, regarded by Ranjitsinhji as the most dangerous of all fast bowlers. In the English season of 1893 he took 14 Australian wickets in two Test matches; but when picked for AE Stoddart's contingent to invade Australia, 1894–95, Lockwood's Test match performances told of nothing so much as sweat, toil and empurpled language – 124 overs and 5 balls, 31 maidens, 340 runs, 5 wickets ...

Still, it's better to have played for England, or Australia, and "flopped" than never to have played at all. Which of Lawry's young men of 1968 are about to write fresh and lasting pages in the history? We all know of Walters; we are all on tip-toe of expectation, ready to applaud his batsmanship. Given fair weather, he is pretty certain to do well over here. My own private advices from Australia are to get ready for experiences of rare delight from Paul Sheahan; he carries the special blessing and confidence of Sir Donald

Bradman himself. My own personal "hunch" is for Ian Chappell, who has not yet quite realised promise; there's time for him, he's only 25* ...

I sincerely hope that, whoever individually shines or is eclipsed, the Test matches this year will be seriously and sternly fought, with all the rigour of the game. Each captain will try to win, from the game's first ball, I implore; and will try as hard to save it, if defeat threatens. I am all for the romantic gesture, whenever the moment invites it, but am impatient with the gambler who goes against the odds. A Test match is not yet a Gillette Cup affair; an XI battling to save themselves dourly, with the scoreboard more or less inactive, can thrill the true cricketer's mind and imagination as wonderfully and as memorably as all the "bright" cricket in the world. *The Cricketer, May 17, 1968*

Sheahan scored 303 runs at 30.30 in seven matches against England in England; Walters 745 runs at 25.68 in 18; Chappell 1111 at 46.29 in 14. None of them scored a hundred in 1968.

Real deal: Ian Chappell makes his mark

First blood to Australia. John Woodcock reports from the first and third Tests – a loss and frustration

It would be pleasant to be able to forget all about the first Test match, if its repercussions weren't so relevant. As a result of losing it by 159 runs, England set themselves the task of having to win two of the remaining four Tests if they are to regain the Ashes, and that, needless to say, is a tall order. It was Australia who chose the extra bowler in search of victory, and England who named the extra batsman in search of a draw. The other way round it would have been understandable, for Australia at the time were terribly short of runs and confidence. It was not necessarily symptomatic of Australian cricket that they did the more positive thing; but it was symptomatic of England's that they didn't.

Dreamy drive: Colin Cowdrey at The Oval

Lawry rates this as the best fielding side he has ever played with. At Old Trafford the runs they saved must have amounted to something like half the margin of their victory. All through the series they will hold a considerable advantage over England in this department. It is ironic, at a time when the standard of fielding around the counties is so high, that the England side should be made to look like a lot of slow-coaches.

The Cricketer, June 28, 1968

Rain ruins England's efforts at Lord's – despite bowling Australia out for 78 – then in the third Test the weather intervenes again

The third Test at Edgbaston began a day late, reached a tremendous climax on the fourth evening, then dissolved into a tragic draw. The game began and ended with rain. In between all this gloom and disappointment was sandwiched some of the best cricket of the summer – a legendary 100 in his 100th Test by Colin Cowdrey, a commanding 96 by Graveney, mean and intelligent bowling by Underwood and Illingworth, and some marvellous fielding by the Australians. Monday was a different story. It was Underwood, changing his pace with the wisdom of an older man, who took the vital wickets of Sheahan and Walters. When England batted again they went for quick runs and got them. Edrich and Graveney enjoyed themselves and so did their audience. Alas, for England, it was all in vain. *The Cricketer, July 26, 1968*

The fourth Test is a run-drenched draw, which means Australia keep the Ashes, then comes the final match and its ramifications that had global, political significance. John Arlott's season notebook records the events

August 24–30 This has been the most eventful week of the cricket season. England won the fifth Test to tie the rubber and D'Oliveira was omitted from the MCC team for South Africa.

After England's massive 494 in the first innings of the Test, Lawry batted all day on Saturday for 135 not out with little assistance from anyone except Redpath, the only other Australian batsman to make

more than 14 ... So Australia needed 352 to win and had a maximum of six hours 35 minutes in which to make them. The 35-minute period was on Monday evening and at the start of it Lawry – whose wicket nowadays is England's most important objective – was brilliantly caught by Milburn at short leg off Brown; and, at the end, Redpath was lbw to Underwood: 13 for 2 and England seemed in a position to win ... Mounting an uncompromising attack, ridding themselves of Chappell early in the morning and chipping out Walters and Sheahan, by a moment or two before lunch, England were moving in on the Australian tail with only Inverarity of the recognised batsmen remaining and the score 86 for 5, when a huge thunderstorm broke over The Oval. Within an hour there were pools all over the ground and, although the run-ups were covered, the wicket was soaked. The ground staff were assisted by an amazing number of volunteers – at least 50 of them – from the crowd and their efforts were so successful that it proved possible to restart play at a 4.45pm – with an hour and a quarter left. Cowdrey set such fields as surely have never been seen in first-class cricket before: for Underwood he had 10 men within four or five yards of the bat: for Illingworth, nine but the pitch was placid and slow: Inverarity and Jarman had survived with little trouble for 40 of the 75 minutes when Jarman left alone a ball from D'Oliveira which flicked out the off bail. At once Cowdrey whisked away D'Oliveira and brought back Underwood. Mallett was caught at short leg; McKenzie's forward defensive push was an inch or two off the ground and Brown, at silly mid-on, scooped it up. Gleeson stayed a quarter of an hour before he was bowled by Underwood to which he offered no stroke. Ten minutes left and Connolly pushed and ran dutifully. Five minutes left and Underwood barely straightened the ball. Inverarity, who had promised and deserved to carry his bat, was lbw and England had won the fifth Test by 226 runs. So the rubber was tied and some of the disappointments of Lord's and Edgbaston made good ...

The day after the Test, MCC announced the team to tour South Africa. The omission of D'Oliveira aroused violent controversy. Mr SC Griffith, secretary of MCC, announced

that there had been no political pressure or consultation with the South African Cricket Association. The selection had been made solely on cricketing grounds. There is no reason to doubt his word: they are honourable men. Their naivety, however, is staggering. What was the rest of the world to think when a man who on Tuesday, as one of England's best 11, scored 158 and took the crucial wicket in the only Test of the series which England won, was not included in their best 16 a day later? It is difficult to think of any step ever taken by the "establishment" more calculated to mar its image. If it were a political move, it was a stupid one. If it is argued that "politics should be kept out of cricket", the only reply is that every international relationship, whether in sport or any other field, is part of a pattern of the way people live and behave, which is politics. D'Oliveira's Test record – an overall average of 50; top of England's batting and second in the bowling this year – and his capacity for rising to the occasion were cited in criticism of his omission. This is not the point ... though it may have been a cricketing decision, its repercussions will be political. [E] *The Cricketer Annual, 1968-69*

Political player: D'Oliveira made 158 at The Oval

1968

1st Test June 6-8, 10-11, Old Trafford †Aus 357 (AP Sheahan 88; JA Snow 4-97) and 220 (KD Walters 86; PI Pocock 6-79); Eng 165 (JH Edrich 49; RM Cowper 4-48) and 253 (BL D'Oliveira 87*). Aus won by 159 runs.

2nd Test June 20-22, 24-25, Lord's †Eng 351-7 dec (C Milburn 83); Aus 78 (DJ Brown 5-42) and 127-4 (IR Redpath 53). Match drawn.

3rd Test July 11-13, 15-16, Edgbaston †Eng 409 (MC Cowdrey 104; EW Freeman 4-78) and 142-3 dec (Edrich 64); Aus 222 (IM Chappell 71) and 68-1. Match drawn.

4th Test July 25-27, 29-30, Headingley †Aus 315 (Redpath 92; DL Underwood 4-41) and 312 (Chappell 81; R Illingworth 6-87); Eng 302 (RM Prideaux 64; AN Connolly 5-72) and 230-4 (Edrich 65). Match drawn.

5th Test August 22-24, 26-27, The Oval †Eng 494 (Edrich 164, D'Oliveira 158) and 181 (Connolly 4-65); Aus 324 (WM Lawry 135) and 125 (RJ Inverarity 56; Underwood 7-50). Eng won by 226 runs.

A fresh decade saw a new and angrier version of the Ashes both on and off the field. Led by Ian Chappell with his chief destroyer Dennis Lillee, Test cricket became uncompromising and brutal. It was terrific to watch with superb quick bowling, great batting and controversy all the way

History makers: anti-apartheid marchers, including one-time England captain the Rt Rev David Sheppard, Bishop of Woolwich, second left

The future starts now

The Cricketer asks significant people about their hopes for the 1970s, a decade that began with political turmoil following the D'Oliveira affair and South Africa's banishment from international sport

From the Bishop of Woolwich, the Rt Rev David Sheppard, former England player

First, that cricket will face up honestly to the most important issue it has ever faced – the question of racialism in sport. It takes time to get things changed but I shall be bitterly disappointed if the next 10 years do not see progress in South Africa towards non-racial sport. I don't mean simply bending the rules to let in occasional black cricketers from abroad; my hope is that good facilities and full opportunities to play alongside white cricketers will be given to the majority of South Africans. Then we could begin to talk of cricket "building bridges". I hope that English cricketers will make it plain where we stand on this issue and I hope that those who, like me, protest against playing all-white teams from South Africa will avoid violence. The cause for which we are arguing can and should be promoted by reason, not violence.

From Colin Cowdrey, England player

I have the highest respect for the young player of today – fitter and keener than ever before. I beg him to remember that, in his search for technical ideals in an ultra-professional world, cricket is still a game to be enjoyed and that the crowd's fun is wrapped up in his.

From GO Allen, MCC treasurer

My main hope for the '70s is that administrators and players will co-operate in their efforts to "open up" the game. But one can achieve little without the other. Ruthless efficiency, a phrase often used nowadays to excuse stalemate, is a poor substitute for aggression. Supporters demand and must be given entertainment and without aggression there is unlikely to be either entertainment or success.

From Sir Donald Bradman

My great hope is that the players of today will realise they are the people who will decide cricket's destiny. The public expect them to provide cricket of purpose and character. To prod and push to an ambiguous victory is not enough. We must have cricket which is obviously purposeful and which will cause spectators to want to come and see more.

From Jack Cheetham, South African administrator and former Test captain

My wish is that cricket will progress through all countries where the game is played and that the spirit of the game will transcend the sporting relationships between the various countries. If the ideals in this great game can be the guiding light for those who take part or support it as a game, only good can emerge from its continued participation throughout all lands. *The Cricketer,* February 1970

Snow and brimstone

England, led by Ray Illingworth, headed to Australia with hope and experience and came back with the Ashes. One controversy followed another. **EW Swanton** previews

To take the merit first, the best of the side will probably be found at the top in both departments: Boycott, Edrich and Cowdrey heading the batting. Snow and Ward using the new ball. Knott's wicketkeeping will surely be a plus factor also. If the captain can begin to repeat his 1969–70 Test form as a batsman, and that of his best years of the 1960s with the ball, the balance of the team might not be too bad. An awful lot, though, depends on Illingworth being able to sustain the treble burden of all this and captaincy too ...

He has to do it, and D'Oliveira also – both on the shady side of 38 – in a six-Test series in the heat. It's asking a lot. Otherwise England must go into the field dangerously short of either batsmen or bowlers. It will be a case, in that event, of six specialist bats and four bowlers or five of each. True, most of the bowlers can bat usefully but whether against good-class wrist-spin – which is one of the commodities Australia, as usual, is not short of – is an open question. The weaknesses of the side are likely to be limited mobility in the field and lack of punch in the batting ...

High hopes: Lawry **left** and Illingworth toss

Broadly speaking the character of the side reflects that of the English element in the county game. (One has to qualify this statement carefully since the overseas influx.) But it fails signally to do so as regards the fielding, the one department wherein in first-class cricket little fault is to be found. *The Cricketer*, October, 1970

Ray Robinson highlights some of Australia's prospects

Except for a few bookmakers, usually handling other people's money, practically everybody seems to have installed Australia as the underdog in the imminent Test series against England. I feel it should not be taken for granted that England's squad of seamers will put Australia's in total eclipse. It will be interesting to know the opinions of Boycott, Edrich and the others after they have opposed Alan Thomson and Alan Connolly in Melbourne and Graham McKenzie and Dennis Lillee, aged 21, in Perth. After Graveney's forearm was broken in Brisbane last season somebody remarked that he was the only batsman Thomson hit in the match. "Maybe I was the only one behind the ball," Tom commented ...

One who cannot much longer be kept out of Australia's strongest team is Gregory Chappell, 22, whom I think capable of challenging his brother Ian for recognition as the country's top batsman. If anyone can put pressure on a thrifty attack, it is the gifted young cricketer who made the first century in the John Player League as a Somerset allrounder ...

One final thought on prospects for the first six-Test series: the English team's average age on landing in Australia was 30½. From what I know of them, they will not fall short in determination, but at times they may be short of breath. ▷

The Cricketer, Winter Annual, 1970

1970-71

1st Test November 27-29, December 1-2, Brisbane †**Aus 433** (KR Stackpole 207, KD Walters 112; JA Snow 6-114) and **214** (WM Lawry 84; K Shuttleworth 5-47); **Eng 464** (JH Edrich 79) and **39-1. Match drawn.**

2nd Test December 11-13, 15-16, Perth **Eng 397** (BW Luckhurst 131; GD McKenzie 4-66) and **287-6 dec** (Edrich 115*); †**Aus 440** (IR Redpath 171, GS Chappell 108; Snow 4-143) and **100-3. Match drawn.**

3rd Test December 31, January 1-2, Melbourne ☂ **Abandoned without a ball bowled.**

4th Test January 9-10, 12-14, Sydney †**Eng 332** (G Boycott 77; AA Mallett 4-40) and **319-5 dec** (Boycott 142*); **Aus 236** (Redpath 64; DL Underwood 4-66) and **116** (Lawry 60*; Snow 7-40). **Eng won by 299 runs.**

5th Test January 21-23, 25-26, Melbourne †**Aus 493-9 dec** (IM Chappell 111) and **169-4 dec** (Lawry 42); **Eng 392** (BL D'Oliveira 117, Luckhurst 109) and **161-0** (Boycott 76*, Edrich 74*). **Match drawn.**

6th Test January 29-30, February 1-3, Adelaide †**Eng 470** (Edrich 130; DK Lillee 5-84) and **233-4 dec** (Boycott 119*); **Aus 235** (Stackpole 87; P Lever 4-49) and **328-3** (Stackpole 136, IM Chappell 104). **Match drawn.**

7th Test February 12-14, 16-17, Sydney **Eng 184** (Illingworth 42) and **302** (Luckhurst 59); †**Aus 264** (GS Chappell 65) and **160** (Stackpole 67). **Eng won by 62 runs.**

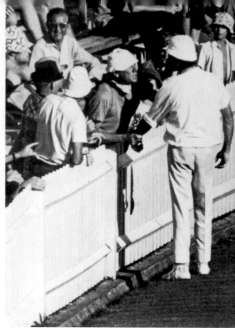

The pain: John Snow hits Terry Jenner during the final Test at Sydney that England won

The anger: a crowd member grabs Snow

EW Swanton continues his tour diary of Illingworth's historic trip, starting with the second Test and a significant contribution from a debutant

Sunday, December 13
Greg Chappell makes history. The tall slim Chappell after a cautious start – his first run after half an hour – reaches 50 and then takes the attack apart. Off Lever 16 in an over, off Snow 12. England mistakenly bowl at his legs and suffer accordingly to the delight of a record crowd of 23,000. Chappell becomes the 11th Australian to score 100 against England in his first Test ... Another draw it was, though England were not in the clear until after lunch. All praise to Edrich.

The Cricketer, January 1971

The rain pours at Melbourne – yet out of adversity history is made, the first one-day international

Saturday, January 2
For the third successive day no play – but now a decision. The Australian Board of Control and the Cricket Council concurring scrapped the last two aborted days, agreed a one-day limited-over match on Tuesday and announced a further Test, making seven including this waterlogged one, in place of the return match between MCC and Victoria ... Hooray! Approval of this imaginative move proved universal in Australia and all but so among English critics: not however

among the English team, who decided that their chances of getting back the Ashes had been scuppered and that, for the added strain, they deserved more money.

Tuesday, January 5
History was made today with the first one-day match between the full international strength of England and Australia. England were undone by the spin for which they themselves have so little use. Edrich played very well indeed but it was significant that the Australians hit the ball that much harder: eight fours on one side, 17 fours and a six on the other, if one considers the matter in that way. And now for Sydney and the real testing time. *The Cricketer*, February 1971

So to the fourth Test at Sydney – and a serious England performance

Wednesday, January 13
A day of consolidation for England first, followed by the destruction of the heart of the Australian batting (less the considerable person of Lawry) for 21 runs. Boycott plays monumentally well again ... [His] performance almost disarms criticism – but not quite. To have taken 85 minutes to go from 84 to 100 might have been held as a black mark against him but for the poor Australian resistance. He is at the height of his powers but does not wholly show he appreciates that cricket is a team game.

Thursday, January 14
The 'coup de grace': Two admirable and spectacular slip catches by men who never field there, Lever and Willis, spark the day, [but] Lawry proves immovable ... Snow, bowling fast and straight on a pitch that no one quite trusts, has a famous haul of 7 for 40 and Lawry carries his bat through the innings, only the fifth Australian to do so and the first since WA Brown at Lord's in '38.

On to the fifth Test back at Melbourne and a bad-tempered affair from both players and spectators

Tuesday, January 16
It was a poor game and, though the major part of the blame for this lay at Australia's door, it was adding insult to injury [for Illingworth] to choose this moment to criticise the umpires.

Wednesday, January 27
The Australian press today report that Illingworth described the umpires' action in warning Snow for intimidation and allowing Thomson to bowl short unchecked as "unfair". Apart from the principle of a captain criticising umpires both specifically and by implication, as Illingworth has done, one's view on this particular outburst is that it was ill-timed, injudicious, undignified and unjustified.

The Cricketer, March, 1971

Revenge: Boycott faces Lillee in a state game

At last: Ian Redpath caught for 171 at Perth

Hard practice: eventual captain Ian Chappell

The sixth game is drawn – after a Boycott bat-throwing incident – and only one match remains. Lawry is axed as captain, Ian Chappell begins to change cricket

Saturday, February 13

A day of shame wherein a finely contested match is interrupted by Ray Illingworth removing his side from the field without reference to umpires or batsmen following an accident to Jenner, felled by Snow with a bouncer, an angry altercation with umpire Rowan on the part of the captain and Snow and a demonstration by the crowd.

Snow goes right up to the pickets at long-leg prepared to continue the argument It is too much for some who have seen their men under pretty continuous fire all the series. One grasps Snow's shirt and cans begin to be tossed on to the field, which is the immediate signal for Illingworth's action. The ground is quickly cleared by police and staff and England return to a hail of boos, having been warned by the umpires that, if they remain in the pavilion, they will lose the match by default.

Sunday, February 14

A thoroughly interesting day and thank goodness an agreeable one. Luckhurst plays a quite sparkling innings but after yet another big English first-wicket stand it needs an unbroken 62 by D'Oliveira and Illingworth to keep the balance still level in this intriguing match.

Tuesday, February 16

Illingworth, getting a little turn, bowls 11 successive overs and pins everyone save Stackpole, whom he bowls off his pads sweeping. Where the five best can raise only 123 what hopes of the last five getting 100?

Wednesday, February 17

The answer is none. Illingworth with Underwood's help again commands the scene and it is all over by half past 12. The England side chair their captain home and the Ashes are deservedly back at the sixth attempt and after 12 years. It remains only to count the cost. *The Cricketer, April 1971*

Bill O'Reilly says losing was not all bad for Australia

In descending order of magnitude I rate the benefits [of losing the series] thus: we have once again become importantly aware of the value of spin bowling. We have been fiddling about with it in recent years. In O'Keeffe and Jenner we have two legspinners bound to reap future harvests of English wickets. We have thrown off the shackles of Bill Lawry's captaincy, which happy event has thrown up the green light for these two young spinners to settle down. And that Sir Donald Bradman has decided to call it a day as a national selector. The greatest cricketer that ever walked on to a field anywhere has never laid great claim in this field to the enterprise. *The Cricketer, April 1971*

Fast and fusarium

A bright and entertaining series saw the emergence of an all-time great and the usual dose of controversy. **Ray Robinson** introduces two key players

Dennis Keith Lillee's fast bowling sharpens Australia's attack. Having a high-speed bowler as spearhead reduces the disparity created by John Snow in the last Anglo-Australian series. With lifting outswingers, Lillee, 22, made experienced World XI batsmen look like novices during his once-in-a-lifetime 8 for 29 on a lively Perth wicket last December. The lean, intent West Australian, almost six-feet tall, ripped through the side like a millsaw through a bunch of celery ...

Robert Arnold Lockyer Massie, 24, has developed into Australia's leading into-the-wind bowler since he blackened Cowdrey's toe with an in-dipper two Decembers ago but otherwise did no damage to the English XI. Until last November he had only 26 wickets in nine first-class matches.

The Cricketer, April 1972

Bryon Butler reports the first salvo sent by skipper Illingworth in the newspapers

In the *Daily Mirror* Ray Illingworth described the omission of McKenzie ("even at 30, I put him on a par with Snowy") and Ian Redpath ("he is everything most Australians are not: a model of batting technique") as boobs. "Someone is going to suffer and I don't think it will be us."

The Cricketer, Spring Annual 1972

John Woodcock writes the Test reports for the 1972 series, starting with England's victory at Old Trafford, which came with a scare and some early blood for Dennis Lillee

1st Test June 8-10, 12-13, Old Trafford †**Eng 249** (AW Greig 57) and **234** (DK Lillee 6-66); **Aus 142** (JA Snow 4-41) and **252** (RW Marsh 91; Greig 4-53, Snow 4-87). **Eng won by 89 runs.**

Marsh and Gleeson came together on the last morning, half an hour before lunch, with Australia on the point of a crushing defeat. By three o'clock when Marsh was caught at the wicket there were some furrowed brows among the English fieldsmen. Although a new ball was almost due these two had created visions of what could have been one of the most astonishing victories in Test cricket. Marsh's wonderful hitting – he struck Gifford for four sixes in his three overs – and Gleeson's stubborn defence, as well as the bowling of Lillee and Stackpole's batting, had given Australia reason to hope for better things at Lord's.

The Cricketer, July 1972

After Lord's (see panel right), England grind out a tricky draw at Trent Bridge. Then in the game that decides the destination of the Ashes, England learn a new word – fusarium. The fusarium fungus had attacked the wicket, killing the grass and presenting Underwood with perfect conditions. Woodcock tactfully avoids the 'f' word

3rd Test July 13-15, 17-18, Trent Bridge **Aus 315** (KR Stackpole 114; Snow 5-92) and **324-4 dec** (R Edwards 170*); †**Eng 189** (Lillee 4-35; RAL Massie 4-43) and **290-4** (BW Luckhurst 96). **Match drawn.**

4th Test July 27-29, Headingley †**Aus 146** (Stackpole 52; DL Underwood 4-37) and **136** (AP Sheahan 41*; Underwood 6-45); **Eng 263** (R Illingworth 57; AA Mallett 5-114) and **21-1**. **Eng won by 9 wkts.**

England retained the Ashes at Headingley in one of the most controversial Tests of recent times. They won at five o'clock on the third day, after bowling Australia out for 146 and 136 on a pitch as bare as a ballroom floor. The matchwinner was Underwood, who, in his first Test appearance of the summer, took 10 wickets for 82 runs in 52 overs. The top score for either side was Illingworth's 57

Elegant power: Greg Chappell at Lord's

Raw pace: Dennis Lillee at Trent Bridge

in England's first innings. For him the match was a personal triumph, whatever the state of the pitch. Whichever side Underwood had been playing for would almost certainly have won. When the ball is turning, even as slowly as it was at Headingley, he is the best in the world. This was what made the Australians so suspicious. Without saying so, some of them thought it was a "fix". Had the groundsman taken less grass off we should no doubt have had a more evenly balanced match, giving the Australians less cause for complaint.

The Cricketer, September 1972

And Australia show what might have been with a strong performance in the final Test at The Oval

5th Test August 10-12, 14-16, The Oval †**Eng 284** (APE Knott 92; Lillee 5-58) and **356** (B Wood 90; Lillee 5-123); **Aus 399** (IM Chappell 118, GS Chappell 113) and **242-5** (Stackpole 79). **Aus won by 5 wkts.**

Only the bigots will have felt that Australia's victory in the fifth Test, leading to a drawn series, was a bad thing. The Oval groundsman produced a pitch that lasted well, and the Australians, true to their word, proved themselves just the better side in these conditions. It was a wonderful Test, either side could have won until towards the end of the final partnership – between Sheahan and Marsh. [Chasing 242, they were 171 for 5 till Marsh and Sheahan made the runs] ... With 31 wickets in the rubber Lillee's was a tremendous performance. No fast bowler has ever taken more than that in an Anglo-Australian series. Yet in the run-up to the first Test Lillee was in danger of being discarded, so poor was his form. He runs a tediously long way; yet to see him pounding in to bowl, like a runaway train, and to put oneself in the batsman's shoes, is to know one is watching a man's game. Lillee's first two overs in England's second innings at The Oval were as fast as anyone had seen for a long time ... All told, in fact, it was an interesting series, played in all kind of conditions, from the green of Manchester to the brown of Leeds and the sunshine of Kennington. The Australians are a very likeable side and we shall be sorry to see them go. **K** *The Cricketer, October 1972*

Massie's match

John Woodcock sees an extraordinary entry into Ashes folklore – Bob Massie's Test debut

The second Test at Lord's produced a succession of riddles. How could an Australian side without a Test victory for two and a half years have won it in conditions that were so peculiarly English? How, on a pitch that was described as being "as good as any you'll find in Adelaide", could England, in their second innings, lose nine wickets for 86 runs in 55.2 overs? How could Bob Massie, in his first official Test, achieve the truly wonderful figures of 16 for 137 runs when he was rejected by Northamptonshire a year or two ago? How was it that so many people watched (over 80,000 in three days and a bit) when so few watched the first at Old Trafford?

It was indeed an extraordinary match and when it was over a series which had looked to be in England's pocket after Old Trafford was wide open. Massie carved out a place for himself in history by making the most of the atmosphere, which was heavy and humid for the first three days, and by confounding England's batsmen bowling round the wicket.

Not until the last day, when the sun was coming through, did the pitch behave as good pitches are meant to. And at no time did England's batsmen bat as England batsmen are meant to. Not that this is unusual. It is only three Tests ago that they were bowled out by India for 101. Almost throughout last summer, in fact, against India and Pakistan, runs were short ...

Looking back at the Lord's Test Greg Chappell's 131, which pulled Australia round from 84 for 4, in reply to England's first-innings total of 272, was scarcely less vital than Massie's bowling. It was a superbly judged piece of batting and technically of the very highest quality. Without it Australia's chances of making a fight of the series could well have collapsed – like England's second innings. Marsh, with a boisterous 50, set up the Saturday for the Australians, and his wicketkeeping has improved out of all recognition ...

It was quite like old times to hear that they were queuing at Lord's at four o'clock on the Saturday morning and closing the gates soon after 11. This was followed, quite understandably, by demands for Lord's to be given a second Test each year. *The Cricketer, August 1972*

2nd Test, Lord's, June 22-24, 26 1972
Australia won by 8 wickets

ENGLAND WON TOSS

G Boycott		b Massie	11		b Lillee	6
JH Edrich	lbw	b Lillee	10	c Marsh	b Massie	6
BW Luckhurst		b Lillee	1	c Marsh	b Lillee	4
MJK Smith		b Massie	34	c Edwards	b Massie	30
BL D'Oliveira	lbw	b Massie	32	c GS Chappell	b Massie	3
AW Greig	c Marsh	b Massie	54	c IM Chappell	b Massie	3
APE Knott†	c Colley	b Massie	43	c GS Chappell	b Massie	12
R Illingworth*	lbw	b Massie	30	c Stackpole	b Massie	12
JA Snow		b Massie	37	c Marsh	b Massie	0
N Gifford	c Marsh	b Massie	3	not out		16
JSE Price	not out		4	c GS Chappell	b Massie	19
Extras		lb6 w1 nb6	13		w1 nb4	5
Total	91.5 overs		272	55.2 overs		116

Fall of wickets 22 23 28 84 97
193 200 260 265

12 16 18 25 31
52 74 74 81

Bowling (1st) Lillee 28-3-90-2, Massie 32.5-7-84-8, Colley 16-2-42-0,
GS Chappell 6-1-18-0, Gleeson 9-1-25-0
(2nd) Lillee 21-6-50-2, Massie 27.2-9-53-8, Colley 7-1-8-0

AUSTRALIA

KR Stackpole	c Gifford	b Price	5	not out		57
BC Francis		b Snow	0	c Knott	b Price	9
IM Chappell*	c Smith	b Snow	56	c Luckhurst	b D'Oliveira	6
GS Chappell		b D'Oliveira	131	not out		7
KD Walters	c Illingworth	b Snow	1			-
R Edwards	c Smith	b Illingworth	28			-
JW Gleeson	c Knott	b Greig	1			-
RW Marsh†	c Greig	b Snow	50			-
DJ Colley	c Greig	b Price	25			-
RAL Massie	c Knott	b Snow	0			-
DK Lillee	not out		2			-
Extras		lb7 nb2	9		lb2	2
Total	122.1 overs		308	26.5 overs		81 2d

Fall of wickets 1 7 82 84 190
212 250 290 290

20 51

Bowling (1st) Snow 32-13-57-5, Price 26.1-5-87-2, Greig 29-6-74-1,
D'Oliveira 17-5-48-1, Gifford 11-4-20-0, Illingworth 7-2-13-1
(2nd) Snow 8-2-15-0, Price 7-0-28-1, Greig 3-0-17-0,
D'Oliveira 8-3-14-1, Luckhurst 0.5-0-5-0

Umpires DJ Constant and AE Fagg   Test debuts R Edwards, RAL Massie (Aus)

First of many: Boycott out

King of swingers: Massie   16-Bob: Massie walks off

"If Lillee doesn't get you, Thomson must"

Deadly duo: David Lloyd is caught Jeff Thomson bowled Dennis Lillee

The 1974-75 series was all about one thing – pace. Lillee teamed up with the unheralded Jeff Thomson who bowled quicker, more dangerously and with more hostility. England had no answer – they even called for the 41-year-old Colin Cowdrey – and Australia loved it. **EW Swanton** records his reaction to the first Test

Jeff Thomson will not sweep through the series picking up nine wickets a time but I doubt whether his performances will be a mere flash in the pan. He is lusty and well-built and obviously has the mechanics for the job. It remains to see how he will react to hard work on plumb pitches when he is not encouraged by the abnormal life that was to be had from one end throughout the match.

Fast bowling seems likely to dominate this series if only because neither side is richly equipped with much else. I trust that the Australian Board will react firmly whether in public or private to the words both written and spoken by Dennis Lillee. Lillee in his book *Back to the Mark* makes the astonishing admission that "I bowl bouncers for one reason and that is to hit the batsman and thus intimidate him" ...

A basic difference in attitude greeted the news that Colin Cowdrey had been recalled. Though with fewer first-class cricketers to choose from, the Aussies almost never bring a man back. They get quickly bored with the old hand, eagerly hail the new boy. They were mystified that Cowdrey should want to come under fire again at his time of life. This was the emotion rather than applause at his courage. *The Cricketer, January 1975*

John Woodcock starts his reports with the barrage at Brisbane

1st Test November 29-December 1, 3-4, Brisbane **†Aus 309** (IM Chappell 90; RGD Willis 4-56) and **288-5 dec** (GS Chappell 71); **Eng 265** (AW Greig 110; MHN Walker 4-73) and **166** (JR Thomson 6-46). **Aus won by 166 runs.**

England's batsmen endured their worst battering for a long time in losing the first Test at Brisbane by 166 runs. The reason for this was a treacherous pitch on which Australia's new fast bowler Jeff Thomson took 9 for 105, besides breaking Amiss's thumb and inflicting more bruises upon the England team than their masseur can have cared to count. Against most sides England would have fancied their chance but not against Thomson. What he and to a lesser extent Lillee achieved in the way of lift Lever and Willis were unable to match. Although nasty, England's two never endangered life and limb in the same way as Thomson and

Lillee. There was as much short bowling from both sides as there can have been in an Anglo-Australian Test since Bodyline. It was a bad start to the rubber and for England a disconcerting one. *The Cricketer*, January 1975

Cowdrey's return makes no difference

2nd Test December 13-15, 17, Perth **Eng 208** (APE Knott 51) and **292** (FJ Titmus 61; Thomson 5-93); **†Aus 481** (R Edwards 115, KD Walters 103) and **23-1**. **Aus won by 9 wkts.**

The hero of the second Test was not Thomson, who took another seven English wickets (that made 16 for 243 in the first two Tests); or Walters, who made a magnificent hundred between tea and the close on the second evening; or Ross Edwards, who scored 115 in his home town; or the groundsman, who produced a splendid pitch. It was Colin Cowdrey, for a great-hearted effort in coming to England's rescue in the middle of an English winter. *The Cricketer*, February 1975

A thriller at Melbourne with England drawing leaves the Ashes in the balance

3rd Test December 26-28, 30-31, Melbourne **Eng 242** (Knott 52; Thomson 4-72) and **244** (DL Amiss 90; Thomson 4-71); **†Aus 241** (IR Redpath 55; Willis 5-61) and **238-8** (GS Chappell 61; Greig 4-56). **Match drawn.**

The drawn third Test match in Melbourne was just as close as the scores suggest: England 242 and 244, Australia 241 and 238 for 8. With Australia needing 246 to win, the last day produced a tremendous struggle ... With another 12 wickets between them Thomson and Lillee were the main cause of England's batting troubles. It was only because of his inability to come to terms with their speed that Denness dropped himself after this Test. *The Cricketer*, February 1975

To Sydney and, inevitably, the Ashes head down under. 'Ashes to Ashes, dust to dust, if Lillee doesn't get you, Thomson must ...'

4th Test January 4-6, 8-9, Sydney **†Aus 405** (GS Chappell 84; GG Arnold 5-86) and **289-4 dec** (GS Chappell 144, Redpath 105); **Eng 295** (Knott 82; Thomson 4-74) and **228** (Greig 54, AA Mallett 4-21). **Aus won by 171 runs.**

The fourth Test in Sydney saw the efforts of Thomson and Lillee crowned by Australia's recovery of the Ashes, with England's batting on the last day showing just how much their resistance had been lowered by the events of earlier Tests. Although it was a good pitch, and in spite of having all their wickets intact with only five and a half hours left for play, England still lost the match – by 171 runs in the 11th of the last 15 overs ... It was the speed of Thomson and Lillee that prepared the way. The same umpires who had stood in the first three Tests lacked the conviction to follow the procedure laid down in the Laws for dealing with persistent short-pitched fast bowling. *The Cricketer*, March 1975

"Coming fresh to this Test series is like walking into a pitched battle between the Mafia and the IRA. You knew they'd been at each others' throats but you couldn't believe it was this uncompromising, this violent or this uncouth. Practically none of the traditional courtesies of cricket survived this fourth Test." **Ian Wooldridge** as quoted from the *Daily Mail*

In the next Test England lose comfortably but by the final game at Melbourne Thomson and Lillee are injured and, with a huge sigh of relief, England win

5th Test Jan 25-27, 29-30, Adelaide **Aus 304** (TJ Jenner 74; DL Underwood 7-113) and **272-5 dec** (Walters 71*; Underwood 4-102); **†Eng 172** (MH Denness 51; DK Lillee 4-49) and **241** (Knott 106*; Lillee 4-69). **Aus won by 163 runs.**

6th Test February 8-10, 12-13, Melbourne **†Aus 152** (IM Chappell 65; P Lever 6-38) and **373** (GS Chappell 102; Greig 4-88); **Eng 529** (Denness 188, KWR Fletcher 146; Walker 8-143). **Eng won by an inns and 4 runs.**

If proof were needed that the one ruling difference between England and Australia was the bowling of Thomson and Lillee, it was provided at Melbourne in the sixth Test. Thomson was unfit, Lillee broke down after bowling only six overs and England won by an innings and four runs. Apart from Greg Chappell and Redpath, Australia's batsmen are no more reliable than England's ... Thanks to Thomson and Lillee cricket in Australia is booming. ⚄ *The Cricketer*, April 1975

Aussie welcome: Cowdrey facing Thomson

No respect: Cowdrey ducks Lillee

False start: Gooch makes a pair in his first Test   Mettle detector: Steele shows fight   Return fire: Thomson bowls at Lord's

Fighting fire with Steele

Australia returned to England instantly and did not find the softer conditions so much to their liking. But they did enough. **Tony Lewis** kept a journal of the season

Week ended July 11

I have a shattering tale to recall. Mike Denness won the toss at Edgbaston and, presumably after seeking opinion from senior players, put Australia in to bat. The weather was chill, cloudy and rather unsettled and Australia's attack was bulging with the sort of bowlers who can take advantage of those conditions. It was the time too when Arnold, Snow, Old and Greig might upset Australia's front-line batting. Perhaps the disaster which followed emphasised more than anything else the professional's unwritten law: "Never put in the opposition if there is rain about." Mike Denness has soldiered through increasing criticism of his leadership and I admire his tenacity. He will need a few friends to ride this latest decision, yet if it had come off would he have received the credit? He has led Kent long enough to understand the risk he was taking. It amounts to an immensely brave decision if not the most fortunate.

Week ended July 25

Jack Fingleton writes in the *Sunday Times*, July 20: "For many years it has seemed a national English pastime to make merry mayhem of their skippers. Peter May got it, Dexter also, and Mike Denness has copped it

in copious doses, particularly so in the columns of this newspaper. I wonder how many of us sitting in the press box would even take on the job, let alone do it as well as those who have willingly put their head on the block? Let me quote the sage words of Michael Melford in the *Daily Telegraph* last week: 'Meanwhile, best wishes to all those, including myself, who in pub and power station, sauna bath and supermarket, must go on captaining England impeccably from a distance and with hindsight. It is a difficult job, but thank heavens our prescience, practical genius, powers of leadership and spirit of aggression are up to it.' I would have loved to have written that."

Mike Denness loses his job. Tony Greig comes in as captain for the second Test

Week ended August 1

There were five new names announced in the England party for the Lord's Test, which began yesterday. David Steele is possibly the most surprising because he is winning a Test cap at the ripe age of 33 and this is his benefit year. David Steele quickly proved why he was chosen. England were again heading for disaster, 49 for 4, Dennis Lillee taking the wickets of Amiss, Edrich,

Wood and Gooch ... Steele, however, marched in to lunch to a hero's reception, 36 not out. The one difference in his play from others is that he plunges forward on the front foot. Lillee, Thomson and Walker in Australia may sort him out but on this wicket at Lord's, which had no special bounce, he had the confidence to recognise that he could play forward to balls well up to him. Amiss, Edrich and Wood rather lingered on the back foot. Yet the balls dug in short Steele hooked downwards and in fact was as quick as anyone to move on to the back foot. Why has he been in the background so long without being chosen for England? Is this one innings, which he extended after lunch to 50 exactly, a chance affair? I suppose he has never looked an outstanding player. His runs have often been grafted cheerlessly.

The second Test is drawn as England fail to bowl Australia out

Week ended August 8

Maybe the victory was for the Lord's pitch, placid throughout. Australia were left 484 to win and Tony Greig left himself 500 minutes in which to bowl them to defeat. England trooped off the pitch an exhausted,

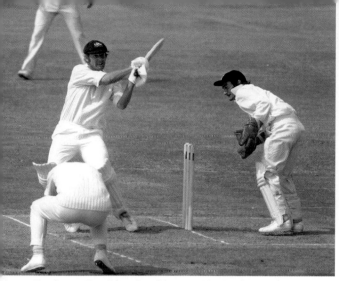

Nearly man: Ross Edwards on his way to 99 at Lord's; Knott keeps

Innocent victims: Tony Greig, Ian Chappell and the Headingley pitch

frustrated but inwardly satisfied team with the tourists 329 for 3 at the close. Still, it is a joy to tell a tale of English ascendancy after the previous winter of humiliation and the Edgbaston debacle. Greig made the most of it. He interrupted batsmen at the crease to adjust fielders, so upsetting their concentration. He took up his position at silly point and gave them as much verbal pressure as they are renowned for handing out. There are many opinions expressed of how regrettable it is that it takes a South African to sort out England's problems. Tony Greig has gone to war far too many times for England for his birth to make a scrap of difference. His Scots father would be very proud of his leadership in this Test. David Steele scored 45 in the second innings but the honours go to John Edrich, who got 175.

For one who suffered the physical terrors of the winter in Australia, it was a performance of character born of long experience ... Others looked shattered by the old traumas down under, Edrich, Greig and Knott have emerged as the men of special aptitude for the game at the top.

Vandals ruin a great finish at Headingley and cost England the Ashes

Week ended August 22
George Cawthray, the groundsman at Headingley, pushed back the covers from the Test wicket on Tuesday morning to find that lumps of soil had been gouged out from the creases and oil poured on to the part of the pitch where the ball would bounce just short of a half-volley. He talked to the nightwatchman, who had not heard a

whisper all through his vigil, then sent for the police. On the walls outside the ground were painted slogans: "George Davis is innocent." The name of George Davis does not appear in *Wisden*, though he is certain of a place next year. He is, in fact, a man convicted of armed robbery and serving a 20-year jail sentence. Cricket has again been used for political purposes. The Test was abandoned; Australia retain the Ashes.

Week ended September 5
England staged a massive rearguard action at The Oval and the fourth Test was drawn. Of course, once Australia had batted so well in the first innings there was never a way we could square the series. Jeff Thomson sent the ball down quicker than at any time on tour. Here is a bowler who has learned much in this country and has certainly gone back to Australia a better performer for the trip. I do not know how much he has learned from Dennis Lillee, but Lillee is a man who would be in any side in the world. Apart from the enormous courage involved in his fight-back to fitness after those stress fractures of the spine, he has other qualities. He is aggressive, physically and verbally. He has learned the true art of bowling which lifts him far above the ordinary. Variation of pace, length and line are all under his control. His presence has made the Australian side of 1975 a memorable one. I also believe that the wicketkeeping of Rod Marsh has enhanced it too. Apart from the acrobatics which he was required to go through to take Jeff Thomson, he moved and took the ball with great certainty; simple keeping with no frills. 🏏 *The Cricketer*, November 1975

1975

1st Test July 10-12, 14, Edgbaston **Aus 359** (RW Marsh 61); †**Eng 101** (DK Lillee 5-15; MHN Walker 5-48) and **173** (KWR Fletcher 51; JR Thomson 5-38). **Aus won by an inns and 85 runs.**

2nd Test July 31-August 2, 4-5, Lord's †**Eng 315** (AW Greig 96; Lillee 4-84) and **436-7 dec** (JH Edrich 175); **Aus 268** (R Edwards 99; JA Snow 4-66) and **329-3** (IM Chappell 86). **Match drawn.**

3rd Test August 14-16, 18-19, Headingley †**Eng 288** (DS Steele 73; GJ Gilmour 6-85) and **291** (Steele 92); **Aus 135** (PH Edmonds 5-28) and **220-3** (RB McCosker 95*). **Match drawn.**

4th Test August 28-30, September 1-3, The Oval †**Aus 532-9 dec** (IM Chappell 192, McCosker 127) and **40-2**; **Eng 191** (Thomson 4-50, Walker 4-63) and **538** (RA Woolmer 149; KD Walters 4-34, Lillee 4-91). **Match drawn.**

HERO No.6

Dennis Lillee

Tests

Batting

Matches	70
Runs	905
Highest score	73*
Average	13.71
Hundreds	0
Fifties	1

Bowling

Balls	18467
Runs	8493
Wickets	355
Average	23.92
Best bowling	7-83
5-for inns	23
10-for match	7

First-class career

Batting

Matches	198
Runs	2377
Highest score	73*
Average	13.90
Hundreds	0
Fifties	2

Bowling

Balls	44806
Runs	20695
Wickets	882
Average	23.46
Best bowling	8-29
5-for inns	50
10-for match	13

v England

Bowling

Matches	29
Balls	8516
Runs	3507
Wickets	167
Average	21.00
Best bowling	7-89
5-for inns	11
10-for match	4

Dennis the Menace

David Frith celebrates one of the all-time aggressive greats who overcame adversity to create adversity. It was written in 1976

There have been faster bowlers than Dennis Lillee, but not many. There have been more hostile fast bowlers, but not many. Spofforth, Ernie Jones, Constantine, Charlie Griffith, Andy Roberts, Jeff Thomson – all have brought menace, even terror. Lillee concedes nothing to any of them. He is one of the great fast bowlers of the 20th century, possessing a full set of gear changes, a knowledge of aerodynamics equal to Lindwall's, an abundance of stamina and determination, and more courage than most.

He needed that courage in 1973 and '74 when he set about achieving one of sport's most impressive comebacks. The four stress fractures in the lower vertebrae would have finished many a career. Lillee, having dramatically bowled his way to fame, was faced with six weeks in plaster and a long fight to full fitness. He withstood the punishment and handsomely repaid those who had worked with him and believed in him. At the end of the 1973-74 season his hopes were as high as the highest of his bouncers.

England arrived next season to defend the Ashes in six Test matches. Lillee pronounced himself fit and dismissed Ian Chappell two or three times in early-season fixtures. Australia selected him again. And in the first Test a new extermination firm was formed: Lillee and Thomson. It was devastating.

Australia's opening pair took 58 wickets in the series out of 108 that fell to bowlers – this despite Thomson's withdrawal through injury halfway through the fifth Test and Lillee's after six overs with a damaged foot in the final match.

The full force of this controlled cyclone was felt in the 1975 series, though England's sleeping pitches absorbed some of the energy. This is when Lillee's other bowling skills asserted themselves. As in the 1972 series, when he took a record 31 Test wickets, Lillee beat batsmen by change of pace and with his wicked away-swinger. Rod Marsh and the ever-expectant slips cordon did the rest. He had more support now: from the tireless Walker, from Gilmour (who would have strolled into any other Test team in the world), and from Thomson whenever he had his rhythm.

Dennis Lillee's inspiration, when only a boy, came from a West Indian: Wes Hall, the genial fast-bowling giant. The young fellow from Perth, born on WG Grace's 101st birthday (July 18, 1949), clambered with all the fervour of a Beatles fan into the members' enclosure at the Waca ground just to be near his idol. There was also Graham McKenzie, the pride of Perth, to fan the flames of his ambition. And Fred Trueman. And Alan Davidson.

Not that this was enough. There had to be an inherent talent. The tearaway with long sideburns, who stormed in over a long distance and hurled his wiry body into delivery with every ounce of his might, eventually played for Western Australia. By 1970–71 he was considered good enough to play for Australia – one of the hopes in a reshaping of the national XI. He took 5 for 84 against England at Adelaide in his maiden Test, opening the attack with another young aspirant, Thomson – Alan ("Froggy"), not Jeff.

He was learning all the time, especially when trying to bowl to Sobers during his indescribably brilliant 254 at Melbourne, when straight-drives came bouncing back from the boundary before the bowler had raised himself upright in the follow-through. Yet he continued to harass the tourists, not by any means now trying to bowl every ball at top speed, and if England in the spring of 1972 thought Australian claims of Lillee's bounce and penetration were exaggerated, the threat was soon a vivid reality.

He has sometimes attacked batsmen with his tongue – and been denounced for it. Brian Statham used to let the ball do all his talking. Fred Trueman's ripe language was somehow not the antithesis of geniality. Dennis Lillee's "verbal aggression" has been something else in its spirit of near-hatred. Lillee was a central figure in Australia's re-emergence as a formidable side and a great deal has continued to be expected of him. The chanting of the crowds, the inescapable typecasting, the need to transpose celebrity into a real-world security – all this must take a man away from himself, at least in part.

A truth that will remain is that Perth has given to cricket a fast bowler, of hawk-like countenance and perfect physique for his purpose, whose flowing approach and superb athletic action have been a thrilling spectacle for young and old, male and female, pacifist and warrior. *The Cricketer, March 1976*

On Lillee's Test retirement in 1984, Frith writes

The long-haired tearaway of the early 1970s turned into a master of his art, equipped with swing, cut, pace-change, bouncer and yorker – all packaged in facial and verbal hostility in the grand Spofforth manner, with the rare grin à la Keith Miller. When he reached 200 Test wickets everyone applauded and thought that was just about that. Yet he bowled on and on, into a maturity which seemed greater because of his loss of hair and lined face. Roared on by his fans, he gave everything for his country and pushed his wicket tally to a staggering 355. Lillee had the stamina of a Tom Richardson, the repertoire of a Ray Lindwall, the speed of a Wes Hall – and self-control little greater than John McEnroe's. The former memorable qualities, in the eyes, surely, of the majority, far outweigh the blemishes. In all probability Lillee was the best fast bowler, all things considered, that the world has ever seen. Now, unless Lillee should succumb to the temptation to come back, we have seen the last of him. Lillee may well invest in that Western Australian ranch, where he might sometimes imagine, above the thunder of the hooves, the chant of 'Lil-lee. Lil-lee, Lil-lee!' ⚡ *Wisden Cricket Monthly, February 1984*

Best of times, worst of times

By 1977 the revolutionary spirit of the sixties and early seventies arrived in the form of
Kerry Packer – a media mogul who bought the world's best players, creating divisions.
In the winter before Packer's summer **David Frith** touches on creeping commercialism

At last a settlement is at hand in the matter of players wearing manufacturers' emblems on the field of play. We can be sure that the Test and County Cricket Board will permit only the most discreet adornments, and quite rightly the manufacturers' payments will benefit the game. The dangers of overlooking things are obvious ... The BBC is sensitive to attempted abuses of its "non-commercial" mandate, such as advertising boards and banners positioned unblushingly in camera range and even interviews conducted at angles advantageous to some commercial organisation or other. *The Cricketer, January 1977*

Ray Robinson, in his season round-up, also highlights commercial disputes

Money, money, money – Australia's 17 touring Britain will each be paid $6,000

100 years on: Greig and Greg Chappell toss

Flash & grab: Keith Fletcher c Marsh b Walker

(about £3,750), the largest rise ever granted cricketers for a tour. This more than doubles the allowance on the Australians' last full tour of England in 1972. On paper it would be up 125 per cent. The new scale reflects a noteworthy advance in understanding reached [between] states' captains [and] leading board members. *The Cricketer, April 1977*

But before the full emergence of the Packer story England and Australia play a celebratory, non-Ashes Test at Melbourne – 100 years after the first official Test. It is a heady five days, which Australia win by exactly the same margin as in the inaugural encounter. David Frith reports

The quaint pattern of play throughout its five days of surprises ensured that the celebration Centenary Test between England and Australia will forever be remembered as an unparalleled happening on the field as well as off it. Australia were humbled – with the gruesome legacy of a smashed jaw for McCosker – only for England to fall well short when put to the test by Lillee and Walker. Australia were then reassured by contrasting but high-quality innings by the youngsters Davis and Hookes, and Marsh, having passed Grout's record of 187 wickets for Australia, then became the first wicketkeeper to make a century for Australia against England. That might have been the end of the excitement, with England expected by the majority to exceed their dismal first innings but not to come anywhere within sight of their target of 463. Now, though, it was the turn – so long-awaited – of a young English batsman to set the cricket world abuzz. Randall, just 26, from Nottingham, not only became the 14th England batsman to record a hundred on debut against Australia – the first since John Edrich in 1964 – but he brought gusts of fun

and animation as well as vibrant strokeplay into the game. When his luck finally ran out and when later the gallant England innings ended – the highest fourth innings in an England-Australia Test – the margin was 45 runs, identical to that in the first-ever Test match, on this Melbourne ground precisely 100 years ago ... The morning session had seen Randall to his hundred, reached off Lillee's bowling; within minutes the bowler had hit him on the skull and caught the rebound. Then when the new ball was taken Lillee thought Marsh had caught Randall, who pointed to his shoulder. Words were exchanged. The batsman managed to carry on grinning. When he fell out of the way of another bouncer he did a backward roll and shot to his feet again. It was one of the most stirring and lengthy personal duels in the 225-match history of these Tests, and everyone loved it ... Lillee, the 11-wicket hero, was carried off shoulder-high, and Randall, after receiving his man-of-the-match medal, thanked everyone for coming and Lillee for the bump on the head. *The Cricketer, May 1977*

Australia come to England, the Packer storm breaks and, as solicitors sharpen their pens, the Ashes produces an engaging series. Tony Greig, heavily involved in recruiting for Packer, loses the captaincy to Mike Brearley. John Woodcock writes

The first Test match at Lord's, known as the Jubilee Test (although the Queen was unable to make her customary visit), confirmed that the fight for the Ashes was likely to be a close-run thing. Only the loss of most of the second day to bad light and rain prevented a result, though who would have won, but for that, was anyone's guess ... There was really nothing to choose between the two pace attacks: Australia's was the faster but not importantly so ...

Centenary centurion: Rod Marsh makes a hundred in the Centenary Test at Melbourne

When it ended both sides were probably happy enough with a draw.

The Cricketer, August 1977

So to Old Trafford and a triumphant England take a lead in the series – the first time in a while

England had had a long wait for their victory by nine wickets in the second Test match at Old Trafford. Their last success at home was in 1974 when they beat India at Edgbaston. When it ended, Brearley warned that, whatever the result might indicate, the sides were evenly matched. England have it comfortably within their powers to bat just as poorly as Australia did at Old Trafford – even if, without Lillee, not to mention Ian Chappell, Australia no longer have that world-beating look.

Boycott returns from a three-year self-imposed exile and there's a glimpse of a half-decent English allrounder

The third Test at Trent Bridge was an unqualified success – for everyone, that is, except Australia. There were four full houses; the pitch was a good one, though not too good to prevent England from winning by seven wickets; there was a record partnership between Boycott and Knott and some match-winning fast bowling by Willis ... Boycott's return to Test cricket, after three

years in his northern fastness, was pure theatre. His scores at Trent Bridge were 107 and 80 not out and he batted all told for almost two full days ... To play in a winning side against Australia is the ambition of every young English cricketer. Having contributed appreciably towards Australia's decline from 100 for 2 to 155 for 8 in their first innings, by taking 5 for 74, Ian Botham, upon coming in to bat, was immediately dropped. He won't always have it so good.

The Cricketer, September 1977

England dominate and Boycott scores his hundredth first-class hundred. At Headingley. Against Australia. As England recover the Ashes. You couldn't script it. (The final Test was a wet draw.)

With good reason Headingley was the scene of unconcealed joy when England won the fourth Test by an innings and 85 runs and so regained the Ashes. Greg Chappell soon announced that the last Test at The Oval would also be his last. With characteristic lack of emotion he accepted Australia's defeat and praised England's victory ... Not since 1886 had England won three successive Test matches against Australia in England. Only twice before in this century had they regained the Ashes in England ... England played with a toughness, a determination and a know-how acquired in their years of defeat. *The Cricketer,* October 1977

1976-77

Centenary Test March 12-14, 16-17, Melbourne **Aus 138** (GS Chappell 40) and **419-9 dec** (RW Marsh 110*; CM Old 4 104); **†Eng 95** (DK Lillee 6-26) and **417** (DW Randall 174; Lillee 5 139). Aus won by 45 runs.

1977

1st Test June 16-18, 20-21, Lord's **†Eng 216** (RA Woolmer 79; JR Thomson 4-41) and **305** (Woolmer 120; Thomson 4-86); **Aus 296** (CS Serjeant 81; RGD Willis 7-78) and **114-6** (DW Hookes 50). **Match drawn.**

2nd Test July 7-9, 11-12, Old Trafford **†Aus 297** (KD Walters 88) and **218** (Chappell 112; DL Underwood 6-66); **Eng 437** (Woolmer 137) and **82 1** (JM Brearley 44). **Eng won by 9 wkts.**

3rd Test July 28-30, August 1-2, Trent Bridge **†Aus 243** (RB McCosker 51; IT Botham 5-74) and **309** (McCosker 107; Willis 5-88); **Eng 364** (APE Knott 135, G Boycott 107) and **189-3** (Brearley 81, Boycott 80*). **Eng won by 7 wkts.**

4th Test August 11-13, 15, Headingley **†Eng 436** (Boycott 191; LS Pascoe 4-91); **Aus 103** (Botham 5-21) and **248** (RW Marsh 63; M Hendrick 4-54). **Eng won by an inns and 85 runs.**

5th Test August 25-27, 29-30, The Oval **†Eng 214** (MF Malone 5-63, Thomson 4-87) and **57-2; Aus 385** (Hookes 85). **Drawn.**

England and Packer victorious

By the next series many Test players from both sides had received bans for signing up to Packer – Australia were the harder hit and it showed as England romped home. It left a sour taste, which inspired **EW Swanton** to write this 'lament for the batting art'

Press Packer: Kerry Packer discusses his World Series Cricket that weakened Australia

Star signing: Dennis Lillee

Rolled over: Rick Darling faces Willis in the third Test

Back in England after the fourth Test had been won and the Ashes safely retained, I found myself frequently at a loss for the apt comment when friends and acquaintances, one after the other, came up with remarks saying was it not an unadmirable series, and how lucky had I not been to see as much as I had. These were not the sentiments of the most knowledgeable, certainly, but they were – and no doubt are – widely held for all that.

As I say, I found myself in a difficulty and I regret to say hedged and prevaricated a bit. How can one come home with a sun-tan and tell people who have just endured some of the bitterest weather for years, and with the certainty of paralysing strikes and shortages to come, that their sole source of comfort in the darkest days of winter was something of a mirage, that the cricket had been deplorably slow and most of the batting woefully poor?

What had given the cricket public at home such a rosy picture of this most crucial of series between England and Australia was surely not the press or the radio version in the early morning but the half-hour "highlights" of each day's play shown nightly on TV. When 360 minutes of cricket is reduced to 30 the result, photographically, can only be an impression of animated action, of runs being scored and wickets tumbling. *The Cricketer,* March 1979

England dominate the Test series except at Melbourne and despite Rodney Hogg's wicket-taking; the loss of world-class players to Kerry Packer is too much to bear. John Woodcock reports on the first four Tests

In winning the first Test against Australia in Brisbane England had one great stroke of luck: they lost the toss. But for that they would almost certainly have batted first, as Australia did, in conditions which, on the opening day, were ideal for bowling. Within 85 minutes of the start of the match Australia were 26 for 6 and more or less doomed to defeat. To survive after that until 3.15 on the fifth and final afternoon represented a great, albeit unavailing, recovery.

Before the series started Hogg was something of an unknown quantity, in spite of having bowled Brearley's side to defeat in their opening match. In Brisbane his bowling in England's first innings drew from Randall the observation that he hit the bat at least as hard as Lillee had in the Centenary Test. Willis matched Hogg: with blistered, sometimes bloodied, feet, he was still England's most successful bowler, as indomitable a trier as ever wore an England cap ...

In the second Test in Perth, as in the first in Brisbane, England's bowlers found the sort of conditions which, much more often than not, they turn to their advantage ... In nine and a half hours' batting in the match, Boycott never once reached the boundary. Even so, without Boycott's first innings of 77, during which he shared a fourth-wicket partnership of 158 with Gower, England would have been harder pressed to win ... When they left Perth, Australia were badly in need of a victory to bring back the crowds. *The Cricketer, February 1979*

And Australia get the victory in the third Test at Melbourne. Woodcock continues

Australia's first day score of 243 for 4 was the basis of their victory. The contrast between that first day and the next was remarkable. On the second day 14 wickets fell in six hours for 122 runs ... The target of 283, which England were left to win, proved, almost inevitably, too great, though at 122 for 3, and then at 163 for 4, they had their noses just in front. To see Australia win, some 10,000 people turned up on the last day, although England had only two tail-end wickets left when it began. There was no charge for admission. All round the country a sigh of relief went up that the siege had been lifted and England had been beaten at last. Australia's young side were clearly coming on. What their batsmen needed most was the application and

concentration to go with their undoubted promise. Too many of them were getting out when they were "in".

The picture is a less happy one in the fourth Test at Sydney as England retain the Ashes

To be bowled out for 152 by 4.45pm on the first day of the fourth Test at Sydney, as England were, and yet to go on and win it represented a great recovery. Australia's inexperience and the length of their tail were factors in the result but more than anything it was the calculated way in which England planned the escape that brought it about ... *The Cricketer, March 1979*

Alex Bannister, the *Daily Mail*'s cricket correspondent, takes over from Woodcock for the final two Tests. The rout continues

The fifth Test at Adelaide began with a local football coach trying to motivate Yallop and his team with a blood-and-belief policy and ended with headlines like 'Sad, Sad Aussies', and 'Here We Go Again'. Perhaps the most significant reaction came from South Australian members at the prize-giving when Phil Ridings, chairman of selectors, claimed there was not a great deal of difference between the teams, though England had gone into a 4-1 lead. As Hansard might have reported – cries of 'No, No, Rubbish and Ah!' ... England certainly owed much to their Derbyshire triumvirate of Hendrick, Miller and Taylor.

If any batsman other than Mike Brearley had made the winning hit in the sixth Test at Sydney it would have appeared as an unseemly intrusion into a singularly personal achievement. No England captain, or for that matter any captain, has gained five victories in Australia. He may have been carried on the tide of Australia's sad domestic confusion, pitches below accepted standards and splendid pace and spin bowling, but equally he has emphasised his qualities of leadership and shrewd tactical know-how. Brearley was the inspiration of a magnificent team spirit and, by common consent, the fittest, most disciplined and best fielding side to tour Australia from England. ◼ *The Cricketer, April 1979*

Lightning Rod: Hogg at Perth

1978-79

1st Test December 1 3, 5 6, Brisbane †**Aus 116** (RGD Willis 4-44) and **339** (KJ Hughes 129, GN Yallop 102); **Eng 286** (DW Randall 75; RM Hogg 6-74) and **170-3** (Randall 74*). **Eng won by 7 wkts.**

2nd Test Dec 15-17, 19-20, Perth **Eng 309** (DI Gower 102; Hogg 5-65) and **208** (Hogg 5-57); †**Aus 190** (PM Toohey 81*; Willis 5-44) and **161** (GM Wood 64; JK Lever 4-28). **Eng won by 166 runs.**

3rd Test December 29-30, January 1-3, Melbourne †**Aus 258** (Wood 100) and **167** (Hughes 48); **Eng 143** (Hogg 5-30) and **179** (Gower 49; Hogg 5-36). **Aus won by 103 runs.**

4th Test January 6-8, 10-11, Sydney †**Eng 152** (IT Botham 59; AG Hurst 5-28) and **346** (Randall 150; JD Higgs 5-148, Hogg 4-67); **Aus 294** (WM Darling 91) and **111** (AR Border 45*; JE Emburey 4-46). **Eng won by 93 runs.**

5th Test January 27-29, 31-February 1, Adelaide **Eng 169** (Botham 74; Hogg 4-26) and **360** (RW Taylor 97; Hurst 4-97); †**Aus 164** (Botham 4-42) and **160** (Hughes 46). **Eng won by 205 runs.**

6th Test February 10-12, 14, Sydney †**Aus 198** (Yallop 121; Botham 4-57) and **143** (B Yardley 61*; G Miller 5-44); **Eng 308** (GA Gooch 74; Higgs 4-69) and **35-1. Eng won by 9 wkts.**

From the anger of the 1970s came the glamour and excitement of the 1980s. Following Packer's revolution England played a kiss-and-make-up series, controversially not for the Ashes, and a forgettable Centenary Test at Lord's. But then came 1981. The Ashes was reborn for the rest of the decade, switching hands, providing great entertainment, great characters and great stories – even if both countries had produced better teams

You're fired: Dennis Lillee with the aluminium bat he used in the first Test. The bat was eventually banned. Allan Border is his cheerful target

Reconciliation – revenge

The three-Test series in 1979-80, played alongside an Australia-West Indies rubber, did not have the Ashes at stake – not that this decision was universally welcomed, especially when a strong Australia flexed its muscles. **David Frith** previews

So the Ashes will not be at stake in the coming Australia-England Test series. The TCCB, supported by the Cricket Council, have declared that their decision was taken because the 1979-80 tour programme "is of an exceptional and experimental nature", and because of the absence of "the normal and necessary build-up before or during the three-Test series".

While there may be some sort of logic about this, the thinking behind the decision reveals a notable shortage of public relations awareness just when the game's "image" needs not only all the stimulation it can muster but all possible adherence to traditional values in the face of

gimmickry and expediency. If the Ashes are withheld because of any suspicion about the series, why accredit the matches with Test status in the first place? ... [Despite many difficulties and threats] the show has gone on and always the Ashes have been the coveted prize. Suppose England manage to hold off the Australian challenge – and decimate the charges of "chicken"? Will all concerned not feel that this was the finest achievement by the Test side since the days of Ray Illingworth's iron rule? *Wisden Cricket Monthly*, December 1979

The tour is far from satisfying. England lose heavily, Dennis Lillee uses an aluminium bat and

An England fan writes

Banners at Australian grounds with witless and inane insults will not, I hope, lead to retaliation when Australia come here. It would be advisable to fill all space round our grounds with adverts. It is far more distracting to look at a badly printed and often ungrammatical banner than a properly produced advert, even if the latter does advise you to drink keg beer.
JE Butcher, Malvern
The Cricketer, May 1980

Peter McFarline reports on the first Tests since the return of the Packer players

First Test, Perth

... The second day was dominated totally by Dennis Lillee. He began by bringing an aluminium bat to the crease to resume his innings. A firm straight-drive brought only three runs. Chappell considered it should have been four and dispatched 12th man Hogg with two conventional bats. At the same time Brearley complained to umpires Max O'Connell and Don Weser that the bat was damaging the ball. They agreed, then went through the farce of a 10-minute public argument. Lillee insisted that he was entitled to use the bat under the present Laws of the game. He sought confirmation from the dressing room, then threw the bat away in anger as he lost the argument ... Later Lillee was to admit in a radio interview that he had used the bat in an effort to boost Christmas sales for the bat company, of which he is a co-director. Lillee's actions in that melodrama did cricket no good ... The final day belonged to Geoff – Dymock or Boycott, depending on your inclination. Dymock, 34, returned a match-winning performance of 6 for 34 from 17.2 overs. Boycott showed a masterly technique while others crumbled, finishing the Test with 99 not out – the first man to be left so stranded. The Australians were victors by 138 runs.

Second Test, Sydney

When the coin was tossed, Brearley called incorrectly and effectively

Law bender: Lillee defends his bat

lost the match and the series. Chappell was later to complain that no match should be decided on the turn of a coin. England were sent in and, in the 148 minutes available, lost seven for 90 ... Eventually England left Australia 216 to win the series. Hughes was superb in his 47. Chappell, edgy at first, blossomed in the latter half of his innings of 98 not out. He had a chance to reach his 16th Test century when Botham gave him a beach-cricket lob on the last ball of the match. It landed 10 metres inside the fence ...

Third Test, Melbourne

With the series already won, the Australians still managed to find the enthusiasm to maintain their superiority in a match that contained many disappointing performances by the tourists.

Wisden Cricket Monthly, February 1980

Packer's shadow looms too large for many traditionalists. John Woodcock provides a postscript to England's tour

However distasteful in some respects and unsettling in others the England tour to Australia was, at least it was better than the alternative would have been, namely another winter of bitter strife between the traditional game and Mr Packer's well-organised and highly paid mercenary force ... No side can expect to beat Australia with a middle order that supplies virtually no runs. Take away Botham's 119 not out in Melbourne and Gower's 98 not out in Sydney and this is what you are left with: in 22 innings these two, together with Randall, Willey and Larkins, scored 211 runs. These, reputedly, are the best batsmen in England we are talking about or, to be more precise, the best English batsmen, and they are being paid big money. However ghastly an itinerary they were subjected to in Australia, there can be no excuse for such impoverishment as this. 🄻

The Cricketer, April 1980

It would be nice to be able to say that the great jamboree which was the Centenary Test Match at Lord's was an unqualified success. Off the field it was, except for anyone unlucky enough to pick up the virus which laid low a number of the old Test players, Harold Larwood and Ray Lindwall among them; on the field it misfired, almost from start to finish ... On the last morning Chappell's declaration left England to score 370 in 350 minutes. To have come anywhere near, Gooch would have had to show the way but, having started as though he might, with two boundaries in Pascoe's first over, he was soon out. When Athey failed, England had to decide whether to risk defeat in a bid for an improbable victory or to play out time. They chose the duller option and achieved it thanks to Boycott, Gower and Gatting ... With Gower, Gatting, Willey and Botham all capable of scoring fast, there was much disappointment at England's tactics ... In the 100 years of Test cricket, though, which the occasion celebrated, the fear of defeat has often been paramount, and this was, don't forget, a Test match.

The Cricketer, November 1980

1979-80

1st Test December 14-19, Perth **Aus 244** (KJ Hughes 99; IT Botham 6-78) and **337** (AR Border 115; Botham 5-98); **†Eng 228** (JM Brearley 64; DK Lillee 4-73) and **215** (G Boycott 99*; G Dymock 6-34). **Aus won by 138 runs.**

2nd Test January 4-8, Sydney **Eng 123** (Lillee 4-40, Dymock 4-42) and **237** (DI Gower 98*); **†Aus 145** (IM Chappell 42; Botham 4-29) and **219-4** (GS Chappell 98*). **Aus won by 6 wkts.**

3rd Test February 1-6, Melbourne **†Eng 306** (GA Gooch 99; Lillee 6-60) and **273** (Botham 119*; Lillee 5-78); **Aus 477** (GS Chappell 114) and **103-2** (GS Chappell 40*). **Aus won by 8 wkts.**

1980

Centenary Test August 28-September 2, Lord's **†Aus 385-5 dec** (Hughes 117, GM Wood 112) and **189-4 dec** (Hughes 84); **Eng 205** (Boycott 62; LS Pascoe 5-59) and **244-3** (Boycott 128*). **Match drawn.**

Botham's Ashes

The summer of 1981 has become synonymous with Ian Botham and his epic Ashes-winning performance. But it does not start so well. **Christopher Martin-Jenkins**, editor of *The Cricketer*, is not exactly bursting with anticipation

The prospect of an Australian touring team arriving in England to contest another series for the Ashes should tingle the blood. If it does so less than normally this summer it is because familiarity breeds contempt. This is the fourth Australian side in five years to make an official tour of England, of one kind or another, and the fifth in seven. There used to be genuine excitement in seeing for the first time players whose exploits one had only read about and sometimes men one had hardly even heard of. But of the 16 chosen this time only Martin Kent, Terry Alderman and Dirk Wellham have not played cricket in England.

It is sad in a way that Greg Chappell decided not to come to England for family and business reasons. He is a very great batsman and his absence gives England a better chance of retaining the Ashes they won in the Jubilee year of 1977.

It is a measure of the prosperity of the leading players, engendered by the Cricket Revolution wrought by Mr Packer in that momentous year, that Chappell should be able to refuse lucrative terms for this tour. Chappell's absence, however, means that the side will be led by Kim Hughes, whose attractive personality as well as his dashing batting should give to this team an image less tarnished than some recent Australian sides. We wish them a happy tour, a warm, dry summer and memorable cricket. If Dennis Lillee remains fit and the younger fast bowlers, Hogg, Lawson and Alderman, bowl to their potential, England's batsmen may be only slightly more at ease than they have been against the remorseless West Indians in their last two Test series. There should not be much between the two sides, so there is much to look forward to. *The Cricketer, May 1981*

David Frith's editorial in *Wisden Cricket Monthly* has other concerns

The curiosity of this 1981 England-Australia series is that for the first time ever, elements of both sides believe they have the Ashes in their possession. The Ashes were originally the product of a newspaper jibe. The concept belongs to the people – specifically to the people of both countries. The TCCB proclaimed that the Ashes were not for competition in the 1979-80 series because of the nature of the series. Many Australians were satisfied, after the 3-0 victory, that the Ashes had been regained.

Wisden Cricket Monthly, June 1981

The series starts at a swinging Trent Bridge. The ball moves, the batsmen nick it and the Aussies win. David Frith reports

1st Test June 18-21, Trent Bridge Eng 185 (MW Gatting 52; TM Alderman 4-68) and **125** (DK Lillee 5-46; Alderman 5-62); **†Aus 179** (AR Border 63) and **132-6** (GR Dilley 4-24). **Aus won by 4 wkts.**

For the second year running England came away from Trent Bridge the losers in a match dominated by bowlers and this time they were beaten at their own game. Both teams fielded four pace bowlers. In conditions which suited seam and swing England's [bowlers of the past] have shown how it should be done. Now it was the Australians Lillee, Alderman and Hogg ... These were four engrossing days. England's misfortune was to have batted twice under cloud cover to Australia's once. There were complaints of shortfall in

Blasted out: England captain Botham is bowled by Alderman for 1 at Trent Bridge

quality but it was a contest from which one dared not avert one's eyes – and that could not have been said of every Test of recent years.

Next Lord's and Botham bags a pair. David Frith describes

2nd Test July 2-7, Lord's **Eng 311** (P Willey 82 ; GF Lawson 7-81) and **265-8 dec** (DI Gower 89); †**Aus 345** (Border 64) and **90-4** (GM Wood 62*). **Match drawn.**

The Lord's Test [was] the last for England – for the time being anyway – with Ian Botham at the helm and had the taste of a draw about it almost throughout. The match was always short on expectancy, apart from the matter of Boycott's 100th Test appearance ... Australia's unlikely target was 232 in 170 minutes, including the 20 overs in the last hour ... Within an hour of the close all was forgotten in the sensation of Botham's departure from the captaincy. [Botham resigned before he was sacked] At least half-a-century will have passed before England beat Australia at Lord's again following the 1934 victory, remembered with increasing nostalgia. *Wisden Cricket Monthly*, August 1981

Botham resigns – he would have been sacked anyway – and Christopher Martin-Jenkins writes

At Lord's on the gloriously sunny evening of July 7, Ian Botham resigned the captaincy after 12 Tests in charge of England. His record in 13 hectic and traumatic months was eight draws and four defeats. His successor was also his predecessor, Mike Brearley, who lost three of his last four Tests as captain. It struck one as poignant that he should lose the England captaincy on the ground where he had first made a modest name for himself as a member of the groundstaff. For that boisterous, carefree teenager, the rise and the fall had been amazingly quick ... For a long time the England captaincy has been an obsession for the press and for the cricket public too. Rightly or wrongly this is unlikely to change. The job therefore demands maturity, balance and a thick skin, as well as luck and skill. The original choice of Botham at the age of 24 was a gamble which always seemed likely to fail. Ironically, it was on Botham's brilliance as an allrounder but especially as a match-winning bowler that many of Brearley's successes as a captain were based. *The Cricketer*, August 1981

The most astonishing match in the history of the Ashes as seen through the eyes of *The Cricketer*'s new editor Christopher Martin-Jenkins

I an Botham, magically transformed in his first match away from a captaincy that had weighed more heavily than Frodo's ring, stole the third Test from Australia in two hours of thunderous driving. Coming in at 105 for 5, with England still 122 behind, his brilliance, bravado and, in Kim Hughes's words, his "brute strength" gave England's bowlers 129 runs to play with. At 56 for 1 their cause seemed hopeless but Bob Willis took eight of the last nine wickets, Mike Gatting and Graham Dilley held crucial catches and the daylight robbery was complete. In the end Mike Brearley's return as captain was triumphant. He gave Botham a much longer first-innings spell than the former captain would have given himself and, in the tense final stages, he kept the right balance between attack and defence. His opposite number, Hughes, was admirably gracious and generous in defeat. For three and a half days his team had outplayed England and the Ashes were as good as regained. Defeat must have seemed like a sudden, unexpected bereavement. For England it was the first win in 13 Tests, ending a spell equal to the most barren in their history. At tea-time on the Saturday Ladbrokes offered odds of 500 to 1 against an England victory. ▷

Leading captain: Kim Hughes heads out for the first Test at Trent Bridge, a Test he wins

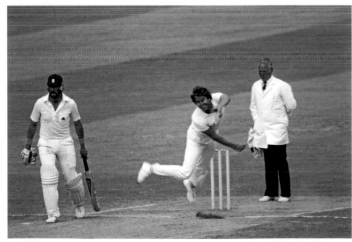

Smiling assassin: Terry Alderman bowling at Lord's as Graham Gooch backs up

The finisher: Bob Willis bowls at Headingley

The hitter: Ian Botham on his way to an unbeaten 149; Rod Marsh is the wicketkeeper

Wayward England bowling had allowed Australia to crawl to 401 for 9 declared. Then Alderman got to work ...

Lillee, Lawson and Alderman made embarrassingly better use of the uneven bounce, and only a heroic counter-attack by Botham gave England a chance of saving the follow-on. Botham's 50 came off only 50 balls. He hit eight fours, magnificent shots all. Once he skied over extra-cover: if the Gods had not returned their favours he would have been caught ...

The astounding turnabout in a momentous fourth day's cricket began shortly before tea when Bob Taylor was caught off a glove at short-leg to make England [following on] 135 for 7, still 92 runs behind. By tea Botham and Dilley had taken the score to 176 for 7. Between tea and the close Botham added a further 106 off his own bat out of 175. John Woodcock compared his spectacular controlled hitting to Gilbert Jessop; Peter West said it was as if the village blacksmith had taken charge of a Test. Botham himself, launching his 16-stone frame towards the ball with joyous abandon, just smiled his way through one of the most amazing innings of all time. Murderous drives and square cuts brought him 19 fours in his personal century, reached off 87 balls.

Dilley actually outscored Botham with a series of rasping off and cover drives. He never seemed to move his feet – nor, very often, did Botham – but luck had changed sides with a vengeance and both players seemed either to middle the ball or to miss it altogether. Chris Old managed to keep the attack going, adding a further 67

before he was yorked by Lawson. England's lead was still under 100 when Willis strode out, but with Botham hitting commanding fours and then collecting a single off the last ball of most overs, the advantage was 124 when stumps were drawn. In the heady euphoria of the moment it seemed England could win ...

Brearley gave Willis five overs into the breeze and up the hill and then brought on Willey, switching Willis to the Kirkstall Lane end at 48 for 1. With his Test career in doubt for the umpteenth time, Willis, of the big heart and vicious bounce, gave it everything he knew. Brushing aside the cost of regular no-balls, he bowled at fierce pace to a shorter length and a straighter line than in the first innings. And suddenly Australia's foundation crumbled ... Alderman walked out with 20 still needed and it was the inspired Willis who knocked out Bright's middle-stump with a ball of full length to complete a victory that saved a moribund series. *The Cricketer, September 1981*

Bob Willis tells how it felt in *Wisden Cricket Monthly*

The Bob Willis who walked off the field at 2.20pm on that amazing afternoon at Headingley was a totally different man from the chap who switched on his radio at 5pm. Not until Henry Blofeld's fruity tones regaled me with the details of the Test did I realise what had happened: it was me he was talking about. I had taken 8 for 43. It slowly dawned that I had played my full part in the most astonishing few hours.

Our victory was the lead story on both radio and TV news that evening. The Stock Exchange closed early. Was it really RGDW – the man with the wonky knees and the no-ball problems – who had helped send the men in pinstripe suits home from the City with light hearts? Did the mandarins of Whitehall really postpone their high-powered meetings to listen to the progress of the Australian innings?

Friends tell me the effect on morale in factories, pubs and offices was astonishing – that incalculable psychological thing is something a sportsman can never really understand. We are on a plateau of self-absorption during a day's play such as that – and I am in a cocoon of concentration. It is very difficult for me to stand aside from the emotional commitment of bowling for England and to be able to appreciate the sheer enjoyment of bowling well.

Even now, some weeks later, I am only starting to come to terms with the Headingley Test. How I envy Ian's ability to say to himself "This is great. I'm loving this" at the actual moment rather than hours later ... [On the final day after lunch] we came out breathing fire at the Aussies – a quality for which [they] are noted. The batsmen did not quite know whether to play normally or in the Botham style. The memory of Bright's middle-stump cart-wheeling out of the ground will warm me when I'm grey, stoop-backed and nodding off by the fireside. Yes, I loved that day. I shall never forget every ball of that dramatic Tuesday.

Wisden Cricket Monthly, September 1981

▷

The allrounder: Botham takes six wickets

The hero: Botham after the fourth day *above*; how *The Cricketer* celebrates the Test *below*

Ian Botham
6 for 95, 50 & 149 not out

'The Test Match of the Century'

At Headingley, Leeds. July 16th to July 21st 1981. Third Test match, England v Australia
After being invited to follow on, England defeated Australia by 18 runs.

AUSTRALIA WON TOSS FIRST INNINGS

J Dyson		b Dilley	102
GM Wood	lbw	b Botham	34
TM Chappell	c Taylor	b Willey	27
KJ Hughes*	c and	b Botham	89
RJ Bright		b Dilley	7
GN Yallop	c Taylor	b Botham	58
AR Border	lbw	b Botham	8
RW Marsh†		b Botham	28
GF Lawson	c Taylor	b Botham	13
DK Lillee	not out		3
TM Alderman	not out		0
Extras	b4 lb13 w3 nb12		32
Total	155.2 overs		401-9d

Wicket 55 149 196 220 332 354 357 396 401

Bowling Willis 30-8-72-0, Old 43-14-91-0,
Dilley 27-4-78-2, Botham 39.2-11-95-6,
Willey 13-2-31-1, Boycott 3-2-2-0

ENGLAND FIRST INNINGS

GA Gooch	lbw	b Alderman	2
G Boycott		b Lawson	12
JM Brearley*	c Marsh	b Alderman	10
DI Gower	c Marsh	b Lawson	24
MW Gatting	lbw	b Lillee	15
P Willey		b Lawson	8
IT Botham	c Marsh	b Lillee	50
RW Taylor†	c Marsh	b Lillee	5
GR Dilley	c and	b Lillee	13
CM Old	c Border	b Alderman	0
RGD Willis	not out		1
Extras	b6 lb11 w6 nb11		34
Total	50.5 overs		174

Wicket 12 40 42 84 87 112 148 166 167

Bowling Lillee 18.5-7-49-4, Alderman 19-4-59-3,
Lawson 13-3-32-3

ENGLAND SECOND INNINGS

GA Gooch	c Alderman	b Lillee	0
G Boycott	lbw	b Alderman	46
JM Brearley*	c Alderman	b Lillee	14
DI Gower		b Alderman	9
MW Gatting	lbw	b Alderman	1
P Willey	c Dyson	b Lillee	33
IT Botham	not out		149
RW Taylor†	c Bright		1
GR Dilley		b Alderman	56
CM Old		b Lawson	29
RGD Willis	c Border	b Alderman	2
Extras	b5 lb3 w3 nb5		16
Total	87.3 overs		356

Wicket 0 18 37 41 105 133 135 252 319

Bowling Lillee 25-6-94-3,
Alderman 35.3-6-135-6,
Lawson 23-4-96-1, Bright 4-0-15-0

AUSTRALIA SECOND INNINGS

J Dyson	c Taylor	b Willis	34
GM Wood	c Taylor	b Botham	10
TM Chappell	c Taylor	b Willis	8
KJ Hughes*	c Botham	b Willis	0
GN Yallop	c Gatting	b Willis	0
AR Border		b Old	0
RW Marsh†	c Dilley	b Willis	4
RJ Bright		b Willis	19
GF Lawson	c Taylor	b Willis	1
DK Lillee	c Gatting	b Willis	17
TM Alderman	not out		0
Extras	lb3 w1 nb14		18
Total	36.1 overs		111

Wicket 13 56 58 58 65 68 74 75 110

Bowling Botham 7-3-14-1, Dilley 2-0-11-0,
Willis 15.1-3-43-8, Old 9-1-21-1,
Willey 3-1-4-0

Umpires **DGL Evans and BJ Meyer** Man of the match **IT Botham**

Bob Willis
8 for 43

BREARLEY

GOOCH

GOWER

GATTING

WILLEY

TAYLOR

OLD

DILLEY

BOYCOTT

David Frith then watches the extraordinary Edgbaston finale for *Wisden Cricket Monthly*

4th Test July 30-August 2, Edgbaston †Eng 189 (JM Brearley 48; Alderman 5-42) and **219** (RJ Bright 5-68); **Aus 258** (KJ Hughes 47; JE Emburey 4-43) and **121** (Border 40; IT Botham 5-11). **Eng won by 29 runs.**

To have two Test matches snatched away within a fortnight is enough to drain all the exuberance even from such a bouncy chap as Australia's captain Kim Hughes; and it showed as he bravely faced the press half an hour after Ian Botham had stolen the match for England with a 28-ball spell of five wickets for a single run. He could not easily explain his side's collapse from just as much a match-winning position as at Headingley. Any team would have been shuddering still long after such a reversal. A target of 151 would normally have been approached as a formality. Instead, on a pitch that gave less help to the bowlers than that at Leeds, there was exaggerated caution ...

On Saturday evening, while hardly any English supporters were optimistic, Australians in several quarters were prone to give the match up as lost. The requirement

151, after all, was 21 more than at Headingley; and Wood was already out ... The ending was hardly close. Marsh lost his middle-stump as he tried to pound Botham straight, Bright was lbw next ball and, after Taylor had secured a catch from Lillee, a near-impossible burden fell on Kent's shoulders. He was bowled off his pad by a Botham who would not be denied. Nothing was more certain now than that Botham would pull England to victory. He found a straight one for Alderman, followed through to grab a souvenir stump, and 20 minutes later received another man-of-the-match award. *Wisden Cricket Monthly*, September 1981

Bob Willis reacts to Edgbaston

I've never seen such crowds there – or heard such noise! They had turned up to see England repeat their Headingley victory and that roar from the terraces was unforgettable. It keeps you going. It is worth runs and wickets, and it lifts you, even if it isn't exactly a replica of the "Kill, kill, kill!" roar we've known on some Australian grounds, particularly when Mr Lillee is operating.

Wisden Cricket Monthly, October 1981

Then comes Old Trafford and with the game in the balance, Botham

takes it firmly away from Australia with his most dynamic display of the summer. Christopher Martin-Jenkins watches

5th Test August 13-17, Old Trafford †Eng 231 (CJ Tavaré 69; Lillee 4-55) and **404** (Botham 118; Alderman 5-109); **Aus 130** (MF Kent 52; RGD Willis 4-63) and **402** (Border 123*, GN Yallop 114). **Eng won by 103 runs.**

From a dreary morning struggle the game was lifted to Olympian heights by the bionic man. Never can any Test crowd have seen such a contrast as the 21,000 people packed inside Old Trafford. In the morning England managed 20 scoring strokes and 29 runs against tight bowling and fielding. Tavaré remained in passive occupation. Boycott and Gatting were lbw to Alderman and Gower caught, hooking to mid-wicket.

When Botham came in, England's lead was 205. He played himself in sensibly but had begun to flex his muscles when the second new ball was claimed. Suddenly was mayhem. In Alderman's first over Botham (then 32) miscued for almost the only time in his staggering innings and Whitney running back from mid-off just misjudged a devilish catch. In the next over from Lillee, Botham hooked two sixes over backward square-leg, clubbing the ball high on the bat from just in front of his unprotected head. Next he square-cut superbly and drove back over Lillee's head with awesome force. 22 runs came from the over. Another superb drive over Alderman's head was followed by perhaps the best stroke of all, an apparently effortless pull yards over mid-wicket for six into a delirious crowd. There was no stopping Botham. Interrupted only by the tea interval (when he was 94, Tavaré 67) he moved from 28 to 100 in 37 minutes, reaching the landmark off his 86th ball with a sweep off Bright, his fifth six. He celebrated with a classical straight-drive over the sight-screen.

Mega-star: Ian Botham, with souvenir stump, after the Old Trafford Test

Making Manchester happy: Mike Whitney on debut drops Botham during his 118

No one in Ashes Tests had ever hit six sixes before. *The Cricketer, October 1981*

David Frith adds for *Wisden Cricket Monthly*

The match, which reached into the last session of the final day, contained all the elements of fluctuating drama experienced in the previous two contests, and by now so stretched had public credulity become that Australia's eventual target of 506 was thought by many to be attainable. For excitement and unpredictability no other series since the 1960–61 Australia-West Indies rubber has matched this one and few ever in England have so arrested the public imagination. *Wisden Cricket Monthly, October 1981*

With England 3-1 up in the series and the Ashes safe, Botham took another 10 wickets in the drawn final Test at The Oval, just to ensure the man-of-the-series award

6th Test **August 27-September 1, The Oval †Aus 352** (Border 106*; Botham 6-125) and **344-9 dec** (DM Wellham 103; M Hendrick 4-82, Botham 4-128); **Eng 314** (G Boycott 137; Lillee 7-89) and **261-7** (Knott 70*; Lillee 4-70). **Match drawn.**

John Arlott appraises Mike Brearley's captaincy and his studious approach to people

Brearley's main characteristics are the ability to assess himself objectively; the automatic sympathy for – and virtual need to study – other people; and an immense mental hunger ... Often highly gifted cricketers' play has been thrown out of gear by the demands of captaincy: that they should think of, and for, other players. Cricket, especially top-class cricket, is a lonely game; individually successful cricket must, quite essentially, be selfish. When they are not batting or bowling, many players like to relax in some undemanding fielding position.

For Brearley, though, that would be mental starvation; his brain demands fodder. Without captaincy sheer boredom would have driven him from the first-class game by now. Many people set out to motivate others, often as the best way to their own success. Mike Brearley, however, instinctively studies other people; if that enables him to fire them to the greater effect of the team he leads, that is an inner, as well as a material, reward ... Much of his strength as a captain lies in the fact that cricket is not the be-all and end-all of life for him. Brearley has always been able to stand back and look at cricket and cricketers as from the outside; few at Test level have had that capacity. 🄰 *Wisden Cricket Monthly, October 1981*

Battling on: Border at Old Trafford

Final fling: Gatting bowled Lillee

Is Botham so good?
So *WCM* has jumped on the "Bothamitis" bandwagon too? What is it about the man that makes everyone think he's so incredibly good? At Headingley and Old Trafford, he slogged bad Australian bowling, pitched halfway down the wicket at him. Gooch or Gower would have done likewise. At Edgbaston, he was lucky enough to have five tailenders bring about their own demise while he was bowling at them. Botham will inevitably win all the awards in the cricketing world this year; he may even win the Sports Personality of the Year. But he's a long way down on some people's list of cricket greats.
John Drummond
Stoke-on-Trent, Staffs
Wisden Cricket Monthly, November 1981

Yes, Botham is that good
I felt it my duty to reply to Mr Drummond's letter regarding Ian Botham. Ian was the prime factor in winning the Ashes for England with some incredible feats. Last summer his performances with the bat outshone those of any of his England colleagues. It is only natural that such explosive match-winning centuries should spring to mind more readily than the less effective but nevertheless well-deserved and possibly more "correct" ones. Ian's five-wicket haul at Edgbaston included Bright, Marsh and, most significantly, Kent – hardly genuine tailenders. He was pulled apart when he failed [as captain] and I cannot understand why, after statistics one could only dream about, there are still those who want to pull Ian down.
Mark Stansfield
Boston, Lincs
Wisden Cricket Monthly, December 1981

Mea Maxima Culpa! I already know the years will embellish the white lies that my mischievous brain has already started to sponsor. And not only white, Father, but great black whoppers. "Oh, yes," I found myself saying to some gawp in the pub the other day, "of course I was there when Botham scored his centuries, and not only was I there but on both occasions I was the last man other than the crossing batsman to wish him good luck," …

Unless I get this off my chest here and now, my wide-eyed great grandchildren are going to be left in no doubt at all that I was there in person for every meaningful ball bowled in that epic and crazy, long ago Ashes series of 1981. And the truth is, that while I had a job and a boss that positively encouraged my attendance, I was never once there when it mattered. Indeed, I publicly wrote off the 1981 Test series at around two o'clock on Monday, July 20 when England were 130-odd for seven in the follow-on. I phoned through the usual "death of English cricket" waffle to the office – and went out to the pub ... Now I cannot wait for the books of the series to come out. I have to learn what happened, chapter and verse. Learn it as though I was there in person. Well, my grandchildren will want to know all about it, won't they?
The Cricketer, October 1981

HERO
No.7

Ian
Botham

Test
Batting

Matches	102
Runs	5200
Highest score	208
Average	33.54
Hundreds	14
Fifties	22

Bowling

Balls	21815
Runs	10878
Wickets	383
Average	28.40
Best bowling	8-34
5-for inns	27
10-for match	4

First-class career
Batting

Matches	402
Runs	19399
Highest score	228
Average	33.97
Hundreds	38
Fifties	97

Bowling

Balls	63547
Runs	31902
Wickets	1172
Average	27.22
Best bowling	8-34
5-for inns	59
10-for match	8

v Australia
Batting

Matches	36
Runs	1673
Average	29.35

Bowling

Wickets	148
Average	27.65

The Colossus

On Botham's retirement in 1993 **Simon Hughes** paid tribute to his one-time team-mate and the man who had dominated English – and Ashes – cricket for the last 16 years

There is a range of toys called Boglins: sort of tough looking monsters that burp or spit coarsely when you press their stomach. In his next life, Ian Botham will probably return as one – he's the most monstrous burper and spitter the world has ever known. But that characterises his whole life – everything carried out with the utmost vigour, whether unleashing a brutal tee shot, marching down the pavilion steps whirling a three-pound bat round his head, or taking pot shots at crows that steal his goslings.

Even in his cricketing dotage he bowled 'a heavy ball' and was capable of interrupting those wobbling seamers to propel a surprise bouncer. Batsmen saw it as a long-hop, and it often was, but many perished anyway ...

Throughout an extraordinary career Botham's enormous self-belief was both his greatest asset and most significant shortcoming. This was the factor that translated the innocuous looking ball into a wicket-taking delivery, that persuaded a spiralling top edge over long leg for six. His lazy hands-on-knees slip-fielding posture confounded all the coaching manuals but his catching at very close second slip was out of this world. His methods were raw and muscular but based on sound technique and massive reputation.

As with most phenomenal sportsmen, he had a fantastic line in excuses if things went awry. "A bloke by the sightscreen was flashing a mirror in my eye," he said once after missing a straight one at Hartlepool. Officials were swiftly dispatched to flush out the culprit; none, of course, was found. At other times he would return complaining of an inswinger that pitched leg and hit off, or of a fluttering tarpaulin that caused him to miss a straightforward slip catch. Kicking at unreliable footholds was a familiar ploy if he dragged a delivery down and it was walloped to the boundary.

No one begrudged him these escape clauses though, because everyone admired him and acknowledged him as the greatest matchwinner the game has known. In that sense he was very un-English – we are a nation of participants and good losers. Botham taught us how to win, forging paths to unlikely victories, retrieving situations others would have considered out of reach.

Burning aggression was often prevalent in the dressing room before major matches, and some younger team-mates found his presence daunting. This was either because they lacked confidence, or suspected he did not value their ability. Often they were right and their form faded. That and the odd tendency to flout authority were negatives to his influence.

They were far outweighed by the positive; the invigorating confidence his name on the scorecard generates in the team, the inhibitions it instils in the opposition (how many times did he receive a juicy four-ball after taking guard?), the power, the dominance, the swagger. He did not spend time analysing a youngster's technique, attitude was far more important. He was frugal with compliments so they meant more when they were offered.

But he is a generous man. He opened doors, organised parties, took us to places we wouldn't otherwise have gone. Towards the end of his career the county circuit became a culinary tour of Britain as he sought out the class of eating establishment that served Chateau Lafite '61. Fortunately he paid for (and drank) most of the wine.

Occasionally he invited entire teams to his exquisite 17th-century farmhouse for a barbecue. Everyone made the trip to this gorgeous valley in the North Yorkshire dales – only a fool refused his hospitality. While he supervised the poaching of wild salmon or the braising of local steak, drinks appeared from all directions – an important by-product of these evenings was to lure leading members of the 'oppo' to excess so they'd be below par next morning. Peter Roebuck noticed an improvement in the Taunton performances of visiting Test stars once Botham had left Somerset ...

Never mind the 383 Test wickets, he's made 14 Test centuries. Fourteen. Batting at No.6. That's phenomenal in anyone's book. One year he hit 80 sixes in the season, 14 more than the next best ever. He has taken five wickets in an innings 59 times. All right, he might have a knack of trapping batsmen with innocuous deliveries, but 1,172 scalps can't all have been flukes.

His retirement underlined perhaps his most striking feature – loyalty. Not to establishments or counties but to individuals. Who else would have cast aside a 12-year association with a county in sympathy with two sacked West Indians? Who else would have flounced out of the pre-World Cup final dinner when the Queen was ridiculed? It's not the team Botham cares about so much as the players in it, imbuing them with the will to win. There was a stir of expectancy when he played. Once he realised he was unable to provide that, and was placing extra burdens on other players, he packed it in ... Few players felt his equal, and rightly so, but at least we had cricket as a common denominator and the game gave him the perfect stimulus. It was a privilege to be on the same field as Ian Botham – no one could fail to be profoundly influenced by his enjoyment, his skill and his achievement. Durham players had lumps in their throats as he left the field for the last time. "That's part of my childhood gone," the wicketkeeper Chris Scott said sadly. We will miss him enormously, apart from the burps. But he might miss us just as much. *The Cricketer,* November 1993

Old Australia's last fight

England, now led by Bob Willis, travelled down under with the euphoria of 1981 still ringing in their ears and with the Australians squabbling, as **Peter McFarline** writes

The battle for the captaincy of Australia this summer became an ugly, public issue. The three candidates, Kim Hughes, Greg Chappell and Rod Marsh, all stated they felt they were the best man for the job. The issue was first raised by Chappell, in an interview on the BBC's *World* programme, which was heard by the Australian team during their disastrous tour of Pakistan. Chappell had declined to make

Stretcher bearers: Alderman at Perth

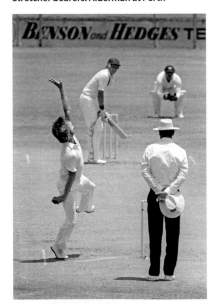
Full stretch: Thomson bowls to Gower

the tour because of business and family reasons. Hughes immediately answered Chappell's claims by saying that the job should go to the player who was prepared to take it on full-time. Chappell has missed two overseas trips recently and has indicated that he will not be available for future tours, although he would like to play three or four more domestic seasons. Then Marsh launched a trenchant attack on Hughes in an interview published in Australian *Playboy* magazine. Marsh, Australia's most-capped player, described Hughes variously as "naive", "impetuous" and always capable of doing "silly things", "whether he had in his hand a bat, a golf club or a pack of cards". Marsh effectively disqualified himself by his criticism of Hughes and a statement that he had been in effect captaining the side for the last four years anyway.

On a less tempestuous note, David Frith wishes all night-time England fans well with a bed-time story

As Gower sweeps towards his double-century or Chappell approaches his third consecutive hundred of the series, the nocturnal listener might spare a sympathetic thought for the Australian listening to Hutton advance to his 364 in 1938. "Cripes," said Jackie, "how good would this fella be if he ever batted in daylight!" Merry Christmas, everyone.
Wisden Cricket Monthly, December 1982

The series kicks off at Perth but crowd trouble resulting in a serious injury to Terry Alderman mars the opening encounter. Matthew Engel reports from a shocked Waca ground at Perth

1st Test November 12-17, Perth Eng 411 (CJ Tavaré 89; B Yardley 5-107) and **358** (DW Randall 115; GF Lawson 5-108); **†Aus 424-9 dec** (GS Chappell 117; G Miller 4-70) and **73-2**. **Match drawn.**

There is a hospitable winery just outside Perth which traditionally marks a Test in the city by inviting the players, officials and journalists to a barbecue. Just as traditionally, very few of the journalists who are not normally averse to invitations from wineries, ever turn up. They are far too busy dealing with the implications of another Perth tradition: the annual Test match sensation. This year, following Lillee and the aluminium bat and Lillee and Javed, the fracas at the Waca was the pitch invasion on the Saturday afternoon and the bizarre injury to Terry Alderman that resulted ... It will be unfortunate if the first Test were forever remembered just for the incident. Although it ended in the blandest of draws, it produced a lot of interesting cricket and at the start of the final day England were in very real danger of defeat.

The disturbances end in court

The invasion of the playing area on the second day, which led to the injury to Terry Alderman, and the ensuing fighting on the terraces between rival supporters, resulted in 26 people appearing in court. Sentences ranged from fines for "urinating in public" to a month in jail for three young men ... Gary Donnison, 19, born in York, an unemployed machinist, pleaded not guilty to unlawfully assaulting Alderman and to disorderly conduct. Telephone threats, believed to be by some who had large bets on Australia winning and who felt Alderman's absence endangered their money, were made to Donnison's home, which was placed under police protection. Donnison has apologised to Alderman in a public statement.
Wisden Cricket Monthly, January 1983

The second game at Brisbane was a batting disaster for England as Lawson and their old nemesis Jeff Thomson cleaned up. Christopher Martin-Jenkins reports

2nd Test Nov 26-Dec 1, Brisbane **Eng 219** (AJ Lamb 72; Lawson 6-47) and **309** (G Fowler 83; JR Thomson 5-73, Lawson 5-87); **†Aus 341** (KC Wessels 162; RGD Willis 5-66) and **190-3** (DW Hookes 66*, Wessels 46). **Aus won by 7 wkts.**

Australia went one-up in the series at the Gabba after a riveting Test in which the standard was patchy. Australia dropped 10 catches on a ground apparently difficult for sighting the ball and their captain ran himself out twice, once officially, the second time unofficially, presumably because the umpire too was unsighted. But in the end it was Chappell who was smiling, Willis the one having to put a brave face ahead of a churning breast. His sportsmanship in defeat was admirable and his acceptance of setbacks during the match exemplary.

The Cricketer, January 1983

Henry Blofeld watches England bounced and bowled to defeat at Adelaide

3rd Test December 10-15, Adelaide **Aus 438** (Chappell 115; IT Botham 4-112) and **83-2**; **†Eng 216** (Lamb 82; Lawson 4-56) and **304** (DI Gower 114; Lawson 5-66). **Aus won by 8 wkts.**

The shortcomings of the England party in Australia were shown up even more sharply in the third Test at Adelaide. Once again England's batting threw the match away although by accident they found themselves up against Australia's best pace attack so far.

The Cricketer, February 1983

Blofeld describes England's terrifying three-run win at Melbourne, which equalled the narrowest margin of victory ever in an Ashes match

4th Test December 26-30, Melbourne **Eng 284** (Tavaré 89) and **294** (Fowler 65); **†Aus 287** (KJ Hughes 66) and **288** (Hookes 68; NG Cowans 6-77). **Eng won by 3 runs.**

England won one of the most exciting matches in the history of Test cricket an hour and a half into the fifth day by three runs. Australia, who had been set to score 292 to win, were bowled out for 288 after a remarkable last-wicket stand of 70 between Jeff Thomson and Allan Border. For the first four days the game had fluctuated

Final stand: Botham to Border at Melbourne in the 4th Test with Jeff Thomson backing up

dramatically and yet all through it remained the most even of contests. All four innings ended within 10 runs of each other: 284, 287, 294, and 288 ... Then, after 85 minutes' play, Botham began an over to Thomson with Australia needing four to win and three to tie which would still have given them the Ashes. The first ball was short. Thomson followed it and it flew from the edge to Tavaré at second slip who got both hands to a straight-forward catch but agonisingly the ball bounced out. Then, suddenly, Miller appeared behind Tavaré from first slip to hold the rebound and set off like a hare for the pavilion followed by the exhilarated England fielders and the two dejected Australian batsmen. After five tense and thrilling days it had all come down to this. It was evidence if any more was needed of the superiority of Test cricket over one-day cricket. *The Cricketer, February 1983*

With the Ashes alive, Henry Blofeld writes on the last Test

5th Test January 2-4, 6-7, Sydney **†Aus 314** (AR Border 89) and **382** (Hughes 137); **Eng 237** (Gower 70, Randall 70; Thomson 5-50) and **314-7** (EE Hemmings 95). **Match drawn.**

It was too much to expect the fifth Test to live up to the excitement and dramas of the fourth. Australia obtained the draw that was enough to win the Ashes. At the end of the match Chappell announced his retirement from the Australian captaincy after leading his country a record 47 times. ◾

The Cricketer, February 1983

Dressing-room tales

After the thrilling finish at Melbourne, star columnists offered a glimpse of the emotions in the dressing room

England vice-captain David Gower

After we had nearly snatched defeat from the jaws of victory, the relief, satisfaction and enjoyment of winning were the highlight of the tour. Simply, though, Test cricket is still the most satisfying game to be involved in and it is there that all our highest hopes and ambitions lie.

England captain Bob Willis

It is a measure of the tremendous interest in cricket that we have found throughout the trip that 18,000 turned up to see what could possibly have been only one ball bowled on the final morning. It was perhaps just as well that we got there in the end. It was as tense a contest as I have ever played in.

Wisden Cricket Monthly, March 1983

England spinner Vic Marks

After the game was over, many of the players, including old hands such as 'Both', Geoff Miller and the captain simply collapsed into chairs exhausted. Derek Pringle did muster the energy to bring out his camera, yet again, to capture a picture of Tavaré's throbbing thumb, the thumb which thankfully managed to parry the ball upwards. It was exhausting watching as well. The manager has no fingernails left for Sydney, Norman Gifford almost swallowed his most expensive pipe and Robin Jackman remained grateful that Benson & Hedges were sponsoring the series. Otherwise his weekly allowance would have disappeared in smoke. *The Cricketer, February 1983*

Weak and wet

Australia were at a low ebb, England had suffered a harsh defeat to West Indies the previous summer. But 1985 provided respite, between the rain, with a resounding Gower-led win. Before the start **David Frith** warns against complacency

A message for Englishmen everywhere from one who has seen many of the 1985 Australian touring team in action and on TV, and spoken to dozens of people involved in cricket out there: Allan Border, the captain, is worn to a frazzle, blitzed perhaps beyond recall by his gallant resistance to the West Indian fast attack. Kepler Wessels can't get the ball off the square, and is as vulnerable as a

tailender if you pitch leg stump. Greg Ritchie and David Boon are very overweight, and would have been lucky to get into an Australian 3rd XI. Dirk Wellham's century at The Oval in 1981 was a fluke, set up by an England skipper who didn't fancy batting in poor evening light. As for the bowling, Geoff Lawson puts more energy into the 'verbals' these days than into his bowling and Craig McDermott's only medium-pace.

Key moment: David Gower catches Wayne Phillips off Phil Edmonds via Allan Lamb's boot in the fifth Test at Edgbaston

Simon O'Donnell – well, he's so raw he isn't even in all the reference books yet. Another so-called allrounder, Greg Matthews, bowls more full-tosses per over than Vic Marks; while Bob Holland will find the pitches so slow that batsmen beaten first-up will be able to play a second stroke at him and survive. And as for Rod McCurdy, he was one of the bowlers operating when David Hookes hit his 34-ball century – enough said? Wayne Phillips? So he's made a few Test runs but probably he's no more than an acrobatic stopper behind the sticks.

And if you believe all that, you'd believe anything. It's an Ashes series, folks. It puts all else in the shade; 108 years of feverish rivalry, with "strongest ever" teams being overthrown and "weakest ever" astounding the pundits. The return of old favourites blended with bright new faces is the essence of the ongoing challenge.

Wisden Cricket Monthly, May 1985

Christopher Martin-Jenkins profiles the Australian squad and has this to say about the skipper

BORDER, Allan Robert (Captain) Born July 27, 1955. Queensland.

It looks increasingly as though the Australian selectors got it right when they chose Allan Border to succeed the hapless Kim Hughes as captain when the West Indians had reduced the latter to tearful resignation. Border has frequently shown himself to be as sturdy and determined as a terrier, for example when making a courageous 123 not out with a broken finger against England at Old Trafford on the last tour, 1981. He fought a lonely battle with the West Indies fast bowlers in the Caribbean in 1984 when his 521 runs at an average of 74 proved not just his toughness but his skill. He now leads a young side going in the right direction after their stretching on the Caribbean rack.

The Cricketer, May 1985

Top scorer: Gower (215) at Edgbaston

Run machine: Gooch (196) at The Oval

England started the series with a dynamic win at Headingley with Botham the inspiration, naturally. Christopher Martin-Jenkins writes

Although [Tim] Robinson was rightly the man of the match after a wholly admirable example of how to play every ball on its merits – including dismissing the bad ones, of which there were many, for four – Ian Botham's role was almost as important in the victory. His thunderous innings on the Saturday afternoon bought England valuable time (they had only half an hour to spare in the end) and he bowled as well as he has done for England since the Lord's Test last year. Emburey, with seven wickets in the match and two from only six overs in the first innings, was the other essential ingredient in England's heartening start to the series.

It was by no means a match without hope for the touring team but they will not win the Ashes without holding their slip catches. The hard chance missed by Ritchie when Robinson was only 22 proved embarrassingly expensive.

The Cricketer, August 1985

David Frith adds his observations

The final day was in so many ways the most exciting. When Cowans

bowled Boon off his boot with the sixth ball, the end seemed imminent. But O'Donnell supported Phillips, who played some exquisite shots. The arrears were cleared. Australia were up off the canvas, and the England camp's frustration returned. They put on 80 before Botham – who else? – broke through ... Still, the outcome was finely balanced: would the weather deny England, or would Australia reach the fulcrum point where the target they set would stretch England on a suspicious pitch? ... So England needed 123 – just under Australia's target in that intrusively unforgettable Test here four years ago – with 200 minutes of play possible. And England's luck with the weather returned at this crucial time ... The circumstances of the winning hit were shameful and unsettling. Lamb cracked a hook over Lawson at fine leg, and as the fielder turned and ran under it, swarms of spectators ran gormlessly on to the field. Their action denied Lawson any realistic chance of sizing up the catch properly and, as the crestfallen fielder squatted on the turf, the mob charged past him, some of them to embark on hyena-like tussles for the stumps and bails.

Wisden Cricket Monthly, August 1985

Bob Willis, now a full-time writer and commentator, reflects on

Australia's win in the second Test, as the Lord's jinx continues

There used to be a nightclub in Scarborough called The Two Bs which festival cricketers would frequent after their fish-and-chip supper. Perhaps MCC should sketch one into their new ground development plans under the same name in honour of AR Border and IT Botham after their efforts in the Lord's Test. It would be easy to run out of superlatives in describing their enormous contribution to this second superb Test ...

Border is a great batsman. Players who average over 50 usually are. In both innings at Lord's he stood out as a towering pillar of strength to the Australian cause. His quickness of eye and sureness of shot make him a daunting proposition for any bowler. Seamer or spinner are murdered if their length strays a matter of inches. He and his management team have certainly got this touring side all working together, which is never easy. AB might not thank me for it but this new 'father figure' image suits him. I don't mind eating my words about legspinners being a luxury in Test cricket. It was a delight to see Bob Holland make such a vital contribution to his side's victory. Rarely can a genuine wristspinner have had such good control. McDermott continues to blossom, highlighting even more England's bare fast-bowling cupboard.

But out of that cupboard sprang Botham. He hates the 'third seamer' tag and on Saturday afternoon threw it off for a few Tests to come. Excuse me eulogising about my old mate, but I do believe he is the greatest advertisement this game has ever had. Now he's given me another 'former' prefix – England's leading wicket-taker. All I can say is it was a pleasure doing business with him. He was Guy the Gorilla in those days; now he's Beefy, and didn't he look like a taunted bull as he charged the Aussie matadors and gored them to ▷

1985

1st Test June 13-18, Head **†Aus 331** (AMJ Hilditch 119) and **324** (WB Phillips 91; JE Emburey 5-82, IT Botham 4-107); **Eng 533** (RT Robinson 175, Botham 60; CJ McDermott 4 134) and **123-5. Eng won by 5 wkts.**

2nd Test June 27-July 2, Lord's **Eng 290** (DI Gower 86; McDermott 6-70) and **261** (Botham 85; RG Holland 5-68); **†Aus 425** (AR Border 196; Botham 5-109) and **127-6** (Border 41*). **Aus won by 4 wkts.**

3rd Test July 11-16, Trent Bridge **Eng 456** (Gower 166; GF Lawson 5 103) and **196-2** (Robinson 77*); **Aus 539** (GM Wood 172, GM Ritchie 146). **Match drawn.**

4th Test, Aug 1-6, Old Trafford **Aus 257** (DC Boon 61; Botham 4-79) and **340-5** (Border 146*; Emburey 4-99); **†Eng 482-9 dec** (MW Gatting 160; McDermott 8-141). **Match drawn.**

5th Test Aug 15-20, Edg **Aus 335** (RM Ellison 6-77) and **142** (Phillips 59; Ellison 4-27); **†Eng 595-5 dec** (Gower 215, Robinson 148, Gatting 100*). **Eng won by inns and 118 runs.**

6th Test Aug 29-Sep 2, The Oval **†Eng 464** (GA Gooch 196, Gower 157); **Aus 241** (Ritchie 64*) and **129** (Border 58; Ellison 5-46). **Eng won by inns and 94 runs.**

the quick? There was also a bit of rump, rib and sirloin about his knock on Monday, though this was refined cuisine after the hamburger heaves of Headingley.

Wisden Cricket Monthly, August 1985

England spinner Phil Edmonds rounds up the next Tests in *The Cricketer*

The main feature of the following three Tests at Trent Bridge, Old Trafford and Edgbaston was the slow, low nature of the wickets. The seeming inevitability of the English batsmen plundering any number of runs quickly against a blunted Australian attack became more and more debilitating for the whole Australian team. In all three Tests the Australians found themselves under pressure fighting to save each match. Had the wickets at Trent Bridge and Old Trafford had a degree more pace and bounce England would have won crushing victories. As it was Wood and Ritchie at Trent Bridge and Border at Old Trafford ensured the Australian survival through dogged and determined batting, Border and Ritchie, in particular, never being frightened to attack.

By the fifth Test at Edgbaston their tactical appreciation was in total disarray. Having succumbed to some magnificent swing bowling by Richard Ellison for a mediocre 335, the Australians now allowed England to race to an unbelievable 595 off

134 overs, putting themselves under immense pressure. Robinson, Gatting and particularly Gower were all brilliant for England and only the incomparable Botham would phlegmatically crash his very first ball back over the bowler's head for six, particularly when that bowler is McDermott. Batting a second time to save the match, Australia succumbed to a combination of

66 Australia's tactical appreciation was in total disarray 99

Botham's devilment (he really is blessed when it comes to taking wickets), Ellison's swing and seam and a degree of bad luck in Wayne Phillips' demise courtesy of Allan Lamb's boot. *The Cricketer*, November 1985

This Edgbaston game turns the series. Australia are heading for safety when a decision goes England's way. Frith writes

The bruise on Allan Lamb's instep lasted no more than two days, thanks to persistent applications of ice-packs. But if England were to go on to regain the Ashes, that bruise would rank with a few others which glow and throb still in cricket's long history. He got it while taking evasive action. One of a covey of close fieldsmen as England tried to prise out the last five Australians on a

shortened final day, he jumped and turned away from Wayne Phillips' square slash off Edmonds, and the ball popped up off his boot for Lamb's neighbour, David Gower, to hold what umpire Constant deemed a fair catch. Umpire Shepherd, from the bowler's end, had consulted because his own view was obscured. Television offers no clear proof and the Australian captain was visibly upset at the end that England's final surge to victory was inspired by such a controversial incident. *Wisden Cricket Monthly*, October 1985

The final Test, with the Ashes still live, is one-way traffic. Bob Willis writes

Thursday's slaughter in the sun sealed Australia's fate. Gower and Gooch were simply magnificent. Methodically Gooch took the attack apart, while Gower rode his deserved good luck with salvoes of blistering boundaries. The seamers to a man were treated with total disdain. I have rarely seen better batting in partnership. They even put the Gower-Robinson effort at Edgbaston in the shade.

The Australian reply never had any real purpose. Caught between attempting quick runs and playing themselves in, in very different conditions, they achieved neither. The happy hookers were at it again. When will they ever learn? Border was not in the mood to give in easily but the rest looked as though they were ready for the Qantas flight. So in many departments it is back to the drawing-board for the tourists ...

In the ruins of their tour stand firm two pillars: a slightly scarred McDermott and an erect, unscathed Border. David Gower will long remember the aftermath at The Oval and the old wheel of fortune; nadir and zenith at the same venue inside 12 months.

Wisden Cricket Monthly, October 1985

David Gower shares his euphoria

This has been a season to enjoy and savour, in spite of the traumas of the first month and a half. The turnaround on a personal level could not have been more emphatic – for someone who, by all accounts, had lost the manufacturer's instructions that came with the bat and yet finished with a best-ever tally for a home Ashes series. 🅰

Wisden Cricket Monthly, October 1985

Golden summer: Gower holds up a replica Urn after England's win – Border grits his teeth

The Grand Slam

The England side was ridiculed and written off before the first Test following feeble warm-up games. But they held the Ashes and there was an optimism, which flourished when real battle recommenced. **Christopher Martin-Jenkins** previews

England have chosen an experienced team for a tough tour. Whether it will be successful will depend very much on the ability of the captain, Mike Gatting, to get the best out of the men chosen and there is no avoiding the importance of Ian Botham's ability to get down to the job as the pivot of the side. Neither he nor any of the team must give the news-hounds any scent at all. *The Cricketer, October 1986*

England spinner Phil Edmonds writes for *The Cricketer*

A quietly confident tour party leaves for Australia determined to do well – and why shouldn't we? Most of the players have been before and enjoyed themselves. Sun, sea and steaks and the common culture make it a most appealing tour for the majority of players. The restriction on players' wives touring (in the name of team spirit) makes it even more appealing for others ...

There seemed to be a good deal more depression among journalists than there was in the England team as we prepared for the first Test. Positive thinking was, we felt, the key to success ... Micky Stewart made a memorable statement about the new ball. In Australia, he said, you have to treat the new ball in the field like a bride – touch the bride as little as possible until she has become a little more familiar. *The Cricketer, November and December 1986*

Australian writer Alan Shiell keeps a diary on the fluctuating hopes of Border and his crew in *Wisden Cricket Monthly*

November 12 In Australia the television advertisements for the "Clashes for the Ashes" are in full swing, and the marketing hype suggests it might be tough but, really, England are doomed. Queensland seem to put the issue beyond doubt when they dispose of Mike Gatting's

team by five wickets. Over in Perth, England have the worst of a drawn match with Graeme Wood's Western Australia. The quote-backs from Fleet Street are predictably damning. One of them will be immortalised: "There are only three things wrong with England – they can't bat, they can't bowl and they can't field." That's it fellas, give 'em heaps! ... Gatting and Border chat to the media in Brisbane. Gatting reads out his team and, to the surprise of no one, that the Test matches are what count and, yes, he is confident his boys can do the job. Border, trying not to sound too confident, warns that this is not a bad England side after all, and this is a Test match after all. So it's not going to be easy. Oh yeah!
November 19 England win the first Test by seven wickets. Nearly 16 million Australians (well, a lot of them, anyway) see their team's loss as a national disgrace. Gatting, smiling, says I told you so, and Border, fuming, and with a captaincy record of three wins from 22 Tests, says it was only the press who wrote England off. Border snarls his way through a lecture to the written media after having refused to attend Channel 9's official presentation of trophies by big Tony Greig. He has been in this mood since early in the match when, after ordering England to bat, he sees his inexperienced bowlers fail to deliver the goods and has to admire privately the thunderous way his old mate 'Both' belts them all over the Gabba for another never-to-be-forgotten century that deservedly wins him the man-of-the-match award and plants England on course to retain the Ashes. Australian cricket is in mourning and its grief is sustained by fears that Border has had a gutful again and will quit the captaincy. He doesn't, much to everyone's relief. *Wisden Cricket Monthly, January 1987*

Can't catch, can't bowl: Gladstone Small has Steve Waugh caught behind at Sydney

England's all-conquering southern winter kicked off in Brisbane in the first Test with a familiar name leading the charge. Matthew Engel writes

The first Test of the 1986-87 Ashes series contained a fluctuation of fortune, in its way, as huge as anything that happened in the famous 1981 series. Not in the game itself, you understand; that took off in England's direction on day one and stayed there right through. But a Test match can never be seen in isolation. Before the game began, England were widely seen as inept, out of form, unhappy, wrongly-chosen, tired and divided; Australia were regarded as young, fit, spirited, well-led, improving and together. Almost before the first day was out, these impressions started to alter; by the end it was as though a 10-ton weight had been slipped on to one side of the scales.

People now began to see the defects of Border's leadership, the failings of his inexperienced attack and the special weaknesses of modern Australian cricketers when faced with high-class spin or anything to do with Ian Botham. England suddenly seemed a different set of animals. Of course, a team containing Botham, Gower, Gatting, etc, etc could not be beaten. It was 1985 all over again. Why did so few people see it?

The realisation that the Australians had still not emerged from the years of strife was the hardest thing for the country's cricket-followers and for Allan Border to take. The tour of India – a tie and two draws – had given them hope. That evaporated in Brisbane. In the very room where Kim Hughes tearfully resigned the captaincy, Border, after spending two years winning a reputation for candour and courtesy in his public dealings, gave his most graceless performance since he inherited the job.

Wisden Cricket Monthly, January 1987

So to Perth where Christopher Martin-Jenkins watches a powerful batting display by the tourists, even if they cannot force the win

The combination of a superb pitch for batting and some wayward Australian bowling, especially but not exclusively in the crucial early stages, enabled Chris Broad and Bill Athey to put on 223 for the first

wicket, the fourth largest opening stand by England against Australia. From this cast-iron base, due especially to Broad's commanding innings, England were able to declare just short of 600, 40 minutes from the end of the second day. But David Gower, pulling, cutting and cover-driving his way back to mental happiness – and to his sixth Test hundred against Australia – found an unexpectedly confident ally in Jack Richards who, in only his second Test innings for his country, rubbed stinging salt into Australian wounds with an innings of belligerence, bottle and brilliance.

The Cricketer, January 1987

After England dominated the first two Tests, a docile Adelaide wicket produces a docile draw with Border cashing in. Christopher Martin-Jenkins again

England went into the crucial Melbourne Test after Christmas still clinging resolutely to their 1-0 lead in the series after another very predictable draw at Adelaide. On a pitch even closer to perfection than the one at the Waca, neither side possessed the depth or quality of bowling to get the other one out twice and even the West Indians might have struggled to do so. There were four individual hundreds of which Broad's was the most important for his side, Boon's the most significant for his own career, Border's the most predictable and Gatting's by some way the most brilliant. He savaged Matthews and, to a lesser extent, Sleep in a three-hour innings of almost disdainful confidence.

The Cricketer, February 1987

John Woodcock begins to worry for the state of Test cricket in Australia – and the state of Botham

With one-day cricket being hyped up in the way it is, and there is a regular glut of it to come on this tour, there is an instability within and around the traditional game in Australia that is not evident in England. I hope I can say without seeming to be patronising that it is becoming desperately important for the good of the game in general, not only in Australia, that the Australian team should find the winning habit again ... I suppose there was never a more popular English

Dream tour: England celebrate winning the Ashes at Melbourne main; Peter Taylor surprises at Sydney as Australia have a consolation win above left; Elton John sprays Mike Gatting below; new man Phil DeFreitas claims an Australian wicket in the second Test at Perth above right

1986-87

1st Test November 14-19, Brisbane Eng **456** (IT Botham 138)
and *17-3*; †Aus **248** (GR Marsh 56, GRJ Matthews 56*; GR Dilley
5-68) and **282** (Marsh 110; JE Emburey 5-80). **Eng won by 7 wkts.**

2nd Test November 28-December 3, Perth †Eng **592-8 dec**
(BC Broad 162, DI Gower 136, CJ Richards 133; BA Reid 4-115) and
199-8 dec (MW Gatting 70; SR Waugh 5-69); **Aus 401** (AR Border
125; Dilley 4-79) and **197-4** (DM Jones 69). **Match drawn.**

3rd Test December 12-16, Adelaide †Aus **514-5 dec**
(DC Boon 103) and **201-3 dec** (Border 100*); **Eng 455** (Broad 116,
Gatting 100; Reid 4-64) and **39-2. Match drawn.**

4th Test December 26-28, Melbourne Aus **141** (Jones 59;
Botham 5-41, GC Small 5-48) and **194** (Marsh 60); †Eng **349**
(Broad 112; Reid 4-78, CJ McDermott 4-83). **Eng won by an
inns and 14 runs.**

5th Test January 10-15, Sydney †Aus **343** (Jones 184*; Small
5-75) and **251** (Emburey 7-78); **Eng 275** (Gower 72; PL Taylor 6-78)
and **264** (Gatting 96; PR Sleep 5-72). **Aus won by 55 runs.**

cricketer with the Australian public than Ian Botham. I know they loved Hendren and Compton and lots of others; but Botham they cheer like one of their own when he walks out to bat, many having come specifically to see him ... They talk of his becoming a dollar millionaire [through sponsorship] and there are times when he already behaves like one. When Broad got back to his hotel in Perth, after making his splendid century, he found a bottle of champagne in his room, a gift from Botham. *The Cricketer, January 1987*

Then in a memorable match at Melbourne in the fourth Test, England win the series and the Ashes. Scyld Berry writes

The Ashes were retained by England at 4-40 on a cool, sunny afternoon in Melbourne when Gladstone Small, the player of the match, caught Australia's last man on the square-leg boundary. It was the first time since 1901-02 that England had won a Test in Australia in only three days. It is only an interpretation but conceivably the potency of the Ashes legend assisted England. Desperate to win them back at any cost, the Australians – starting with the selectors – laid back their inexperienced ears and went all out for victory. It would have been less macho, but more politic, to have aimed simply at squaring the series by drawing at Melbourne, and gambling on winning the toss and the game on a Sydney turner ...

Gatting commented afterwards: "You won't see anyone getting five wickets in a Test in the way Both did." He ambled in at D'Oliveira pace because of his intercostal twinge. His art was to let the batsmen impale themselves.

At the other end, from lunch until the innings expired, Small did an imitation of Hadlee – the short run, the delivery from close to the stumps, the outswinger that made bats twitch involuntarily and the odd one cutting back.

Broad again, for the third Test running, was England's major contributor with another century. His technique against fast bowling – both feet outside the crease, the back foot going back, then the weight transferred to the front – enables him to play forward without having to move his front foot at all. He played within his limitations,

neither hooking, pulling nor sweeping, and only square-cutting if the legspinner Sleep dropped invitingly short.
Wisden Cricket Monthly, February 1987

Australia win the last Test, suggesting a brighter Australian future. By David Frith

Another fairy-tale chapter was tacked on to cricket's history when the Australian Test selectors called up a player almost unknown to the nation at large and then eased themselves comfortably into their chairs with broad grins as their discovery did enough to earn the man-of-the-match award. Peter Taylor's meteoric success was coupled with a drought-breaking Test victory for Australia. And not a moment too soon, because Aussies were starting to turn against the Test cricket that had been so unkind to them for so long, favouring the one-day glitz where the occasional success seems guaranteed ... Certain newspapers seemed to believe that Peter Taylor's selection for the last Test was a case of mistaken identity and one TV station actually sent a crew out to see Mark Taylor, the NSW batsman. *Wisden Cricket Monthly, March 1987*

Christopher Martin-Jenkins offers his verdict of the tour in his editorial

Australian cricket is in pain. The same anxious questions about its health and the chances of a cure are being asked by well-wishers as were being asked of England only a few months ago. In Australia's case, like a sufferer from heart trouble, the only hope of a long life is to start cutting the excesses now. There is too much cholesterol. In other words, too much cricket.

Without wishing to sound smug, one has been saying and writing this for years, and this time one can only pray that the greedy controllers of Australian cricket will accept the truth and have the courage to admit that they have been wrong. Since that uneasy compromise between the Australian Cricket Board and World Series Cricket in 1979 there has been too much butter and cream every year: the flesh gets podgier and grosser with every series of hyped-up limited-over matches and with every rich mouthful, the vital organs, the heart and soul, are becoming rotten. ◪ *The Cricketer, February 1987*

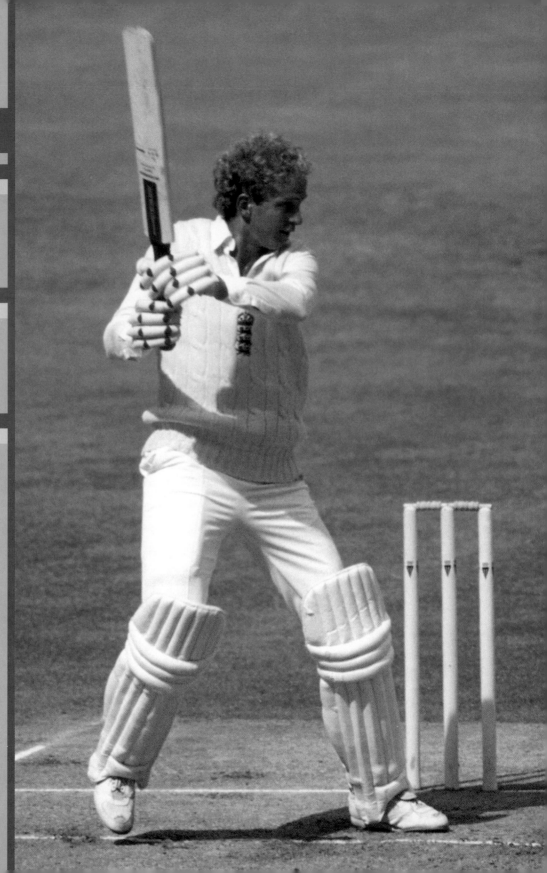

HERO No.8

David Gower

Tests
Batting

Matches	117
Runs	8231
Highest score	215
Average	44.25
Hundreds	18
Fifties	39

First-class career
Batting

Matches	448
Runs	26339
Highest score	228
Average	40.08
Hundreds	53
Fifties	136

v Australia
Batting

Matches	42
Runs	3269
Highest score	215
Average	44.78
Hundreds	9
Fifties	12

Whimsical and wonderful

David Gower scored more runs for England than anyone before him – over 3,000 of those against Australia and always with an unmatched elegance. In his introduction to *TWC*'s *Heroes of Cricket* supplement celebrating Gower, **Paul Coupar** writes

D avid Gower – Tiger Moth co-pilot, Bollinger-lover, heavenly timer of a cricket ball and, as detractors often forget, scorer of more Test runs than any Englishman when he was shoved out in 1992, after 117 brilliantly frustrating Test matches.

Others of the same vintage in some respects achieved more. Gooch eventually scored more Test runs, Brearley (1981) and Gatting (1986-87) won Ashes series in tougher circumstances, and the Botham-show provided the sports story of the decade. However none, I think, was as well-loved as Gower. Many were mucked around by whimsical selectors; only Gower inspired an MCC revolt against them, when he was dumped by the Roundhead Gooch regime in 1992, a decision that was either ruthlessly pragmatic or disastrously blind to genius, according to taste ...

Matthew Engel illuminated another part of Gower's mystique when he wrote: "Other batsmen go in and out of form: Gower always seemed to play the same – beautifully, until the moment he made a mistake. Sometimes, the mistake was put off long enough for him to play an innings of unforgettable brilliance." Gower encapsulated two traits very dear to the English, effortless brilliance and human vulnerability, *Brideshead Revisited* and Del Trotter.

Sometimes Gower the *bon viveur* has distracted from the excellence of Gower the cricketer. No one scores more Test runs than Geoffrey Boycott without determination. Only four other Englishmen have Test averages that never dipped below 40. But perhaps the ultimate endorsement comes from the Caribbean, that archipelago of woe for England in the 1980s. David Gower, said the West Indian captain Clive Lloyd, would be an automatic pick in our side. That will do for me.
The Wisden Cricketer, December 2008

Here are some reactions to Gower's retirement
"Gower has paid the price for one of the great fallacies of sport. This is the belief that a genius could be even better if he put his mind to it." **Simon Barnes in** *The Times*

"At its best, as he drove through the covers, his batting became artistic in that it was sculpture made flesh and animate. If Michelangelo's David had taken to cricket, he might have batted like Gower." **Scyld Berry in the** *Sunday Telegraph*

"He was a key destructive player ... a very tough competitor and bloody difficult to get out." **Sir Richard Hadlee**
Wisden Cricket Monthly, January 1994

One-time team-mate and captain Bob Willis writes
It is a shame, when talking about the retirement of one of the finest batsmen to have graced the cricket grounds of the world, that the emotion closest to the surface is that of anger. The treatment of David Gower by the Dexter-Stewart-Gooch regime was nothing short of scandalous. How did a batsman averaging nearly 45 runs per Test innings ever get left out of the side? ...

From the very beginning it was obvious this was a special talent and he was soon taking Australia by storm. David always had a soft spot for Oz, and their discerning cricket public quickly felt the same. Great players and captains like Allan Border and Ian Chappell remain mystified by Gower's treatment by the England selectors ...

One great innings sticks in the memory, the 1979-80 Sydney Test on a damp, unfit surface. The ball did everything it could off the seam, rattling into batting gloves in front of teeth. Gower's fleetness of foot and quickness of eye combined in innovative strokeplay to get him so close to a remarkable century [he made 98*].

As captain he had a difficult start with the 1984 series against West Indies. The team's fortunes yo-yoed between the heights of 1985 at home to the depths of 1986 in the Caribbean. I remember, in Antigua after West Indies had completed their 5-0 demolition job, David remaining outwardly cool and cheerful when he was burning inside with disappointment. *Wisden Cricket Monthly, January 1994*

England's then rugby union captain Will Carling writes about his favourite cricketer
The name of David Gower evokes a definite image in my mind, one of graceful ability, natural talent and, not to put too fine a point on it, extreme pleasure. David has an ability you would go a long way to watch. It is rather like watching Maradona in the 1986 World Cup, or Seve Ballesteros at his prime. I put him into the same bracket as going to see a fine piece of art, listening to a great piece of music or sampling some magnificent food.

Unfortunately, it would seem that you cannot have this kind of talent, this ability, without also evoking tremendous bitterness and jealousy from other quarters in life. From the moment he hit his first ball in Test cricket for four, David has either been lauded or crucified for the way he plays his cricket.

I admit to many times when I have turned round to punch a cushion when David has been caught, flashing his bat outside off stump. Those moments of exquisite pain and frustration still live with me. The most important thing is to remember the pleasure derived: the graceful cover drives, the neat flick off the leg, the sheer elegance of the man. Five minutes of David, to my mind, is worth an hour or two of many other batsmen. *The Cricketer, December 1993*

THE AUSSIE ERA

1989-2003

England played Australia in a one-off bicentennial match at Sydney – to celebrate 200 years since Australia's settlement – and the home side hung on for a draw after following on. Chris Broad scored his fourth hundred in five Tests down under, then smashed his stumps as he left the pitch. And that was as good as it got for England for the best part of the next 10 years. Border had finally moulded the side he dreamed of, a couple of star performers were breaking through. Australia were becoming the best team in the world and no Englishmen had really noticed

Job done: Allan Border can finally smile at The Oval at the end of the series with the Ashes safe

No more Mr Nice Guy

Allan Border had had enough – he had struggled through the 1980s watching England's glamour boys swagger away with the Ashes. Now he meant business. Despite winning the World Cup and a Test against the unbeatable West Indies, Australia still turned up as underdogs. **Henry Blofeld** writes about that Australia-West Indies series

The Chairman of the Australian Cricket Board, Malcolm Gray, has had his say too, complaining at the over-use of bouncers although, tactfully, he blames both sides, saying that this form of attack has been responsible for killing interest in Test cricket in Australia. I am not certain that it was wise for him as a non-cricketer to become involved in this particular argument. What I am certain of is that there is nothing wrong with the Australian public's view of Test cricket that victory over England in this summer's Ashes series will not put right. In the meantime the Australian authorities need to try to ensure that the West Indian fast bowlers are not given pitches they would normally dream about.

The Cricketer, February 1989

John Woodcock was also concerned about a malaise in Test cricket down under – and he points the finger firmly at one man

So cast your minds back to the middle 1970s. Although the best players were still being underpaid, their lot was slowly improving. The international game was in the pink of health. Test matches across the world were drawing large crowds. When England played in India it was barely possible, for love or money, to raise a ticket. The Centenary Test at Melbourne in 1977 was a great joy. One-day matches had been discreetly and beneficially

introduced as part of a touring team's itinerary. Another World Cup was due in 1979, and keenly awaited. Then came Packer and his fast-sell, and now, barely 10 years on, the game in Australia is fighting for its identity, while Test cricket, there and elsewhere, battles for its life.

The Cricketer, March 1989

Henry Blofeld writes about the touring party – highlighting its limitations – and as good as predicts a convincing England win

The Australian selectors did not have too many alternatives when they came to choose their 17 players for England and the result of the deliberations was predictable enough, give or take 25-year-old Greg Campbell, a fast medium seam bowler from Tasmania who moves the ball away from the right-hander. It is the bowling which will have given them their greatest worry and where they found themselves shortest in options.

Trevor Hohns is accurate and even mild wristspin is these days a language which very few contemporary batsmen understand. For all that, he is not a bowler who should go through a batting line-up as experienced as England's. Offspinner **Tim May** is also not a bowler to give English batsmen sleepless nights and Border's hatful of wickets in the recent Sydney Test will surely never happen again.

A great deal will depend on the

accuracy of **Alderman** as he moves the ball away to the slips, and on the touch of devil within **Geoff Lawson**. But Alderman is 33 and is well known in England while Lawson (31) is no longer the bowler he was. It may be that **Carl Rackemann** who is 29, very keen and as strong as an ox, will be the surprise package among the fast bowlers. The sum total of all this is unlikely to be enough to bowl out England twice which Australia must do on at least one occasion if they are to regain the Ashes. They badly miss one genuine fast bowler.

While the bowling does not look strong enough for the job in hand, the batting is solid and will make the England bowlers work hard. Obviously much depends on Allan Border but **David Boon** and **Geoff Marsh** are very experienced, although I expect **Mark Taylor** to open with Marsh which will allow Boon to go in third. *The Cricketer*, May 1989

Trevor Grant is equally pessimistic about Australia's chances

Only three players – Border, Lawson and Boon – have survived from the last England tour four years ago. Those who recall how easily Australia capitulated in the final two Tests of that series to forfeit the Ashes believe that is no bad thing. But the 1989 Australians, for all their enthusiasm, are only marginally better equipped and will face a huge task to reclaim the Urn this summer. ▷

1987-88
Bicentennial Test
January 29-February 2, Sydney †**Eng 425** (BC Broad 139; PL Taylor 4-84); **Aus 214** (DM Jones 56) and **320-2** (DC Boon 184*). **Match drawn.**

1989
1st Test June 8-13, Head **Aus 601-7 dec** (SR Waugh 177*, MA Taylor 136) and **230-3 dec** (Taylor 60, AR Border 60*); †**Eng 430** (AJ Lamb 125; TM Alderman 5-107) and **191** (GA Gooch 68; Alderman 5-44). **Aus won by 210 runs.**

2nd Test June 22-27, Lord's †**Eng 286** (RC Russell 64*; MG Hughes 4-71) and **359** (DI Gower 106, RA Smith 96; Alderman 6-128); **Aus 528** (Waugh 152*, Boon 94) and **119-4** (Boon 58*). **Aus won by 6 wkts.**

3rd Test July 6-11, Edg †**Aus 424** (IJM Jones 157; ARC Fraser 4-63) and **158-2** (Taylor 51); **Eng 242** (IT Botham 46). **Match drawn.**

4th Test July 27-August 1, Old Trafford †**Eng 260** (Smith 143; GF Lawson 6 72) and **264** (Russell 128*; Alderman 5-66); **Aus 447** (Waugh 92) and **81-1. Aus won by 9 wkts.**

5th Test August 10-14, Trent Bridge †**Aus 602-6 dec** (Taylor 219, GR Marsh 138), **Eng 255** (Smith 101, Alderman 5-69) and **167** (MA Atherton 47). **Aus won by an inns and 180 runs.**

6th Test August 24-29, The Oval †**Aus 468** (Jones 122) and **219-4 dec** (Border 51*); **Eng 285** (Gower 79; Alderman 5-66) and **143-5** (Smith 77*). **Match drawn.**

Aggression: Hughes   Perfection: Steve Waugh at Headingley   Dejection: Gatting falls lbw to Alderman in the second Test at Lord's

And how they got it wrong. David Gower, England's new captain (again) wins the toss at Headingley and that is the last thing to go right for England. All summer. Christopher Martin-Jenkins reports

The first Test was, in cricketing terms, a triumph for the Australian team, a disaster for England. What made it so galling for the home team was not just their inept cricket but also that their captain, David Gower, had given Australia the first use of a benign pitch. Unpalatable though the result may have been for England, it was a rousing start to the series ...

Lamb and Barnett replied in kind for a while, pointing England towards the draw they ought to have achieved with comfort, but in one of those abject batting performances in which England have specialised during six defeats in seven years at Headingley, Alderman, Merv Hughes and Lawson probed and harried to devastating effect as England lost their last seven wickets for 57 ... Only in wicketkeeping were England superior, Russell becoming the first man to keep through a Test innings of 600 in England without letting a bye. This was small consolation indeed to an outplayed team. Had Dilley, Gatting and Botham been fit, it might not have happened, but they were not and, once again, England's lack of quality and technique was exposed ...

Steve Waugh was in such form that singles were hardly necessary to him. Every now and again he played and missed outside the off stump, usually to Foster, but he hit the ball with such classical ease square of the wicket on either side that one felt, long before he got there, that this would be the day that he would finally break the barrier of a Test hundred. At the age of 24 he had already played in 27 Tests, not to mention more than 70 one-day internationals. This,

and that he has generally batted at No.6, helps to explain why such a gifted player has waited so long for a century, but it was a glorious innings when it came.

Waugh batted throughout in a cap. He hit 24 fours. He was quick to judge the length of every ball, going right forward or right back and the impression left in the mind was of a series of clinical square cuts interspersed with firm punches off the toes or impeccable forward defensive strokes ...

Australia, as so often happens to a team on the crest of a wave, held all their catches barring one very sharp one. Their cricket throughout the match had been more positive, thoughtful and efficient. *The Cricketer, August 1989*

The second Test at Lord's is the same story – brilliant Australia, immovable Waugh, England woeful and weeping. Christopher Martin-Jenkins writes

Everything went catastrophically wrong for England on the Saturday. On a golden morning Waugh, 35 not out overnight, carried on in the vein which had seen him twice crashing off stump half volleys to the extra-cover boundary in the last three overs of the previous evening.

Waugh, eschewing the use of a helmet and coolly expressionless, was rather expected to do what he did. If he was beaten, as sometimes he was, notably by the luckless Jarvis, he either missed the ball completely or sent it off the inside edge to the fine-leg boundary. Runs came at the alarming rate of four an over. Waugh's strokes were beautifully clean and crisp, inspired by the occasion, buoyed up by the determination of the entire Australian team, and quite unawed by an England attack still inclined to offer a bad ball an over and, on this disastrous day, devoid of luck.

England ended the day 184 behind with Gower and Gatting, captain and vice-captain, struggling grimly for survival ... Soon afterwards Gower, with a taxi waiting to take him to the theatre, let himself down uncharacteristically by reacting to the hostile array of cameras, microphones and journalists awaiting him in the marquee in the Lord Harris Gardens, by making a few flippant replies and then beating a testy retreat. *The Cricketer, August 1989*

It couldn't get any worse – until it did. Jack Bannister offers his expert view on the third Test at Edgbaston – saved only by the weather

The England outlook is becoming gloomier with every Test. As soon as one department improves another deteriorates under the pressure of the screw Allan Border turns ever tighter as the series unfolds. Headingley seemed a bad dream – before Lord's that is. Get the bowling right and the rest will fall into place: that was the popular theory before the Edgbaston Test. But what now? ... How could England get into trouble after nearly 10 hours of the match were taken out by the weather? Technique and pride were at stake, but it seems nowadays that if West Indies don't get you, the Aussies will. The English game has been all but denuded of the batting arts. *Wisden Cricket Monthly, August 1989*

What had become inevitable happened at Old Trafford. Australia reclaim the Ashes despite an English backbone emerging – but to top this horrendous summer, an old issue reappears. David Frith reports

Beyond the confines of Australia's jubilant Old Trafford dressing room England was in mourning twice over. Not only had the Ashes been lost but 16 of her cricketers, nine of

Precipitation: outside Edgbaston

Celebration: Taylor and Marsh after the Trent Bridge Test

Conclusion: Jones (122) at The Oval

whom had played in this series, had signed to go to South Africa, barring themselves from Test cricket for years to come ...

That England's fading grip on the Ashes lasted into the month of August was mainly Jack Russell's fault. The little Gloucester man, in for his supreme wicketkeeping skills, showed those above him in the batting order what concentration, judgement and courage were all about as he went to his maiden first class century, hauling England away from the second-innings degradation of 59 for 6 on the Monday. Thank God, said the Lion, that the South African Cricket Union got neither Russell nor that other batting saviour Robin Smith ...

Allan Border, for his part, found it hard to express his pride and pleasure adequately, and his small, grey eyes sharpened as he responded to a questioner that, yes, he was glad to make a few critics (Tony Greig among them) who had branded his side the worst ever to leave Australia eat their words.

Wisden Cricket Monthly, September 1989

Christopher Martin-Jenkins on a seminal moment in Ashes history

So much for the "well contested series between two teams of more or less equal strength" that we all predicted. Australia won the Ashes, when they finally confirmed their superiority over England with nine of the last 20 overs of the Old Trafford match to go. It is odd but true that, despite being in complete command each time, Australia won only in the final hour at Headingley, Lord's and Old Trafford. Each time one felt that a little more resolution from all rather than some of the England players might have saved the day; each time, however, one also felt that they would not have deserved to do so. *The Cricketer, September 1989*

The Aussies were in no mood to ease and bask in their Ashes glory. At Trent Bridge the 'surprise of the series' Mark Taylor bats through the whole first day with Geoff Marsh. By Christopher Martin-Jenkins

Alderman, Lawson, Hughes and Hohns each deserved high praise for doing his job to the very best of his ability, but their task was made easier by the exemplary performance of the batsmen and in particular of the openers, Taylor and Marsh, who, by putting on 329 for the first wicket, left behind all previous opening stands in an Ashes Test match. It took England just over seven hours to part them and, although they inevitably needed some luck to bat together for so long, this was nevertheless a superb exhibition of controlled batting, perfectly attuned to the tempo of a five-day Test.

The openers were never negative; certainly not Taylor, who, no doubt to his surprise as well as his immense delight, has taken to Test cricket like a dog to meat. His technique is straight from the text book, head always over the line, footwork positive and precise and his judgement of the ball to hit seems to be impeccable. His 219 was his first double hundred in any class of cricket and I dare say part of him was mildly disappointed that England's batsmen could not manage to force him to have a second innings. *The Cricketer, October 1989*

England draw the final Test but Border declares late – and still fancies his chances. WCM reports the post-series press conferences

Allan Border
It's the highlight of my career. No question of it. I didn't want to give England any hope whatsoever and I thought that we could bowl England out in 67 overs. I didn't think there was any need to declare before lunch. It's happened a couple of times in the series where we've bowled England out in under 60 overs. I didn't want to give them any outside chance whatsoever. I was far more aggressive, positive about my own captaincy and the side responded to that very, very well.

When we get back to Australia, that's when we'll start to realise what we've achieved. I think the first day at Headingley was "crunch day". We were apprehensive about going into a Test series. The wicket at Headingley hadn't been traditionally a very good ground for us. And to play the way we did on that first day gave everyone a huge boost of confidence, and I think we went from strength to strength as a result of that day. I don't know whether the English players were over-confident. I think the media were.

Ted Dexter (chairman of selectors)
My feelings are entirely forward-looking. There's nothing to be gained by looking back. We're looking forward to happier days. I'm not aware of any errors that I have made.

Bob Willis writes in the same issue

The final act was a mirror image of so much that had gone before: willing bowlers toiling honestly but ineffectively for England through the long hot afternoons while their counterparts, with little more natural talent, tore through a succession of inept tentative strokes fathered by that uncaring parent one-day cricket ... Border's late declaration at The Oval was the last humiliation England had to suffer. On the best cricket pitch in the world, Australia were confident of bowling out England in four hours. ⊞ *Wisden Cricket Monthly, October 1989*

Bashed and bruised

Graham Gooch led an ill-fated trip to Australia in 1990-91 and despite some encouraging moments, England were still lagging, even if there were some familiar Australian squabbles, writes **Trevor Grant**

Bobby Simpson, the man who has given worldwide credibility to the relatively new idea of having well-paid coaches travelling every step of the way with Test teams, no doubt spluttered into his muesli the other morning when he picked up his copy of the Melbourne *Age* and read Ian Chappell's declaration that the most appropriate use for a coach in senior cricket was to transport the teams between venues.

Chappell maintains that he objects to all coaches at senior level, not just the Australian Test team supremo. According to Chappellian wisdom, the coach belongs at the lower levels, honing the talents of teenagers so that when they arrive at first-class level they come with a sound technique and a well-balanced

❝ Coaches at Test level are not just useless but harmful❞

mental approach. Perhaps the most stinging part of Chappell's criticism is his assessment that coaches at Test level are not just useless but harmful.

Simpson, who is seen as no less than a saviour of cricket in this country now that we have the Ashes and are already starting to talk about being the best in the world after next year's West Indies tour, has plenty of supporters within his own team to offer as positive evidence of his worth. The public praise and expressions of gratitude for his help from players like Geoff Marsh, Dean Jones and David Boon when they score runs makes excellent reference material. Border is less effusive in his praise. *Wisden Cricket Monthly, December 1990*

Meanwhile Vic Marks warns against too much English optimism

England, having beaten both New Zealand and India this summer, may be on the crest of a wave or at least a substantial ripple, as we contemplate the Ashes series. However, if anyone doubts the magnitude of their task in Australia, ponder this: neither Tom Moody nor Mark Waugh is likely to gain selection for the first Test in Brisbane. Both have decimated county attacks this summer and both would be guaranteed places in any other national side in the world but in Australia they must patiently bide their time. *The Cricketer, November 1990*

The first Test kicks off without the England captain and a now familiar pattern emerges. David Frith writes

There was an unreality in the air. Margaret Thatcher's resignation had been announced overnight and an England team – led unexpectedly by Allan Lamb because of Graham Gooch's awful finger infection – had done little in the tour preliminaries to suggest they would frighten Australia here at the Gabba. And yet the start of any Test series prompts optimistic feelings that the contest will be evenly fought, gripping, enjoyable ... The shadows stretching from England's humiliation in the 1989 series proved to be long. A good first day – a good first Test – would have shoved the shadows firmly back into history. Instead the pattern continued. The Australians, rocked by a first-innings collapse, recovered their poise to take command in the

fourth innings, while England, pathetically short of discipline and critically thin in experience, were made to look impotent before the trio of Australian fast bowlers. *Wisden Cricket Monthly, January 1991*

In Melbourne England show more stomach for the fight until a bean-pole, injury-prone left-arm quick finds rhythm. Christopher Martin-Jenkins reports

Until teatime on the fourth day of a tense, toughly contested and memorable Test match in Melbourne between Christmas and the New Year England were not only playing Australia on level terms but were actually making much of the pace. Then, alas, they threw away their chance – or rather it was, to some extent, seized from them by superb fast bowling by Bruce Reid and, when Geoff Marsh and David Boon followed his second devastating analysis by batting heroically all through what was supposed to be an intensely difficult last day, Australia virtually assured themselves of the Ashes for three more years. *The Cricketer, February 1991*

England at last put up a fight at Sydney with hundreds from Gower and Atherton and five wickets from Phil Tufnell in only his second Test – but only after Australia scored over 500. David Frith writes

No matter how fervently one subscribes to the magical appeal of England-Australia Tests, it is still possible to approach the event with misgivings. Such was the case at Sydney early in January for the third

1990-91

1st Test November 23-25, Brisbane **Eng 194** (DI Gower 61; BA Reid 4-53) and **114** (TM Alderman 6-47); **†Aus 152** and **157-0** (GR Marsh 72*; MA Taylor 67*). **Aus won by 10 wkts.**

2nd Test December 26-30, Melbourne **†Eng 352** (Gower 100; Reid 6-97) and **150** (GA Gooch 58; Reid 7-51); **Aus 306** (AR Border 62; ARC Fraser 6-82) and **197-2** (DC Boon 94*, Marsh 79*). **Aus won by 8 wkts.**

3rd Test January 4-8, Sydney **†Aus 518** (GRJ Matthews 128, Boon 97; DE Malcolm 4-128) and **205** (IA Healy 69; PCR Tufnell 5-61); **Eng 469-8 dec** (Gower 123, MA Atherton 105) and **113-4** (Gooch 54). **Match drawn.**

4th Test January 25-29, Adelaide **†Aus 386** (ME Waugh 138; PAJ DeFreitas 4-56) and **314-6 dec** (Boon 121, Border 83*); **Eng 229** (Gooch 87; CJ McDermott 5-97, Reid 4-53) and **335-5** (Gooch 117). **Match drawn.**

5th Test February 1-3, 5, Perth **†Eng 244** (AJ Lamb 91; McDermott 8-97) and **182** (RA Smith 43; MG Hughes 4-37); **Aus 307** (Boon 64) and **120-1** (Marsh 63*). **Aus won by 9 wkts.**

Moth balls: Gower and Morris prepare

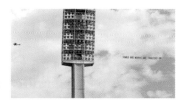
Flying shame: support at Perth

Debut star: Mark Waugh on his way to 138 in the fourth Test at Adelaide – his first

A classic Perth pitch and good quick bowling complete a comfortable win. Christopher Martin-Jenkins writes

Australia's tougher, more resilient, thoughtful and, in the field, aggressive cricket had its reward with a nine-wicket win on a Waca pitch back to its fastest and bounciest. Craig McDermott produced the spectacular figures of 11 for 157 to underline the wisdom of his recall but Mervyn Hughes and Terry Alderman bowled equally well and the absence of Bruce Reid with a sore heel proved to be, remarkably, of no consequence. Australia thus completed a 3-0 win in a series which, despite the ultimate result, was far less one-sided than its predecessor.

The Cricketer, April 1991

The notorious 'Tiger Moth' incident, where David Gower and John Morris hired a plane during a state match and flew over the ground as England batted, highlighted disciplinary issues. An over-reaction from the coach and captain highlighted management issues. Christopher Martin-Jenkins writes

England's last match against a state side had several unfamiliar but desirable aspects, not least the result, and one unusual but undesirable one: what might be called 'The Tiger Moth Affair', starring David Gower and introducing John Morris. This will certainly be a salutary lesson to the whole team that playing professional cricket for England, overseas or at home, is a serious business, demanding unyielding dedication, if consistent success is to be expected. It is a pity the point was not made more forcibly much earlier in the tour after the Lamb-Gower casino visit. Yet one would hate to think that it has become a crime to *enjoy* a cricket tour. *The Cricketer, March 1991*

Test match, the first two having gone heavily Australia's way on the final lap. England seemed a desolate ragbag outfit, dogged by injury, drooping after repeated, crucial failures. And yet the intrinsic talent in the ranks persuaded the pensive that they were worth a final dollar here. A third defeat, though, would leave them as targets for a skyful of vitriolic arrows. This cricket-lover's dread was mercifully unfulfilled. What followed was one of the most enthralling Ashes battles of recent years.
Wisden Cricket Monthly, February 1991

Mark Waugh replaces his brother, makes his debut and makes a hundred – but Adelaide produces another draw. By Martin Blake

Should anyone ever think of running a festival of batsmanship, Adelaide in January would do nicely as the venue. For the sixth year in a row the circus departed the beautiful city of churches with memories of some fine cricket but no result ... Mark Waugh, elevated to the Australian team at 25 after such an extended apprenticeship, smote a debut century so sublime that sages battled to recall a better start to a Test career. David Boon, the pugnacious Tasmanian, bailed the Australians out of strife with 121 in the second innings, but Graham Gooch topped both those players when it came to judgment for the man-of-the-match award. The England captain was inspirational in hitting 87 and 117, yet by the end of the match his side had surrendered the series as well as the Ashes, Australia holding a 2-0 lead with only Perth remaining.
Wisden Cricket Monthly, March 1991

"This ball will live forever"

There was optimism and hope, as always, from the England camp. A young Australian side was coming containing, of all things, a vaunted legspinner called Shane Warne – a breed of bowler long thought extinct. **David Frith** previews

Regular spin is in the hands of the sole South Australian, Tim May, the offspinner who toured in 1989 without playing in a Test, and Shane Warne, the blond legspinner whose lifestyle has got him into most of Australia's colourful women's magazines. Warne, 23, chosen by Australia's cricket writers as Young Cricketer of the Year, already knows what it is like to spin his country to victory (7 for 52 v West Indies, Melbourne), and his big-spinning legbreak, well-concealed googly and nasty 'flipper' may be aimed at spiking England's big guns, Hick and Smith. His target is 20 wickets for the series, and he wants them to come when they are most needed ... A fascinating bunch of players. It is largely up to England's selectors and cricketers whether they go home to a tickertape welcome as in 1989. *Wisden Cricket Monthly, May 1993*

Peter Roebuck anticipates a battle of the ages

It could be dreary, as in 1964 when both teams batted for ever and cricket fell into a deep sleep; it could be epic, as in 1981 when Botham and Willis stunned a poorly led Australian eleven; it could be close as in 1926 when such ancients as Hobbs and Sutcliffe batted for defiant hours upon a gluepot; or it could be easy, as in 1989 when Border's last team trounced their confused and divided hosts. It will be a summer of contrasts. Most of all it will be a struggle between crabbed age and brash youth to see which is the mightier. England will probably rely on its old troopers, some of

them approaching their 40s. Australia's approach will be bold, and they have brought six young cricketers, determined that none of their talents will wither on the vine. *The Cricketer, June 1993*

Mark Taylor starts where he left off in 1989 with a punchy hundred and a bristling opening stand with debutant Michael Slater. But England fight back and are in the game when Shane Warne bowls his first ball in Ashes cricket ... David Frith describes

Gatting, acknowledged as a master of spin bowling, placed his broad self in readiness for Shane Warne's first ball. The ruddy-faced peroxide blond walked four paces, skipped three and flicked the ball apparently too wide to leg to cause havoc. Gatting, shunning the sweep so early in his innings and conscious of the need to avoid being bowled around his chunky legs, played forward in fairly textbook fashion. The buzzing legbreak landed on the fringe of the bowlers' rough and shot 18 inches leftwards to hit the off stump. Unseemly though it was in a slow bowler, Warne clenched his fist and charged down the pitch; whereas Gatting stood dumbfounded, wondering at the bizarre geometry of it all ... Cricket is a game in which much is preserved in folklore while an immense amount of detail is also lost and forgotten, but this ball will live forever, as much for its very nature as its uniqueness. *Wisden Cricket Monthly, July 1993*

> **66** He stood dumbfounded, wondering at the bizarre geometry of it all **99**

Young guns: Graham Thorpe with Nasser Hussain after Thorpe has made his first hundred in his debut Test at Trent Bridge

England lose the Test, Warne takes eight wickets and a psychological hold on the opposition he never loses. Bob Willis moans

Smith cannot play spin, Hick cannot play pace and Stewart averages only 20 when keeping wicket. Gatting's two dismissals were the key to the result of this match. The first turning-point was Warne's first delivery, which left not only the batsman but the whole ground dumbfounded. What a delight it has been to see legspin re-emerge as an art in Test cricket – like a bloom among the stinging-nettles that have been those attacks consisting of four fast bowlers. *Wisden Cricket Monthly, July 1993*

The trouncings continue – this time at the nemesis ground Lord's. David Frith again

Never before had Australia beaten England at Lord's by an innings. Only eight times anywhere in the 276 Anglo-Aus Tests since 1877 had Australia administered a heavier thrashing. And what really hurt the vanquished was that the visitors lost only four wickets in the match and played throughout with 10 men, McDermott having been rushed to hospital on the second evening for emergency surgery on a twisted bowel. *Wisden Cricket Monthly, August 1993*

Panicking selectors continue their scatter-gun tactic but they hit their target with Graham Thorpe. England fight a positive Trent Bridge draw. Bob Willis says

At last the England selectors saw some sense and injected some young blood into their set-up. The presence of these young lions added extra spice. Thorpe played superbly but did not quite have the courage to go after the Aussies' wilting attack between lunch and tea on the fourth day. The Surrey left-hander should be thrilled with his hundred – and relieved that he made his debut at Trent Bridge rather than Headingley.

Not everyone is convinced – media round-up writes

Pragmatists were led by Peter Johnson in the *Daily Mail*: "Somehow the stinging pain of not quite winning seemed harder to bear than the dull ache of constant defeat."

Wisden Cricket Monthly, August 1993

Headingley. 200 from Border, another 600 conceded and Graham Gooch quits. Bob Willis writes

Headingley was a very sad end to Graham Gooch's reign as England captain. He lost a vital toss. The pitch was much slower than in recent years but the surface cracks were always going to make batting more difficult. His four seam bowlers had an especially ordinary first day.

Wisden Cricket Monthly, September 1993

To Birmingham for the next routine defeat – new captain (Mike Atherton), same result. Finally relief and release at The Oval where England's seamers find rhythm. By Richard Hutton

The weight and depth of Australia's batting failed to withstand an unfamiliar England bowling attack on an equally unfamiliar pitch in the final Test. It was a highly eventful match with some thoroughly absorbing and entertaining cricket from both sides. *The Cricketer*, October 1993

The Captain's Log

Mike Atherton – the new England captain – writes a season's journal for *The Cricketer* – starting with the week he got the top job

Week beginning July 26
This week probably constitutes the most hectic of my life. Nothing quite prepares you for the press attention but within hours they had managed to find out where I live and about my girlfriend ... Then it's down to London for my first selection meeting and first taste of the problems selectors face. Meanwhile, Lancashire administer a first defeat to the Australians with John Crawley underlining his potential with an excellent hundred.

Week beginning August 2
As England slip towards another defeat, the chairman of the England selectors Ted Dexter resigns, probably more hurt and battered than he would admit after constant harpooning by the media.

Week beginning August 16
What everyone had dreamed of all summer, an England victory, occurs. Maybe the Australians were tired, maybe Venus was in the right juxtaposition with Mars and maybe we got the rub of the green, but when it came it was an emotive moment, especially for those – and there were many – who had never beaten Australia or even won a Test match ... Graham Gooch calmly passed David Gower's record of Test runs with a trademark off-drive off Paul Reiffel. Gower, true to character, sends Gooch a congratulatory card wishing him well in his new position at short leg, and as a postscript saying well played. *The Cricketer*, November 1993

Who's to blame now? A reader writes about the Whingeing Pommie Press

Why haven't the media, *WCM* included, yet found out what dastardly cheating methods the Australians use to defeat our great cricketers? After all, Gooch and Smith are "the greatest batsmen in the world" (Jack Bannister on BBC TV) After the Pakistanis' tampering with the ball, West Indians bowling wicked head-high bouncers, Indians rigging pitches and bribing umpires and Sri Lankans throwing – allegedly – surely we haven't run out of excuses against the arch-enemy? When we have the sporting sense and guts to admit our cricketers, even those Commonwealth cousins conveniently labelled "English", are lacking in technique and ability compared with other nations, then we may be on the road to regaining competence and respect in the cricket world.
GA Statham
Torrance, Glasgow
Wisden Cricket Monthly, July 1993

1993

1st Test Jun 3-7, Old Trafford **Aus 289** (MA Taylor 174; PM Such 6-67) and **432-5 dec** (IA Healy 102*); †**Eng 210** (GA Gooch 65; SK Warne 4-51, MG Hughes 4-59) and **332** (Gooch 133; Warne 4-86, Hughes 4-92). **Aus won by 179 runs.**

2nd Test Jun 17-21, Lord's †**Aus 632-4 dec** (DC Boon 164, MJ Slater 152, Taylor 111); **Eng 205** (MA Atherton 80; Hughes 4-52, Warne 4-57) and **365** (Atherton 99; TBA May 4-81, Warne 4-102). **Australia won by inns and 62 runs.**

3rd Test Jul 1-6, Trent Bridge †**Eng 321** (RA Smith 86; Hughes 5-92) and **422-6 dec** (Gooch 120, GP Thorpe 114*); **Aus 373** (Boon 101) and **202-6** (BP Julian 56*). **Match drawn.**

4th Test Jul 22-26, Head †**Aus 653-4 dec** (AR Border 200*, SR Waugh 157*, Boon 107); **Eng 200** (Gooch 59; PR Reiffel 5-65) and **305** (AJ Stewart 78; May 4-65). **Aus won by inns and 148 runs.**

5th Test Aug 5-9, Edgbaston †**Eng 276** (Atherton 72; Reiffel 6-71) and **251** (Thorpe 60; Warne 5-82, May 5-89), **Aus 408** (ME Waugh 137) and **120-2** (ME Waugh 62*). **Aus won by 8 wickets.**

6th Test Aug 19-21, The Oval †**Eng 380** (GA Hick 80) and **313** (Gooch 79); **Aus 303** (Healy 83*; ARC Fraser 5-87) and **229** (SL Watkin 4-65). **Eng won by 161 runs.**

Hello world: Shane Warne bowls Mike Gatting at Old Trafford with his first ball

HERO
No.9

Allan Border

Tests

Batting

Matches	156
Runs	11174
Highest score	205
Average	50.56
Hundreds	27
Fifties	63

Bowling

Balls	4009
Runs	1525
Wickets	39
Average	39.10
Best bowling	7-46
5-for inns	2
10-for match	1

First-class career

Batting

Matches	385
Runs	27131
Highest score	205
Average	51.38
Hundreds	70
Fifties	142

Bowling

Balls	9750
Runs	4161
Wickets	106
Average	39.25
Best bowling	7-46
5-for inns	3
10-for match	1

v England

Batting

Matches	47
Runs	3548
Highest score	200*
Average	56.31
Hundreds	8
Fifties	21

The artful stodger

In a team of strugglers and second-stringers one man stood tall and unsmiling against the tide. **Malcolm Knox** worships Allan Border

WHEN Allan Border was playing, he was never my favourite cricketer. I couldn't see past the glittering surfaces of Dennis Lillee, Doug Walters and Ian Chappell; then Vivian Richards, Clive Lloyd and Michael Holding. Experience didn't add depth to my vision. In recent years my favourites have been dashers like Adam Gilchrist, princes of the willow like VVS Laxman, or fearsome athletes like Curtly Ambrose.

But just recently I went back to look at the Australian Team of the Century, voted by the Australian Cricket Board in 2000. Every player in the XI was part of a golden age – from the years before the First World War, or playing around Don Bradman in the 1930s and 1940s, or around Chappell in the 1970s, or around Shane Warne and the Waughs in the last decade.

The 12th man in that side played in no great teams. He came into Australian cricket during World Series Cricket. He survived the reunification in 1979 and was building his name as a batsman when Australian cricket disintegrated in 1984. The team were being smashed. Kim Hughes relinquished the captaincy in tears then fled with a Test squad's worth of players to South Africa.

What did Allan Border do? He had been to the Caribbean and played in Trinidad two of the greatest innings by any Australian anywhere: 98 not out and 100 not out, to earn the most miraculous draw. He'd proved himself as the one man who could stand up to them. So he took the captaincy, and in the next few years stood as the single pillar around which Australian cricket was rebuilt. He scored 11,174 Test runs, which no Australian has yet passed. He averaged over 50! He was the only one to make it into that Team of the Century who had spent most of his career surrounded by strugglers.

Also recently I watched a TV documentary about Australian cricket in the 1980s. Usually any sporting footage more than 10 years old looks inferior. Tennis players dab and slice, footballers walk around the park leisurely, cricket's bowlers look round-arm, and the batsmen – even Bradman – have distinctly dodgy techniques. Everything is slower. If you transplanted any player from the past into the present, they simply couldn't take the speed.

Yet when I watched those West Indian batteries – Holding, Malcolm Marshall, Joel Garner, Courtney Walsh, Ambrose – I saw attacks that were faster, nastier and harder than today's. Pitches were most certainly quicker and bouncier. If you threw a 2006 vintage Ricky Ponting or Mohammad Yousuf or Sachin Tendulkar into a 1984 Test match

> **The attacks Border faced were faster, nastier and harder than today's**

against those West Indians in, say, Brisbane or Barbados, it's the present stars who would suffer.

So my appreciation of Allan Border has increased over time. As it should, I feel that Border's legacy will grow and grow over the years, as will Brian Lara's for similar reasons. Yet while Border developed, under duress, personal leadership skills, which Lara never has, he was never as glamorous as the man who took his world record.

Border stood in a baseballer's crouch, bat raised, ready to hop backwards and pull or cut the short ball. The Trinidad innings of 1983-84 were full of twitching jabs at balls aimed into his armpits. As he aged, he became a plainly unattractive batsman to watch, all punch, no grace.

But this is to forget what a wonderful attacker he was. He was arguably the best player of spin Australia has produced in 50 years. He scored 150 in each innings in a Test at Lahore in 1979-80 against Iqbal Qasim and Tauseef Ahmed. It would have been a dream to see him play Shane Warne.

Though his reputation is built on stodge and defiance, Border was also the finest all-round one-day cricketer of his time, alongside Viv Richards. I was at the SCG in 1984-85 when Border smashed an attack of Holding, Garner, Marshall, Winston Davis and Richards for 127 not out off 140 balls. He was also a brilliant fielder. In his early years he was a wonderful catcher in the hardest position, the wide third-to-fifth slips. His left-arm spinners were always useful and, in typical Border fashion, he under-used himself. In 1988-89 he took 11 wickets in a Test match against West Indies.

Yet the enduring image of Border is from off the field, from the decisive Adelaide Test of the 1992-93 series. Sitting in the dressing room, he clutched a lucky cricket ball in his hands. Finally we were going to beat West Indies. Finally Border was going to beat them. Two runs short, Walsh got Craig McDermott with a lifter. The keeper caught the ball but the cameras caught Border. He sprang to his feet and hurled his ball into the floor. An entire career's worth of frustration captured in a single gesture.

Border retired one year before Australia won back the Frank Worrell Trophy. He never held it. But that's the way life is. It's not a fairytale. And Allan Border was never the fairytale hero. If I'm appreciating him more now, I'm glad. It shows some wisdom is finally getting through. 🄌 *The Wisden Cricketer, May 2007*

Malcolm Knox is a novelist and former cricket correspondent of the *Sydney Morning Herald*

Big Mac: Craig McDermott has Crawley at Perth

Domination continues

Michael Henderson writes on the first part of a tour that set out optimistically but ended in injury and loss

In the days that followed [England's arrival in Australia], with no cricket to think or write about, the hours were full of talk about England's pace attack. Devon Malcolm noted that the Australian batsmen looked scared at The Oval in the final Test of 1993. Darren Gough was being written up as the quickest new kid on the block and there was general anticipation of what Martin McCague might do ... Keith Fletcher did little to adjust the fevered tone of the debate. In terms of pace, he said, Malcolm was faster than Dennis Lillee and almost rivalled Jeff Thomson. It is never wise to seek comparison with genuinely great performers. The fact that Lillee and Thomson were both in town, meant that England did not have to wait long for a reply. Lillee's was not particularly considered: "It sounds like a heap of s**t to me," he said of Fletcher's claims. The early signs, however, are good. This is a happy team, not short of confidence, not short of realism. *The Cricketer, December 1994*

Jonathan Rice records an emerging war of words

Captain Atherton is already in trouble for his words used about Steve Waugh. Waugh, we are told by Atherton, was not only the main culprit in the sledging campaign allegedly masterminded by Old Grumpy himself, Allan Border, but was also routinely "wetting himself" every time he faced up to any bowler faster than Graeme Hick ... Steve Waugh responds: "I don't mind wetting myself if I'm going to average 80 against England." *Wisden Cricket Monthly, December 1994*

Usual service is resumed in the first Test at Brisbane. Warne takes eight in the second innings and Mark Nicholas watches

Ashes cricket is liberally sprinkled with marvellous bowlers who have illuminated the contest for the old Urn and tormented the old enemy. None, though, can have captured cricket's soul in quite the way that Shane Warne has done, or can have had such a single hand in renovating an art long forgotten and much mourned. Australia won the first Test match of this eagerly awaited series because for the most part they were the better, slicker team, and because in the wonderful Warne they have a glittering jewel who transfixes the opposition with his variations and renders them mute with his accuracy. His dismissal of the confident looking Alec Stewart during the England second innings with a wicked flipper left the mouths of the gripped Gabba wide open with its effect. *The Cricketer, January 1995*

Paul Allott watches at Melbourne over Christmas as Warne takes a hat-trick

England arrived in Melbourne on Christmas Eve with hope. Six days later, as

Take hat: Warne takes his third in three balls

the New Year beckoned, they left, hopeless. Quite where the Ashes series and the tour was going from here was obvious – down, down and further down as the horrific prospect of a 5-0 whitewash loomed. It was that bad ... In a hat-trick of extreme simplicity – one flipper and two legbreaks – the blond bombshell wiped away the tail. Warne admitted to nerves before the third delivery to Malcolm but stuck to what he knows best. He shut his eyes and bowled a legbreak and Boon snaffled a diving chance. *The Cricketer, February 1995*

At Sydney England find some form and nearly force a win – despite Mike Atherton declaring with Graeme Hick unbeaten on 98. Allott again

England were valiant to the last, Australia defiant to the end. The Ashes were retained by Australia, England's pride was salvaged, the spectators left breathless by the excitement. It is one of the great attractions of cricket that so much endeavour, spirit, skill, judgement, sweat and intrigue can be crammed into five days and still not produce a winner. Over 100,000 people witnessed this match, they saw England kick-start their tour with a performance which came six weeks too late, they saw Australia prove themselves under pressure and they saw that the gap between the two sides is not a chasm. *The Cricketer, February 1995*

Matthew Engel reflects on what it means

After Melbourne England's performance meant that not just the players but the entire country was turning into something of a laughing-stock. In Sydney the pressure eased. Australians have long since ceased to regard Britain as the Mother Country. The danger is that they are starting to think of

us as simpleton cousins. This is a matter that has repercussions far beyond the cricket field. *Wisden Cricket Monthly, February 1995*

And the casualty list grows and grows

Darren Gough leaves Australia to return to England on January 11 for a complete rest after an X-ray had revealed a stress fracture of his left foot. Gough was the third member of the original tour party to be forced out by injury following the departure of Martin McCague and Craig White. Chris Lewis became the fifth of England's replacements following call-ups for Angus Fraser, Mark Ilott, Jack Russell and Neil Fairbrother. *The Cricketer, February 1995*

Vic Marks watches a dramatic and surprising England win at Adelaide

A wonderful match in Adelaide reminded us that Test cricket at its best remains the most dramatic, romantic and exhilarating form of the game. It was a Test which confounded the critics, stunned the Aussies and sent the swelling ranks of the 'Barmy Army' into frenzied celebrations in the pubs of Adelaide. It cheered Mike Atherton up as well. England won by 106 runs and it is mighty difficult to explain why ... *The Cricketer, March 1995*

The Perth wicket provides pace that suits Craig McDermott (second innings 6 for 38) perfectly. Bob Willis writes

The magnificent Waca pitch provided the third enthralling Test match in succession. England should have had Australia 70 for 5 on the first day, but their woeful catching tossed the advantage to the home team. Although Malcolm bowled at the speed of light and was well supported, Slater's fleet footwork and Mark Waugh's classical stroke-play took Australia to a position of supremacy on day one ... Slater and Shane Warne, along with Darren Gough, are the best things that have happened to world cricket for a long time. These are entertainers and they never forget their obligation to the paying public ... Craig McDermott surely moved in among the top three fast bowlers in the world as he finished the series as he had started it. ■

Wisden Cricket Monthly, March 1995

1994-95

1st Test Nov 25-29, Brisbane †**Aus 426** (MJ Slater 176, ME Waugh 140; D Gough 4-107) and **248-8 dec** (MA Taylor 58; PCR Tufnell 4-79); **Eng 167** (MA Atherton 54, CJ McDermott 6-53) and **323** (GA Hick 80; SK Warne 8-71). **Aus won by 184 runs.**

2nd Test Dec 24-29, Melbourne **Aus 279** (SR Waugh 94*; Gough 4-60) and **320 7 dec** (DC Boon 131); †**Eng 212** (GP Thorpe 51; Warne 6-64) and **92** (McDermott 5-42). **Aus won by 295 runs.**

3rd Test Jan 1-5, Sydney †**Eng 309** (Atherton 88; McDermott 5-101) and **255-2 dec** (GA Hick 98*); **Aus 116** (Gough 6-49) and **344-7** (MA Taylor 113, Slater 103; ARC Fraser 5-73). **Match drawn.**

4th Test Jan 26-30, Adelaide †**Eng 353** (MW Gatting 117) and **328** (PAJ DeFreitas 88; ME Waugh 5-40); **Aus 419** (GS Blewett 102*) and **156** (IA Healy 51*; DE Malcolm 4-39, CC Lewis 4-24). **Eng won by 106 runs.**

5th Test Feb 3-7, Perth †**Aus 402** (Slater 124) and **345-8 dec** (Blewett 115); **Eng 295** (GP Thorpe 123) and **123** (McDermott 6-38). **Aus win by 329 runs.**

On the Waugh path

A very bright start for England in a summer of hope ends in disaster.
Scyld Berry reports first on the stunning Edgbaston win

The best-laid plans of England's men did not go astray. From start to finish English cricket made the most of its resources and the result was one of its most glorious victories in the annals of the Ashes. After underperforming for most of the post-Packer era, we can celebrate the sight of our game finally getting its act together.

Ten days before the first Test the Edgbaston pitch was flooded to such depth that enough moisture remained for the Australian batsmen to be caught with their pads down. The persistent rain ensured a conclusion; and the essential slowness anaesthetised the genius of Shane Warne, who took 1 for 137. Seldom in recent years have a county and its groundstaff responded so fully to England's needs as Warwickshire and Steve Rouse.

Graham Gooch and Mike Gatting, if not chairman Graveney, had seen enough of Australian triumphalism, and Mike Atherton and David Lloyd had started their strategic thinking in New Zealand. Luck did have a part, though. As their seamers had failed to perform in the opening sessions of the last two series, in Bulawayo and Auckland, England were inclined to bat first. Instead the Australians did and were caught cold on a seaming pitch at the English Test ground that most consistently favours swing.

Wisden Cricket Monthly, July 1997

The Aussies spark into life at Lord's thanks to Glenn McGrath – only the rain saving England. An astonishing display by Steve Waugh at Old Trafford draws them level – then Thorpe drops a catch at Headingley ... By Steven Lynch

Did England really win at Edgbaston, only two months or so ago? Australia so dominated this match, to take a 2-1 lead in the series, that that victory seemed as long ago as Botham's Test at Headingley in 1981, the obligatory highlights of which appeared during the numerous rain-breaks. The ghost of Headingley '81 reappeared in another form, too: soon after lunch on the fourth day, the odds on England winning were 500-1. This time there was no stampede from the Australian dressing room – even the coach-driver wasn't tempted. And despite brave resistance from Nasser Hussain and John Crawley there was to be no second miracle ... Australia's big total owed nearly everything to memorable innings from two batsmen of completely differing styles. Matthew Elliott, tall, left-handed, all angles and chin, thumped his second century of the series, living a charmed life on his way to 199. Ricky Ponting, compact and elegant, made his first Test century, and the England bowlers were cover-driven to distraction ... It's harsh to blame England's downfall entirely on Graham Thorpe but, if he had taken that catch, Australia would have been 50 for 5, etc, etc. Elliott, 29 at the time, was dropped twice more.

Wisden Cricket Monthly, September 1997

Big comeback: Australia win again

When it's finally over, Australian keeper Ian Healy, one of the architects behind Australia's record fifth Ashes win in a row looks back at the series with Ken Piesse

England were flattered by their 3-2 Ashes defeat. The set of green, bowler's pitches reduced Australia's superiority but played into the hands of No.1 strike bowler Glenn McGrath, who bowled as fast as anyone in the world. Here's his Test-by-Test verdict:

Edgbaston: "We didn't bat or bowl well and weren't ready for England's onslaught. We let them get about 100 too many."
Lord's: "We had a chance to force a result had there been an extra day. Glenn bowled very fast as he has for a couple of years now. He's as quick as anyone."
Old Trafford: "Steve Waugh's hundreds were a highlight but so was Shane Warne's bowling on a pitch which was wet from day one. They got the best of the conditions but it was Shane who really spun them out."
Headingley: "Jason Gillespie took seven-for. He bowled very fast and swung the ball. He had the Poms really worried."
Trent Bridge: "Being made man of the match was a rare honour for me and meant a lot. Winning the Ashes is always a special feeling."
The Oval: "From the very first ball which popped through the top of the pitch and died on its way through we thought the pitch wasn't going to be as easy as we'd first imagined. The top of the pitch wasn't together at all. It was a very average Test pitch but produced an exciting game." ∎

The Cricketer, October 1997

1997

1st Test Jun 5-8, Edgbaston †**Aus 118** (AR Caddick 5-50) and **477** (MA Taylor 129, GS Blewett 125); **Eng 478-9 dec** (N Hussain 207, GP Thorpe 138; MS Kasprowicz 4-113) and **119-1** (MA Atherton 57*). **Eng won by 9 wickets.**

2nd Test Jun 19-23, Lord's **Eng 77** (GD McGrath 8-38) and **266-4 dec** (MA Butcher 87); †**Aus 213-7 dec** (MTG Elliott 112; Caddick 4-71). **Match drawn**

3rd Test Jul 3-7, Old Trafford †**Aus 235** (SR Waugh 108; DW Headley 4-72) and **395-8 dec** (SR Waugh 116; Headley 4-104); **Eng 162** (Butcher 51; SK Warne 6-48) and **200** (JP Crawley 83; McGrath 4-46) **Aus won by 268 runs.**

4th Test Jul 24-28, Headingley **Eng 172** (JN Gillespie 7-37) and **268** (N Hussain 105; PR Reiffel 5-49); †**Aus 501-9 dec** (Elliott 199, RT Ponting 127; D Gough 5-149). **Aus won by inns and 61 runs.**

5th Test Aug 7-10, Trent Bridge †**Aus 427** (Taylor 76; Headley 4-87) and **336** (IA Healy 63); **Eng 313** (AJ Stewart 87; McGrath 4-71, Warne 4-86) and **186** (Thorpe 82*). **Aus won by 264 runs.**

6th Aug 21-23, The Oval †**Eng 180** (McGrath 7-76) and **163** (Thorpe 62; Kasprowicz 7-36); **Aus 220** (PCR Tufnell 7-66) and **104** (Caddick 5-42) **Eng won by 19 runs.**

Another tour, another drubbing

Australia's dominance continues with the usual consolation England win. Warne misses most of the series through injury but Australia have plenty in hand. **Matthew Engel** writes

For some reason it was put about before the third Test that Adelaide was a lucky ground for England. This was based on two draws and a freaky win on the last three tours. Perhaps any ground where England occasionally escape being pummelled counts as lucky; that's the level of English expectations these days. Excluding 1994–95 and the irrelevant victory over the Packer-weakened team in 1978-79, England have only one other win since Bodyline. Lucky? This time they had no luck at all. That was one factor in their defeat.

Wisden Cricket Monthly, February 1999

Mark Nicholas adds

Australia confirmed their superiority in technique and reiterated the iron will which dominates the tightest match situations. As Mark Taylor said bluntly: "I just don't think they are as good as us at the moment." ... Taylor's men may not be a better side, and are probably not much worse a side, than Bradman's in 1948 or Ian Chappell's in '74-'75. Suffice to say they are extremely good, rather too good at the moment for England.

The Cricketer, February 1999

England claim a consolation win, this time at Melbourne, with Dean Headley and Gough providing the heroics. By Simon Briggs

This was so nearly the Test match of the '90s, the game that had it all. But this time the photo finish won't be the only thing we remember. There was also a revitalised leading role from Alec Stewart, a bustling five-wicket haul for Darren Gough

and a stupendous innings from Steve Waugh, who for once batted with as much style as substance ... So what was missing? The Ashes.

Wisden Cricket Monthly, February 1999

The final game produces further England heroics. Australia's second-string legspinner Stuart MacGill has the final word, despite a Gough hat-trick. By Tanya Aldred

If Melbourne was a tale with a twist, Sydney was a boy's own adventure. For three wonderful days, in front of record crowds, the momentum swung absurdly so much that on the fourth day the hordes half-expected a miraculous England victory, even though only one side had ever chased more than 200 at the SCG to win – and that was Australia. In the end new England, like old England, proved easy pickings for their nemesis – the wristspinner. Stuart MacGill finished as leading wicket-taker in the series, flummoxing batsmen who couldn't bring themselves to attack him. "I would have to say we didn't master legspin in this series," deadpanned Alec Stewart.

Wisden Cricket Monthly, February 1999

John Woodcock reviews another desperate yet hopeful tour

English cricket can never have been in lower water than when Alec Stewart and his team arrived in Melbourne ahead of the fourth Test match.

1998-99

1st Test Nov 20-24, Brisbane **†Aus 485** (IA Healy 134, SR Waugh 112; AD Mullally 5 105) and **237-3 dec** (MJ Slater 113); **Eng 375** (MA Butcher 116; GD McGrath 6-85) and **179-6**. Match drawn

2nd Test Nov 28-30, Perth **Eng 112** (DW Fleming 5-46) and **191** (GA Hick 68; JN Gillespie 5-88); **†Aus 240** (Taylor 61; AJ Tudor 4-89) and **64-3. Aus won by 7 wkts.**

3rd Test Dec 11 15 Adelaide **†Aus 391** (JL Langer 179*; DW Headley 4-97) and **278-5 dec** (Slater 103); **Eng 227** (N Hussain 89*; SCG MacGill 4 53) and **237** (AJ Stewart 63*). **Aus won by 205 runs.**

4th Test Dec 26-29 Melb **Eng 270** (Stewart 107) and **244** (Hick 60); **†Aus 340** (Waugh 122*; D Gough 5-96) and **162** (Headley 6-60). **Eng won by 12 runs.**

5th Test Jan 2-6, Sydney **†Aus 322** (ME Waugh 121; Headley 4-62) and **184** (Slater 123, PM Such 5-81); **Eng 220** (MacGill 5-57) and **188** (Hussain 53; MacGill 7-50). **Aus won by 98 runs.**

They were the laughing stock of Australia. "England face the stinging reality that they no longer deserve a five-Test Ashes series," said the *Adelaide Advertiser*, and, among Australian critics, that was the majority view. A fortnight later they were being acclaimed for their mettle. Could this have been the tide that will lead England on to fortune, we asked ourselves. With so little genuinely penetrative bowling on good pitches, one has to doubt it – but the spirit is there, and that is so much of the battle ...

The first thing to strike visiting cricketers on their introduction to the modern game down under is its abrasiveness. Australians like it that way: those who don't, fall by the wayside. It goes with the heat and the dust and the national persona. The South Africans are the same, though less palpably so. Australia retained the Ashes not because they smiled less and sledged more than England but because they were the more versatile, the less cooped-up and technically the better of the two sides – as well, perhaps, as the luckier ...

Australia always found the bowlers to come to the aid of the party. Put Kasprowicz, Fleming, Nicholson, Miller and McGrath, all of whom played in the Test series, into an English county side, individually if not collectively, and they might be lost in the crowd. Put them in a baggy green cap, surround them with a considerate and positive captain, a brace of Waughs and a Healy, and tell them that nothing beats beating the Poms, and pride and adrenalin, it seems, will do the rest. ∎

The Cricketer, February 1999

Dazzling hat-trick: Gough

An all-time great side

This time England took a beating against an awesome Australia – and claimed that usual consolation win. **Tanya Aldred** watches optimism drain in the first Test at Edgbaston

And so the beat goes on – the insatiable, pounding beat of a truly great cricket team – and England had no answer. The Australians were hypnotically awesome. They tore at England's heart and for the 17th time in their last 19 Tests walked away with the bloody entrails. *Wisden Cricket Monthly*, August 2003

Matthew Engel witnesses the traditional drubbing at Lord's

The appeal of Test cricket as opposed to one-day internationals rests on a simple proposition: that each Test is unique, like a fingerprint, with all kinds of whorls and loops that are never repeated. The vast majority of one-dayers, in contrast, fit into about five or six well-used alternative scenarios, like American cop dramas. Of course, the scores were not precisely the same as at Edgbaston two weeks earlier. In essence the game should have been staged not on the 20th anniversary of Headingley '81 but on Groundhog Day.

Gideon Haigh watches the swift Ashes finale at Trent Bridge

To lose one Ashes series might be characterised as misfortune. To lose seven looks like an awful lot of carelessness. Such was the case at Trent Bridge where Australia's record-breaking sequence was secured, appropriately enough, with a no-ball from Caddick. As so often in recent years, England had their moments: 90 minutes on the first day, perhaps two hours on the second. For the rest, Australia reigned.

Wisden Cricket Monthly, September 2003

Christopher Martin-Jenkins keeps a journal of the season – here are his entries for the last two Tests

August 20

What a day it turned out to be. Australia had set the pace from the start of the fourth Test in the absence of Steve Waugh. Ricky Ponting played two fabulous innings on a pitch with something for everyone. But it was Mark Butcher who stole the game after Adam Gilchrist's declaration, crowning his successful return to the side with an innings of inspired brilliance. Nasser Hussain and Mark Ramprakash lent excellent support but the issue hung on a duel after lunch between Glenn McGrath and Butcher. The batsman won it with a series of rapier thrusts that thrilled yet another capacity crowd and delighted a whole nation.

August 27

Help, I have just realised that I might have watched my last home Test between England and Australia as a daily reporter, although, with a little luck, perhaps not as a commentator. There was a certain symmetry; the first one I reported was in 1972 when Ian and Greg Chappell both scored superb hundreds. This time it was Steve and Mark Waugh. It was amazing that the elder twin should have played after ripping a calf muscle at Trent Bridge.

There was a fine innings too by Justin Langer, getting back into the Test side at Michael Slater's expense and making an almost faultless hundred to set it up for the Waughs and then for Glenn McGrath and Shane Warne to win the game despite a lovely hundred by Mark Ramprakash ... Australia have cherished the spirit of the game, and this could be the greatest legacy of one of the most powerful all-round teams that ever took a field. *The Cricketer*, November 2001

John Woodcock writes his series verdict

Not since Don Bradman in 1948 had an Australian captain returned home to such paeans of praise as Waugh. For some years he has shown himself able to see the bigger picture to an extent that few do when they are still playing the game, and no captain ever asked or expected more of himself. Thanks to Mark Butcher's great innings at Headingley, our tails have not been quite permanently between our legs. Even so, the gap between the two sides is, if anything, wider than when England last went to Australia, in the winter of 1998-99. It is not, I think, that England have gone back since then so much as that Australia continue to raise their game to levels of unprecedented intensity, driven by their captain and the competition for places. 🅻 *The Cricketer*, October 2001

Total batting: Gilchrist at Edgbaston

2001

1st Test July 5-8, Edg **Eng 294** (SK Warne 5-71) and **164**; †**Aus 576** (AC Gilchrist 152, SR Waugh 105, DR Martyn 105). **Aus won by an inns and 118 runs.**

2nd Test July 19-22, Lord's **Eng 187** (McGrath 5-54) and **227** (JN Gillespie 5-53); †**Aus 401** (ME Waugh 108) and **14-2. Aus won by 8 wkts.**

3rd Test Aug 2-4, T Bridge †**Eng 185** (McGrath 5-49) and **162** (Warne 6-33); **Aus 190** (AJ Tudor 5-44) and **158-3. Aus won by 7 wkts.**

4th Test Aug 16-20, Head †**Aus 447** (RT Ponting 144, Martyn 118; D Gough 5-103) and **176-4 dec; Eng 309** (McGrath 7-76) and **315-4** (MA Butcher 173*). **Eng won by 6 wickets.**

5th Test Aug 23-27, T Oval †**Aus 641-4 dec** (SR Waugh 157*, ME Waugh 120, JL Langer 102); **Eng 432** (MR Ramprakash 133; Warne 7-165) and **184. Aus won by inns and 25 runs.**

2002-03

1st Test Nov 7-10, Bris **Aus 492** (ML Hayden 197, RT Ponting 123) and **296-5 dec** (Hayden 103); †**Eng 325** and **79. Aus won by 384 runs.**

2nd Test Nov 21-24, Ade †**Eng 342** (MP Vaughan 177) and **159; Aus 552-9 dec** (Ponting 154). **Aus won by inns and 51 runs.**

3rd Test Nov 29-Dec 1, Perth †**Eng 185** and **223; Aus 456** (White 5-127). **Aus won by inns and 48 runs.**

4th Test Dec 26-30, Mel †**Aus 551-6 dec** (JL Langer 250, Hayden 102) and **107-5; Eng 270** and **387** (Vaughan 145; SCG MacGill 5-152). **Aus won by 5 wkts.**

5th Test Jan 2-6, Syd †**Eng 362** (MA Butcher 124) and **452-9 dec** (Vaughan 183); **Aus 363** (Gilc't 133, SR W'gh 102) and **226** (Cad'ck 7-94). **Eng won by 225 runs.**

Huge hope, big shame

The eighth Ashes series in succession without an England win was agony. Nasser Hussain had built a winning side – but both captain and team froze as soon as they set foot in Australia. **Scyld Berry** keeps a tour diary

November 6

England are so, well, muted as they get off the team bus on returning to the team hotel in Brisbane. They radiate less hope than any England side before the last seven Ashes wallopings. [There was] disarray on their arrival in Perth, when Andrew Flintoff was found to be incapable of running and sent off to the Academy. Australia meanwhile seamlessly evolve: Ricky Ponting to take over from Mark Waugh at second slip and Damien Martyn at No.4.

November 7

First day of the series. Gasps in the main stand when the PA announces that England have won the toss – and will bowl. Soon Matthew Hayden is standing tall and driving down the ground. England appear one or two games short of match fitness – and short of a bit else besides. The rest submerges in the one image, of Hayden standing tall and driving down the ground.

November 10

Gough gone home. England gone, for 79. Sports psychologists being quoted as saying England were too concerned about the outcome, not focused on the process.

November 22

Second Test, Adelaide. Vaughan has batted divinely. Had a bet with Mike Atherton who said that England, 295 for 4, would score more than 380. "My head keeps ruling my heart," he offered by way of explanation after England had disintegrated in the face of another new ball and added that he didn't have any change. There went England's chance of avoiding 5-0.

November 29

Third Test, Perth. If Australia had batted first, England might have taken it into a fourth day, assuming they saved the follow-on. Australia's quicks rip through England's batting in little over two sessions. Before the close Silverwood became the ninth serious injury of the tour, tearing a left ankle ligament.

December 1

Australian journalist Robert Craddock says it has been like two brothers playing in the backyard. The younger one at times has given a bit of cheek, but the older one knows that if he puts his mind to it he can never lose.

December 17

In the one-day series Warne is injured and out for six weeks. Aaah diddums. The Brisbane *Courier Mail* back-page headline: "The selection chaos caused by Shane Warne's injury." I know he's a great bowler but he's only one player and Australia's first injury of the series. England have had to deal with a serious injury every week.

December 26–30

Boxing Day Test at Melbourne. Hayden hooked his first ball from Caddick just over fine-leg's head for four – and that's it, game virtually over, as a pig seems more likely to fly over the MCG than England take a wicket. England fought well, especially Vaughan whose second innings hundred was divine in its timing. England even rattled the Aussies' cage on the last morning, re-creating a bit of their panic in the MCG Test of four years ago, the last home Test the Aussies lost.

January 2

Final Test. At the SCG Australia drop a few chances. The Australians have passed their zenith in this series while England seem fully adapted to the conditions. Without Shane Warne and Glenn McGrath the heat has gone out of the Australian bowling, making it normal.

January 4–6

Vaughan has batted divinely again – he has reached 50 only three times but converted every one. It was the shot of the series by an England player when Brett Lee steamed in with the second new ball and Vaughan took a forward stride and drove him through extra-cover. So simple, so difficult. England win final Test. Australia performed when it mattered; Hussain was right to call it "the same old story". ◪

Wisden Cricket Monthly, January-February 2003

Positive English signs were there …

As much as any England follower I found the rapid series defeat in Australia a sad, if predictable, spectacle. However, the customary vitriolic reactions were equally unwelcome. We should come to fully appreciate the dominance of this Australian side over all rivals. Australia stand not merely head and shoulders but knees and ankles above the rest. England have shown in the past three years that they can compete with every Test nation except Australia. While, as they are our longest standing adversaries, it is galling to lag behind the Aussies, our cricket is not in the parlous state suggested in some quarters.
Paul McNicol
via email

Wrong call: Captains Waugh and Hussain at Brisbane

HERO
No.10

Shane Warne

Tests
Batting

Matches	145
Innings	199
Runs	3154
Highest score	99
Average	17.32
Hundreds	0
Fifties	12

Bowling

Balls	40705
Runs	17995
Wickets	708
Average	25.41
Best bowling	8-71
5-for inns	37
10-for match	10

First-class
Batting

Matches	301
Innings	404
Runs	6919
Highest score	107*
Average	19.43
Hundreds	2
Fifties	26

Bowling

Balls	74830
Runs	34449
Wickets	1319
Average	26.11
Best bowling	8-71
5-for inns	69
10-for match	12

v England
Batting

Matches	36
Runs	946
Average	22.00

Bowling

Wickets	195
Average	23.25
Best bowling	8-71
5-for inns	11
10-for match	4

Bowling's Bradman

Shane Warne changed the modern game, brought light to the darkness of pace and reawakened a hibernating art. On retirement **Malcolm Knox** writes this tribute

During the Ashes Test at Melbourne Sajid Mahmood discovered the essence of Shane Warne. As Mahmood settled in to bat on the first day, he heard a constant nasal badgering from first slip: "Seventeen overs ... seventeen overs ..." Never mind that England were six wickets down and in disarray, that Mahmood's batting posed all the threat of a sick Labrador, that the series was won and that Warne had announced his retirement. He was still harassing an opponent in a special on-field code that only Mahmood's weakest part could decipher. The "seventeen overs" referred to the pitiful bowling contribution Mahmood's captain had asked him to make during the Titanic five days at Perth. In getting into Mahmood's earshot Warne had one objective: to make the young Englishman feel he did not belong.

It is the most potent of sledges because the speaker so clearly did belong. Warne's special talents form a rich catalogue. His accuracy, his stamina, his variety, his legbreak, his flipper, his determination, his competitive force ... But, if you could distil all of these qualities to the single characteristic that really made Warne what he was, it was that in the middle of a Test ground, at the time when the match was there to be won or lost, he was so absolutely, overbearingly, at home.

When Warne talks about his early career one could see he had never forgotten the trauma of starting out, of being yet to belong. He speaks ruefully about striving to "feel comfortable" as a Test cricketer. His advice to young legspinners makes no reference to flippers or wrong 'uns but only to human relations: "You've got to be best friends with the captain, you need a lot of love from everyone and you need to have courage ... "

We all know about Warne's off-field brain snaps. No one with much common sense would have behaved as fecklessly as Warne. He is not that smart, by the usual measures. But there are different kinds of intelligence and Warne is exceedingly "cricket-smart". Even among a generation of cricket-smart Australians – Mark Taylor, Steve Waugh, Ricky Ponting, Darren Lehmann – Warne stands out as having possessed an Einsteinian cricket brain.

What exactly is "cricket-smart"? In Warne's case it is not only knowing how to set his fields, how to plan an attack on a batsman, when to bowl the unexpected ball or even the expected one – though it includes all those things. Above all it is a certain gift of empathy, the ability to think the way a batsman is thinking. In his most candid moments, inside the dressing room, Warne is a gifted mimic, particularly of batsmen. He can 'do' Ian Chappell, he can do Viv Richards, he can do everyone from Arjuna Ranatunga to Jacques Kallis. Terry Jenner, Warne's

mentor, has always said the gift of mimicry stems from Warne having started his cricket as a would-be batsman. He can place himself inside a batsman's skin and detect precisely where the batsman least wants him to bowl next.

He can get under a batsman's skin, too. Mark Taylor said Warne was continually "thinking up new ways to get under a batsman's skin". Or, he added as an afterthought, "just new ways to get them out". How to get under the skin? To say that cricket is played 90% between the ears is a cliché but Warne practised psychology with a shamanistic mastery. Ian Botham, who never played Warne, said he had heard that Warne was "always thinking up new nicknames for opposing players ... they'd go back to Google the name and find out what character Warne was naming them after". It was more than Warne standing at first slip and, as Graeme Smith said, "calling you a f-ing c- all day". It was Warne making them think about him even when he was not bowling: when he was fielding, talking non-stop; when they were in their hotel rooms. Warne knew that much worse than people talking about you was people not talking about you.

Thus he would risk self-exposure by carrying out legspin masterclasses all around the world, showing off his full bag of tricks: exactly how he turned his wrist to deliver each variation. Healy said that team-mates would question the wisdom of this but Warne would shrug them off. "It's not how the ball comes out," he would say, "it's how it arrives." What he meant was: if a batsman can concentrate hard enough, he might pick how each ball will turn but Warne's trick, beyond all of what Bob Woolmer called "Mr Heinz's 38 varieties", was that he could cloud the batsman's concentration. Even when a batsman thought he could master Warne, he was still thinking about him. And the cards were, in the long run, stacked Warne's way. During the course of a contest the bowler could make several mistakes; the batsman could afford only one.

Warne's legacy is not, as is often claimed, that he rejuvenated the art of legspin. There is little evidence that every blond-haired boy bowls over-the-wrist. Warne is inimitable.

His legacy is that he rejuvenated the game itself. The fascination of his bowling, the aura of his personality and the overturning of an old expectation that teams could comfortably bat out draws on the last day ... Warne reset the limits of the game. 🄰 *The Wisden Cricketer, February 2007*

Malcolm Knox is a novelist and former cricket correspondent of the *Sydney Morning Herald*

> 66 Warne made batsmen think about him when he was not bowling ... when they were in the hotel 99

ASHES FEVER

2005-07

At last the Australians looked beatable. England had built a decent side and, coming back from 1-0 down, emerged triumphant from an unbearably tense series. But Australia's star-studded team were not finished, just wounded. In a little over 18 months they reclaimed the Urn emphatically

The Perfect Storm

In 2005 Ashes fever took hold as an England team in peak form met an Australian side full of all-time greats. It was Test cricket at its absolute best – a series of an unparalleled drama

Cricket became the talk of the nation for a brief period in late summer, pushing football from the back pages and news off the front. The media couldn't get enough of it, as players appeared in fashion magazines, financial supplements, health guides, and on children's television. More people watched the last day at Trent Bridge than the *Big Brother* final (a record-breaking 8.4m). Asda sold more cricket shirts than football tops for a short time. Spar supermarket reported a boost in beer and fizzy drinks sales through the series. David Beckham talked Ashes, [England football manager] Sven-Goran Eriksson was due to visit The Oval, before his side's defeat to Northern Ireland made him wary of the spotlight. Tabloids got excited when cricketers were spotted out on the town (Shane Warne and Kevin Pietersen were particularly prominent). Warne appeared on Graham Norton's BBC chat show. And as Channel 4 succumbed to popular demand, moving its highlights package from midnight to a prime-time slot, BBC Radio Five Live broadcast all its day-time programmes from The Oval for the whole of the final Test. **Edward Craig**

The Wisden Cricketer, October 2005

Sing when you're winning: crowds celebrate with England in Trafalgar Square

Letters to the editor

What an Ashes contest. Freddie Flintoff is not only an English hero, he is now an Australian hero. My boys played a backyard Test match here in Melbourne and argued over who would be Freddie and who Brett. Each wanted to be Freddie. The winner then gave the other hell with the ball. Unfortunately, they both tried to bat like him to the amazement of our neighbours who were peppered with tennis balls.
Michael Shatin, Melbourne, Australia

The Ashes series was what older cricket followers have missed for 30 years. It is like the good old days when the players were heroes. Players like Geoff Boycott ruined English cricket with a slow, defensive attitude. Both sides have lived up to the occasion and taken cricket back to what it should be: exciting, tough and fair. Thank you Australia and thank you England.
Philip and Gordon Dowe, Germany

I was privileged to be at every day of the Lord's, Edgbaston and Old Trafford Tests. The cricket was exceptional with mind-blowing tension but I will never forget the genuine good-natured bantering and support for each side and the expressions of goodwill offered to us as visitors to this wonderful country. Huge thanks to the players and umpires who performed so admirably under enormous pressure, surely the image of Freddie Flintoff consoling Brett Lee must go down as one of the all-time great sporting images of any sport let alone cricket
Greg Morrissey, Parkes, NSW, Australia

The Wisden Cricketer, October 2005

Magic moment: Flintoff and Lee

Chasing the tale

From first ball to last **Julian Guyer**, who reported on the whole international summer, charts the sweet agony of success

First day of the Ashes
Thursday, July 21, London
Perhaps the most fevered day I've known at Lord's. Some people have spent all night camping out for a ticket, a scene more reminiscent of Wimbledon than Lord's. The atmosphere is beyond excitement before the match starts and reaches something close to hysteria after Australia are bowled out for 190. Certainly the reception the England players receive as they walk back into the pavilion is so rousing you do fear for the health of some MCC members.

The air of unreality is heightened by news of what appears to be a failed bomb attempt in London just a fortnight after the July 7 attacks. Then, Glenn McGrath runs through England's top order, which is a vaguely reassuring

reminder of how things used to be, even if 17 wickets in a day isn't.

Sunday, July 24, London
England collapse in the face of McGrath and Shane Warne, with only Pietersen – whose background perhaps makes him immune from the dreadful diffidence which seems to afflict so many of his English-born colleagues – making any reasonable stab at defiance. (But why was he taking singles with the tail at the other end?)

McGrath's children join him for the post-match press conference as, we later discover, do a couple of interlopers for whom admission represents part of a 'prize'. Michael Vaughan still refuses to say outright that England can win the Ashes. How significant this is I'm

Do believe the hype: above Kevin Pietersen after his 158 at The Oval that secured the Ashes below Queues at Lord's on day one of the series

not sure. Reminded of the story about the long-serving Chinese premier Zhou Enlai being asked what he thought of the French Revolution. "It's too early to tell," replied Zhou.

Sunday, August 7, Birmingham
The most maddening, tense and infuriating session of cricket – and that was just in the press box. If you ever wanted proof of the professionalism of the Australian press corps it was that they were quite keen for England to win, as they did not want to rewrite the reports they'd already sent through for the first editions of their papers.

My job requires me to send a piece as soon as the game finishes, which means there were three different articles (covering each

Celebrations: top McGrath takes his 500th Test wicket **below** England win

possible result) on my screen and, rather like one of those plate-spinners, I try to keep all of them updated while watching the game at the same time. Andrew Flintoff's consoling words to Lee at the end of the match must rank already as one of the classiest sights of the summer.

Tuesday, August 9, Manchester
England players answer (or fail to answer) your questions; Warne makes statements. Today he tells us that Andrew Strauss is the "new Daryll", after Daryll Cullinan, Warne's famous South African bunny. Priceless.

Monday, August 15, Manchester
Confronted by the bizarre sight of thousands walking away from Old Trafford long before play starts. One of the AWCs (Award Winning Columnist) in the press box loftily pronounces, "Well, what's going to happen today?" To which this AFP reporter, showing previously unknown speed of thought, replies: "I don't know, that's why I've come."

After Edgbaston an almost tame climax. Well, there were only two outcomes possible this time.

Tuesday, August 16, London
Return to the office where I'm greeted by an excited colleague who runs up to me and says: "I know all about Simon Jones and reverse-swing." The colleague in question is French.

Wednesday, August 24, Nottingham
Sledged quite beautifully by Warne at a press conference. When my old tape recorder starts playing rather than recording, Warne turns to me and says: "First day on the job?" I'm a lot better off than one of my colleagues who gets knocked over by a television camera tripod that topples, camera and all, and smashes into his shoulder. "Only 55 more to go," says Warne.

Sunday, August 28, Nottingham
There are still some people out there who think your job finishes more or less when the games does. Today a few of us leave the ground at 10.30pm after hanging on for the result of the Ponting-Katich disciplinary hearings. Whatever happened to "win with grace, lose with grace"?

Anyway it suddenly hits me that these last three matches are the most majestically thrilling I've ever seen and maybe ever will see. And, apparently, I've only been in the job five days.

Tuesday, September 6, The Oval
There are few things more likely to provoke anger than a sports reporter complaining about his working conditions. We, who pay nothing, are on the whole grateful for the positions we hold. Nevertheless there is consternation when we see that the windows of the new press box are covered with a gauze-like substance, white on the outside, after complaints that the bowler's arm was disappearing over the sightscreen. It is like looking through a tea strainer or at one of those magic eye pictures. Your view is slightly improved if you bob your head from side to side like Amir Khan.

Saturday, September 10, The Oval
All of us would be considerably richer if we had a pound for every time someone said: "What do you do when it rains?" In the case of CMJ, my Oval neighbour, he is looking through a copious series of notes and cuttings ahead of a radio interview he is conducting with Michael Grade, the BBC chairman. One piece suggests Grade is a "bit of a schmoozer". CMJ asks me: "What does schmoozer mean?" I try to explain but clearly don't make too good a job because I find myself having to dissuade him from the belief that Mr Grade would be happy to be called a 'schmoozer'. Don't hear if the dread word is used. Anyway that's what I do when it rains. I advise CMJ on Yiddish.

Monday, September 12, The Oval
Be careful of what you wish for. My fondest hope ahead of the Ashes was that the series would still be alive come The Oval. Well, it's the last day and my 'dream' has come true. Wendy Wimbush, the press box scorer, keeps us supplied with a constant flow of statistics despite wanting to avert her gaze (or should that be gauze) every time Pietersen plays and misses. But Pietersen is the cricketing embodiment of Shaw's dictum that the "reasonable man adapts himself to the world, the unreasonable man adapts the world to himself, therefore, all progress depends upon the unreasonable man". Say what you like about his hair, his origins and the rest, the central issue is that Pietersen can play. It's a cruel exit for Warne but he still fronts up afterwards. Eventually leave the ground after 11pm and then it hits me, again. This is the best Test series I have ever covered and probably ever will cover. It's a strange feeling, somewhere between euphoria and loss. ∎

The Wisden Cricketer, October 2005

Julian Guyer is a reporter for Agence France Presse and is based in London

2005

1st Test July 21-24, Lord's †Aus **190** (JL Langer 40; SJ Harmison 5-43) and **384** (MJ Clarke 91, DR Martyn 65); **Eng 155** (KP Pietersen 57; GD McGrath 5-53) and **180** (Pietersen 64*; McGrath 4-29, SK Warne 4-64). **Aus won by 239 runs.**

A staggering 17 wickets on the first day means that the Ashes actually lives up to the hype – at least until day two. Then normal service is resumed – or so it appeared ...

See next page for 2nd Test

3rd Test August 11-15, Old Trafford †Eng **444** (MP Vaughan 166, ME Trescothick 63, IR Bell 59; Warne 4-99, B Lee 4-100) and **280-6d** (AJ Strauss 106, Bell 65; McGrath 5-115); **Aus 302** (Warne 90; SP Jones 6-53) and **371-9** (RT Ponting 156; A Flintoff 4-71). **Match drawn.**

The most exciting match since ... the last one. McGrath and Lee hold out for four overs after Ponting's heroic defiance – but the ball is swinging in England's direction.

4th Test August 25-28, Trent Bridge †Eng **477** (Trescothick 65, Vaughan 58, Flintoff 102, GO Jones 85; Warne 4-102) and **129-7** (Warne 4-31); **Aus 218** (SP Jones 5-44) and **387** (Langer 61, Clarke 56, SM Katich 59). **Eng won by 3 wkts.**

England dominate, Australia follow on but the low target inspires Warne and Lee as England feel the heat. Giles and Hoggard finally see them home. England lead the Ashes for the first time since 1997

5th Test September 8-12, The Oval †Eng **373** (Strauss 129, Flintoff 72; Warne 6-122) and **335** (Pietersen 158, AF Giles 59; Warne 6-124); **Aus 367** (Langer 105, ML Hayden 138; Flintoff 5-78) and **4-0. Match drawn.**

Pietersen guides England to safety on an agonising last day where, with the series still at stake, England totter. Warne takes 12 in the match but drops Pietersen on 15 and England have finally won the Ashes.

The day a nation held its breath

This was the match you could not script – quick runs, great bowling, heroes and villains – with no clear winner till its nail-bitten conclusion. **Scyld Berry** writes

HAS THERE ever been a more exciting match? The drama at Edgbaston began before the start, when news that Glenn McGrath had injured his right ankle in practice swept like a bushfire, interrupting radio programmes. It continued – at four runs an over and in front of capacity crowds who played their part in the action – right through until the climax, which really was like a Greek play, nobody knowing what the gods would decide. Had the agonising tension gone on 21 minutes longer into the fourth morning, no one would have been able to eat a bite of lunch.

If the match lacked anything, it was a piece of great batting. There was great hitting, great spin bowling and great fast bowling, without using the term at all loosely. Great character too. So maybe this game will have to be bracketed with the Brisbane tied Test of 1960-61, which also had a great innings from Garry Sobers. But has any other cricket match surpassed it?

Punter loses gamble

Australia were behind from the moment Ricky Ponting sent England in on a flat pitch which offered seam movement only if the ball was very full, ie driveable. When McGrath was carried off with torn ankle ligaments, why did the captain not play to his strength and bat? He had no doubt decided to bowl in advance; changing plan would have been a vote of no confidence in his new seam attack. Also history helped outweigh Ponting's gut instinct: before 2003

and Graeme Smith's double-hundred, Edgbaston was a bowl-first pitch. From the moment Brett Lee found as little deviation as a sniper's bullet, England sensed they could level the series.

Trescothick's lead

It will always be a different game for England if Marcus Trescothick can survive the new-ball bowlers until Shane Warne comes on. Trescothick's 77 before lunch gave England the advantage which for the rest of the game was like an edged chance to Geraint Jones: it looked as though they might let it slip but never actually lost it. With McGrath absent and the openers going after Warne, Australia leaked runs at both ends and England's first-innings 407 was their highest on the opening day of a Test since World War II. It would surely have been no more than 300 if McGrath had been bowling. In the match England hit 16 sixes – one-sixth of their run aggregate, an amazing proportion. Yes, the boundaries were short but it was the same for both sides, and Australia managed only two.

Super Fred

The crowd was not quite so wildly patriotic as it is when the Birmingham Test is staged at the proper time, the last week of the university term, but it did its job in rousing Andrew Flintoff to the status of a world-class allrounder. He had done serious bowling before but this was the first Test in which he scored substantial runs

Hello ... massive:
Flintoff hits out

against the best: 141 off 148 balls. He began by lunging at Warne but settled in for his first proper partnership with Kevin Pietersen. Their century stand took 66 minutes and, better still, Pietersen did not try to compete with Flintoff: he was a mature enough team-man to be the restraining influence.

The damage Flintoff did with his hitting (nine sixes in the match was an Ashes record) can be quantified fully only at the end of the series. But at the time it seemed possible that his hitting had finished the careers of either Jason Gillespie or Mike Kasprowicz, or both.

Flintoff's next contribution was his reverse-swing bowling. To dismiss Australia in only 76 overs on a flat slow pitch was an outstanding effort achieved largely by reverse-swing. After years of being impotent on flat pitches in the absence of a mystery-spinner, England are now able to dismiss batsmen when well-set: Simon Jones got Justin Langer for 82 with a first-innings in-ducker, and Matthew Hayden – after his first golden duck in Test cricket – for 31 with a second-innings outswinger.

Flintoff took four wickets in two overs spread over Australia's innings: two tailenders in successive balls and then, in his first over of the second innings, Langer and Ponting. He later called it the best opening over he had bowled, and rightly. He reverse-swung the old ball both ways at ferocious pace and had Ponting in trouble every ball. England made sure that Ponting did not set a big example.

Australia's champion

England were 25 without loss in their second innings, 124 ahead and cruising, when Warne came on and did everything expected of him. His dismissal of Strauss with a legbreak turning three feet, if not undermining England's confidence, must have led them to take their eye off Lee on the third morning, when he took three wickets in the first half-hour. Warne was masterful, from over and round the wicket, teasing and tormenting, with legspinner and straight ball. When Warne took his 598th Test wicket, England were reeling at 131 for 9, only 230 ahead. Allowing for the short boundaries, and the Edgbaston pitch's tendency to die for pace bowlers, that lead was not enough – however much rough there was for Giles. Much was made of an lbw reprieve which Billy Bowden allowed Simon Jones when 12, although the umpiring mistakes evened up in the end. But the damage had been done already. If the nine-ball over when Kasprowicz went for 20 wasn't decisive, then Lee's over for 18 was: both of them included two sixes from Flintoff, the pick of them an on-drive on to the roof of the pavilion. Every fielder was placed around the boundary but they still clutched at air. His last-wicket stand of 51 off 49 balls with Jones restored England's momentum.

The denouement

It all seemed over on the third evening when Australia lost Michael Clarke in the extra half-hour and ended on 175 for 8, still 107 short. Again the brilliant reverse-swing of Flintoff and Jones, and the steadiness of Giles, had run through the line-up on a slow pitch. Australia's first eight batsmen in their second innings scored 134 runs between them. If nothing changed, it would be impossible for three tailenders to reach 282, far higher than the previous highest successful run-chase in an Edgbaston Test, 211 for 3 by England against New Zealand in 1999.

But something did change: England's tactics. On the last morning, after a brief go with Giles, Vaughan relied on his two heavyweight fast bowlers Harmison and Flintoff. They bowled very straight. The normal line of just outside off stump, and normal length, went out the window. Aggression usurped thought, and who can blame England? They were so intent on winning, so tense, so motivated, so desperate, that they threw the kitchen sink at Warne, Lee and Kasprowicz – and the runs flowed. Australia's last three batsmen and Extras put on 145.

It was like two heavyweight boxers slugging each other into the 15th round, but better than that, for no sport could have been more compelling than the fourth morning here. In such situations, like Melbourne in 1982-83, the last pair score freely when there is nothing to lose but clam up and get out when they come close to winning and the pressure transfers. But the gods still did not know what was happening after Simon Jones spilled a diving chance at third man with 15 wanted.

Australia needed only five runs to go 2–0 up and end the summer. Flintoff bowled one last mighty over, more on off stump this time and leaked one run. Harmison, from the pavilion end, bowled a full toss wide of off stump which Lee – battered and bruised under England's assault – must have climbed into a thousand times since in his sleep but which he only pushed to deep cover for one. Kasprowicz had been shovelling every short ball to leg but in extremis he did not attack. He went for caution or survival, ducked and only gloved down the leg side. And say what you like about Geraint Jones but he never shirks a challenge.

The Wisden Cricketer, September 2005

Scyld Berry is cricket correspondent of the *Sunday Telegraph* and *Wisden* editor

2nd Test, Edgbaston, August 4-7
England won by 2 runs

ENGLAND

Batsman	1st innings			2nd innings	
ME Trescothick	c Gilchrist b Kasp'wicz	90		c Gilchrist b Lee	21
AJ Strauss	b Warne	48		b Warne	6
MP Vaughan*	c Lee b Gillespie	24	(4)	b Lee	1
IR Bell	c Gilchrist b Kasp'wicz	6	(5)	c Gilchrist b Warne	21
KP Pietersen	c Katich b Lee	71	(6)	c Gilchrist b Warne	20
A Flintoff	c Gilchrist b Gillespie	68	(7)	b Warne	73
GO Jones†	c Gilchrist b Kasp'wicz	1	(8)	c Ponting b Lee	9
AF Giles	lbw b Warne	23	(9)	c Hayden b Warne	8
MJ Hoggard	lbw b Warne	16	(3)	c Hayden b Lee	1
SJ Harmison	b Warne	17		c Ponting b Warne	0
SP Jones	not out	19		not out	12
Extras	lb9 w1 nb14	24		lb1 nb9	10
Total	79.2 overs	407		52.1 overs	182

Fall of wickets 112 164 170 187 290 293 342 348 375 — 25 27 29 31 72 75 101 131 131

Bowling (1st) Lee 17-1-111-1, Gillespie 22-3-91-2, Kasprowicz 15-3-80-3, Warne 25.2-4-116-4
(2nd) Lee 18-1-82-4, Gillespie 8-0-24-0, Kasprowicz 3-0-29-0, Warne 23.1-7-46-6

AUSTRALIA WON TOSS

Batsman	1st innings			2nd innings	
JL Langer	lbw b S Jones	82		b Flintoff	28
ML Hayden	c Strauss b Hoggard	0		c Tres'hick b S Jones	31
RT Ponting*	c Vaughan b Giles	61		c G Jones b Flintoff	0
DR Martyn	run out Vaughan	20		c Bell b Hoggard	28
MJ Clarke	c G Jones b Giles	40		b Harmison	30
SM Katich	c G Jones b Flintoff	4		c Tres'hick b Giles	16
AC Gilchrist†	not out	49		c Flintoff b Giles	1
SK Warne	b Giles	8	(9)	hit wicket b Flintoff	42
B Lee	c Flintoff b S Jones	6	(10)	not out	43
JN Gillespie	lbw b Flintoff	7	(8)	lbw b Flintoff	0
MS Kasprowicz	lbw b Flintoff	0		c G Jones b Harmison	20
Extras	b13 lb7 w1 nb10	31		b13 lb8 w1 nb18	40
Total	76 overs	308		64.3 overs	279

Fall of wickets 0 88 118 194 208 262 273 282 308 — 47 48 82 107 134 136 137 175 220

Bowling (1st) Harmison 11-1-48-0, Hoggard 8-0-41-1, SP Jones 16-2-69-2, Flintoff 15-1-52-3, Giles 26-2-78-3
(2nd) Harmison 17.3-3-62-2, Hoggard 5-0-26-1, Giles 15-3-68-2, Flintoff 22-3-79-4, SP Jones 5-1-23-1

Umpires BF Bowden (NZ), RE Koertzen (SA), JW Lloyds
Match referee RS Madugalle (SL)   Man of the match A Flintoff

Early aggression: Marcus Trescothick

The series in a flash

The 2005 Ashes had much magic, big turning points and huge performances
– eight writers pick their favourite passages and key moments

First Test, Lord's
Day 1, 11.24am
Harmison hits Ponting
Steve Harmison had already cracked Justin
Langer's elbow and clanged Matthew
Hayden's helmet but this was a more
symbolic achievement. Australia have made
it a long-standing policy to attack the
opposition captain but have never
experienced such a sharp taste of their own
medicine. Ricky Ponting aimed a pull at
Harmison but the ball crashed through the
grille of his helmet and drew blood. England
might have lost the match but Australia
knew then that their opponents would not
be intimidated and Ponting was left dazed
and confused for the first of many times in
the series. Patched up by the physio, he was
dismissed 10 balls later and fielded with
butterfly clips over the cut before an
appointment with a plastic surgeon for eight
stitches. Harmison had hammered the first
blow and no amount of antiseptic cream
could make it disappear. **Peter English**

Second Test, Edgbaston
Day 3, 4.04pm
Flintoff gets Ponting
When Andrew Flintoff came on to bowl the
13th over of Australia's second innings they
were nearer to winning the second Test –
and with it for sure the Ashes – than at any
moment until the later stages of that
improbable final morning. Shane Warne
had bowled them back into contention on
the Saturday morning and only Flintoff's
uninhibited hitting had enabled them to
set a sufficiently demanding target. But
Australia were 47 for 0, almost a fifth of the
way to their target of 282. Langer kept out
the first ball of Flintoff's seminal over, but
the second bowled him off his arm. Enter
Ricky Ponting. The third and fifth balls
nipped back sharply into his pads. Both
were narrow lbw not-outs but Ponting
could feel the hound's hot breath. He was
harried by the fourth and the sixth, a
no-ball. The seventh had to be played but it
lifted, left him and took the edge. Best
batsman gone: match transformed.
Christopher Martin-Jenkins

Cutting edge: Ponting is hit by Harmison

No cigar: Glenn McGrath bowls Michael Vaughan with a no-ball at Old Trafford

Day 4, 12.10pm
Jones's winning catch

Q What do Michael Jackson and Geraint Jones have in common? A They both wear gloves for no apparent reason. Jones tells this joke against himself. Sometimes it does not seem funny. Had England fans been told on Saturday evening that England's victory the next day depended on Jones taking a catch, there would have been a collective churn of the stomach. Steve Harmison was bowling his heart out but Australia needed only three to win. England's Ashes summer was about to go down the drain when Michael Kasprowicz fended off a short, straight ball. It clipped the glove and looped up towards leg slip. Showing both alertness and agility, Jones ran forward to his left and dived to take the catch inches from the turf. There had been a nanosecond of disbelief and then an eruption of joy, on the field and off it. That's why Jones wore gloves. **Stephen Fay**

Third Test, Old Trafford
Day 1, 1.27pm
Vaughan's charmed life

Michael Vaughan came to Old Trafford longer on confidence than runs, believing he had a big innings in him despite contrary statistical evidence. The shadow of Glenn McGrath, who had not been expected to play after his mishap at Edgbaston, then fell across his path. Vaughan had compiled a promising 41 when it looked as if a cut shot would cut short his comeback but Adam Gilchrist parried the catch wide of first slip Shane Warne. McGrath responded with a ball close to perfect for a batsman whose feet had been anchored all summer, removing off stump with the precision of a dentist extracting a tooth. The distance between it and perfection, however, was the centimetre or so by which the bowler had overstepped. Vaughan obtained his big innings, 166, McGrath went wicketless, 0 for 86, and the balance of power in the series tilted further. **Gideon Haigh**

Day 5, 6.28pm
Ponting's defiance

The mutterings about Ricky Ponting's leadership grew louder with every England batsman's flourish. There were signs of hesitation, as he lingered between overs in huddles with his bowlers, and as Shane Warne slung an arm around his shoulders. Here was an Australian captain, nails chewed to the quick, facing the sternest test of his 18 months in the job. He responded with the most substantial innings of his career. His team-mates' confusion at the angling, reversing deliveries of Andrew Flintoff and Co was their undoing. Yet the captain kept a clear head and blunted them with majestic drives and defiant pulls. He thought all was lost when, with four overs remaining, he lightly gloved a nasty Steve Harmison ball down the leg side and was caught behind for 156. Ponting's head dropped at the thought of what these brutish fast bowlers might do to No.11 Glenn McGrath, and in the privacy of the dressing room he threw a "little tantrum". McGrath and Brett Lee held their nerve for an epic draw, but it was Ponting's monumental, rearguard innings that saved Australia from a more desperate position in the series. **Chloe Saltau**

Fourth Test, Trent Bridge
Day 3, 11.28am
Strauss catches Gilchrist below

Andrew Strauss is reckoned to be a useful wicketkeeper and this was a great gloveman's catch. Adam Gilchrist may not have felt moved to appreciate it. There was just the hint that the real Gilchrist was making an appearance after he had started climbing into Matthew Hoggard. That was until Andrew Flintoff squared him up with fractional seam movement. Strauss leapt to his left, at first going for the ball with two hands before realising it had to be a one-hander. The ball was almost behind him when he caught it and he still had to

negotiate a safe landing. Gilchrist was gone for 27 and Australia were 163 for 8, contemplating the full horror of their first follow-on since 1987-88. **John Stern**

Day 2, 1.57pm
Flintoff's century

Andrew Flintoff's innings have a way of matching his surroundings. At Lord's he is subdued, at Edgbaston explosive and at Headingley his stats are as ugly as the encircling stands. So it was fitting that this sumptuous innings, easily the most classical century of Flintoff's career, should have graced England's loveliest arena. Up until a rustic heave that brought about his downfall, his 102 was the work of a pukka No.4. Reassured by the fluency he found at Old Trafford, he decided he was good enough to play whatever hand he was dealt. And the winnings, at Trent Bridge, made a rare old pile. **Simon Briggs**

Fifth Test, The Oval
Day 5, 11.51am
Warne drops the Ashes

To claim that this was the instant when Australia finally surrendered the Ashes is to discredit the passages of play before and after. But its poignancy was undeniable. Shane Warne was the man who had perpetually kept England guessing and usually persuaded them to guess wrong. Now here he was, at first slip, where he is barely less assured. Brett Lee lured Kevin Pietersen, on 15, into the drive with a full-length ball outside off stump. Pietersen is drawn to these as a moth to a flame and, early in his innings, his bearings are about as steady. He duly edged around throat height, a regulation chance if such could exist in the circumstances. The ball squeezed from Warne's upturned hands and, as it hit the ground, many people swore that it took on, briefly, the shape of an urn. **Stephen Brenkley**

The Wisden Cricketer, October 2005

HERO No.11

Michael Vaughan

Tests

Batting

Matches	82
Innings	147
Runs	5719
Highest score	197
Average	41.44
Hundreds	18
Fifties	18

Bowling

Balls	978
Runs	561
Wickets	6
Average	93.50
Best bowling	2-71

First-class career*

Batting

Matches	264
Innings	460
Runs	16192
Highest score	197
Average	37.13
Hundreds	42
Fifties	68

Bowling

Balls	9342
Runs	5245
Wickets	114
Average	46.00
Best bowling	4-39

v Australia

Batting

Matches	10
Innings	20
Runs	959
Highest score	183
Average	47.95
Hundreds	4
Fifties	1

* Up until May 5, 2009

The modern hero

Michael Vaughan played in two Ashes series. In one he excelled with the bat, in the other he led England to an astonishing win, their first Ashes victory for 18 years

Mike Atherton on Vaughan's batting

Throughout the wreckage of the [2002-03] Ashes defeat Michael Vaughan has stood tall. His bold and aggressive strokeplay has won legions of admirers in a land where dour defence is not enough. Hundreds at Adelaide and Melbourne and the second highest number of runs in a calendar year confirmed his growing reputation as a match-winning batsman. If only England can find some bowlers. He scores his runs at a decent lick, forcing the opposition on to the defensive and giving the captain enough time in a match to bowl the opposition out twice, as he proved at Sydney with his 183.

It was not always so. As a young man he had to cope with the vagaries of the Headingley pitch and the ghosts of Yorkshire's past, neither of which has been conducive to an easy entry into first-class cricket. He struggled to impose himself for a while, threatening to become another county player who fell short of expectations and failed to fulfil his talent and potential.

His subsequent rise to prominence started when he was plucked out of county cricket by Duncan Fletcher and selected for the 1999-2000 South African tour. Immediately Fletcher sensed something special – an orthodox technique supplemented by a strong mind – although injuries and selectorial conservatism meant he did not command a regular place until 2001-02.

When a player steps up to a higher grade he must improve to survive. Vaughan had the toughest of introductions: on a spiteful pitch, in murky light at the Wanderers, and with England 2 for 4, Vaughan was joined by another newcomer, Chris Adams, at the crease. What impressed me immediately was not the quality or range of strokeplay but his unflappable temperament. Neither the situation nor the ball regularly passing his bat made any impression. He simply settled in for the next delivery.

Since assuming his position at the top of the order with Marcus Trescothick, Vaughan has simply flourished. It is not just the volume of runs but the style in which he has scored them that has impressed. I think he just stopped complicating the game and began to pare batting down to its bare essentials. Instead of tinkering with technique and looking to defend first and score second, now he watches the ball intently and looks to hit it. He plays the ball, not the name sending it down. It is a simple philosophy, almost Australian. *Wisden Cricket Monthly*, February 2003

Mike Atherton captained England in 54 Tests and is chief cricket correspondent for *The Times*

Nasser Hussain on Vaughan's captaincy

When we were all hiding behind our sofas in 2005, praying for that final wicket at Edgbaston, praying for KP at The Oval, Michael Vaughan stayed calm. That was his greatest asset, his greatest skill. He had retained that calmness right till his resignation. His captaincy had not diminished, he was still his normal, composed self.

But captaincy starts affecting your batting, it starts affecting your life and suddenly you get this gut feeling that your time is up and it is somebody else's turn. Vaughan will have realised it just as I realised it in 2003.

Vaughan was an iron fist in a velvet glove, a tough man with a cool, calm exterior. It was that calmness that allowed a young team to express themselves without fear of failure.

England would not have won the Ashes in 2005 under my captaincy. They did not need someone barking at them all the time. You need different captains at different times. When I took over in 1999 we were under-achieving and I had to be tough with people. When I gave it up in 2003, the team no longer needed that. They were doing all the right things and the fault was not with them, it was with me.

When Vaughan first played for England he was a typical opening batsman: he would sit in the corner, Boycott-like, concentrating on his own game.

And that was fine, that is what I wanted from him. He was a good man to have around the dressing room and he would offer advice from time to time.

But by the end there was something telling us that he had more to give, though not so much tactically. That has been the biggest eye-opener for me, how tactically astute and brilliant he became. It is a lesson to us all that captains are not necessarily born, they can be made. Vaughan got better with each game.

There are three key elements to being a successful modern captain. You need a coach who knows how to get every player in the opposition out and Vaughan had that in Duncan Fletcher; you need a bowling attack to put those plans into action, which he had in 2005; and then you need the gut feel and the tactical nous and Vaughan was increasingly brilliant at that.

Whatever plans had been discussed, he was astute enough and confident enough to change things. *The Wisden Cricketer*, September 2008

Nasser Hussain captained England in 45 Tests between 1999 and 2003. He now commentates on Sky Sports

> **"Vaughan was an iron fist in a velvet glove, a tough man with a cool, calm exterior"**

Hammer blow: Mike Hussey hits Alastair Cook during the Adelaide run chase; **below** Collingwood celebrates his double-hundred with Pietersen

The ultimate revenge

The most highly anticipated Ashes series in history – the return match after 2005's epic – was either a monumental disappointment or thumping vengeance, depending on whether you're an Aussie or Pom. Australia 5 England 0. The crucial game was the second Test at Adelaide where Australia turned a routine final-day draw into an astonishing victory. **Matthew Engel** writes

I N THE EARLY HOURS of December 5, 2006, a well-built, blond-haired man in his late 30s was observed taking the lift up to the executive floors of the Hyatt Regency Hotel, Adelaide. There he infiltrated himself into each room occupied by members of the visiting England team, either by limboing under the door or inveigling himself through the spyhole. Once inside he placed a droplet of a potion as yet unknown to the World Anti-Doping Agency into the ears of sleeping players.

The effect of the drug was to cause an attack of self-doubt, whereby the victims suddenly had no faith in their own ability, or in anything else except that their destiny was to be subjugated to the

will of the perpetrator. The above may not be correct in every detail but as an explanation of the mysterious happenings that Tuesday at Adelaide, it is as good as any and rather more plausible than anything offered by the England coach. What we know is that England lost a match that had "draw" stamped all the way through it for its first four days and 43 minutes. At once their quest for the Ashes shifted from the "difficult" column into the "improbable, going on impossible".

The horror! The horror!

Against much competition the day can safely be nominated as one of England's Ghastliest Ever. We can also safely reject Shane Warne's assertion that it was the greatest Test match he had ever played in. It was never totally boring – there were too many subplots for that – but for most of its length it was perhaps the most meandering England-Australia contest since the bicentenary Test of 1987-88. The main fault belonged to the wicket, which had the pace of a traffic jam. If you can't get hard, fast bouncy wickets in Australia in the middle of a drought, where can you?

But then Andrew Strauss was given out (sawn off, actually) by Steve Bucknor and Warne's potion began to work. Yes, the pitch was offering some turn; yes, there was some reverse swing for Brett Lee – if the batsman thinks it is turning and reversing, it is turning and reversing. England veered between dither (Ian Bell) and what looked like ineptitude (Andrew Flintoff and Kevin Pietersen, sad to say). Just a few more whacks, or several more blocks, and the game would have been beyond Australia's reach. But it was not.

However ineptly Flintoff batted, he was compelling when Australia set out to get their 168 in 36 overs. He would have preferred to be resting not bowling; if we knew the full truth about his ankle, we might think he should be ordered to rest.

But he would not give in. He kept rallying his troops like the last officer left amid the wreckage of the conquered city. Smoke rose from the rubble; women in rags hid in the ruined cellars; one by one his starving soldiers were forced to surrender to the brutal enemy, gloatingly repeating their marching song: "Aussie, Aussie, Aussie! Oy! Oy!

Oy!" At the end England vanished into the pavilion, as if being led away in chains. Bloody right, too.

Where it began

The events-leading-up-to all seemed very distant on the Tuesday afternoon. But what happened at the start was critical. The decision to play James Anderson ahead of Monty Panesar was dogmatic and ill-judged, not because Panesar is a young Warne but because he could have offered control – crucial at Adelaide, of all grounds. It was one of the most shocking selections in memory – and that is not hindsight.

Paul Collingwood's double-century was a triumph for a player who just goes out and does the business. He has cricketing as well as great battling qualities. Pietersen scoring 158 is hardly news – he knows it, hence, presumably, his twitchy rush to get 159.

It would be good to spend more time celebrating the pair of them. But it all meant nothing in the end. Among the many other factors Flintoff declared too early. England had not scored quickly enough to put the game beyond reach inside two days. That was no crime on this pitch but he needed to grind them into the dust until Sunday, aiming for 650. And that is not hindsight either.

Did anyone really believe Australia would crumble against a wounded Flintoff, an uncertain Harmison, a non-spinning Giles and an inadequate Anderson? They got three wickets between them. Dear old Hoggy had to get the others on his own.

Yes, it would have helped if Giles had not dropped Ricky Ponting on 35, 107 less than his final score. But this was not a collapse pitch, certainly not then. The first wicket attributable to anything other than the new ball or batsman-error was Warne at teatime on the fourth day.

Then came the fifth morning. For that, you do not want a cricket writer. Try a mystic. ◼ *The Wisden Cricketer, January 2007*

2nd Test, Adelaide, December 1-5
Australia won by 6 wickets

ENGLAND WON TOSS

AJ Strauss	c Martyn	b Clark	14	c Hussey	b Warne	34
AN Cook	c Gilchrist	b Clark	27	c Gilchrist	b Clark	9
IR Bell	c and	b Lee	60	run out Clarke/Warne		26
PD Collingwood	c Gilchrist	b Clark	206	not out		22
KP Pietersen	run out Ponting		158		b Warne	2
A Flintoff*	not out		38	c Gilchrist	b Lee	2
GO Jones†	c Martyn	b Warne	1	c Hayden	b Lee	10
AF Giles	not out		27	c Hayden	b Warne	0
MJ Hoggard			-		b Warne	4
SJ Harmison			-	lbw	b McGrath	8
JM Anderson			-	lbw	b McGrath	1
Extras	lb10 w2 nb8		20	b3 lb5 w1 nb2		11
Total	168 overs		551-6d	73 overs		129

Fall of wickets 32 45 158 468 489   31 69 70 73 77
491   94 97 105 119

Bowling (1st) Lee 34-1-139-1, McGrath 30-5-107-0, Clark 34-6-75-3, Warne 53-9-167-1, Clarke 17-2-53-0
(2nd) Lee 18-3-35-2, McGrath 10-6-15-2, Warne 32-12-49-4, Clark 13-4-22-1

AUSTRALIA

JL Langer	c Pietersen	b Flintoff	4	c Bell	b Hoggard	7
ML Hayden	c Jones	b Hoggard	12	c Coll'wood	b Flintoff	18
RT Ponting*	c Jones	b Hoggard	142	c Strauss	b Giles	49
DR Martyn	c Bell	b Hoggard	11 (5)	c Strauss	b Flintoff	5
MEK Hussey		b Hoggard	91 (4)	not out		61
MJ Clarke	c Giles	b Hoggard	124	not out		21
AC Gilchrist†	c Bell	b Giles	64			
SK Warne	lbw	b Hoggard	43			
B Lee	not out		7			
SR Clark		b Hoggard	0			*
GD McGrath	c Jones	b Anderson	1			*
Extras	b4 lb2 w1 nb7		14	b2 lb2 w1 nb2		7
Total	165.3 overs		513	32.5 overs		168-4

Fall of wickets 8 35 65 257 286   14 33 116 121
384 502 505 507

Bowling (1st) Hoggard 42-6-109-7, Flintoff 26-5-82-1, Harmison 25-5-96-0, Anderson 21.3-3-85-1, Giles 42-7-103-1, Pietersen 9-0-32-0
(2nd) Hoggard 4-0-29-1, Flintoff 9-0-44-2, Giles 10-0-46-1, Harmison 4-0-15-0, Anderson 3.5-0-23-0, Pietersen 2-0-7-0

Umpires SA Bucknor (WI), RE Koertzen (SA); SJ Davis
Match referee JJ Crowe (NZ)   Man of the match RT Ponting

Pulling power: Captain Ponting on his way to 142

Ashes post-mortem

Mike Selvey picks over the bones of the England carcass and realises, quicker than most, that Duncan Fletcher has had his day

EACH TO his own: where Australia's coach, John Buchanan, takes his maxims from the Chinese warlord Sun Tzu, England for the purposes of this Ashes campaign have adhered firmly to the dictates of Murphy, whose law states that anything that can go wrong will.

It has not been edifying to watch England systematically destroyed, day-by-day and match-by-match, as if suffering death by a thousand cuts. But there has been an inevitability about it since Steve Harmison began the whole thing by firing the opening shot of the most hyped series in history straight towards second slip. If too much can be made of that one ball, it was still a horrible manifestation of a fear that England were no more

❝England were, day-by-day, destroyed, suffering death by a thousand cuts ❞

adequately prepared to take on a ferocious and focused opponent than the Jumblies in their sieve would be for the America's Cup.

Fail to prepare and you prepare to fail is one of sport's clichés but it carries a truth. Despite protestations to the contrary, England arrived for the first Test in chaos. The build-up had been inadequate and ill-conceived, with key players such as Harmison and Ashley Giles woefully short of hard match-bowling (none for a year in Giles's case). Duncan Fletcher's faith in the professional ability of Giles to pick up where he had left off was a leap too far as it transpired. Still,

subsequent batting performances, once Giles made way for Monty Panesar after two Tests, only strengthened the coach's rationale that there had to be significant runs scored down the order. Earlier the loss of Marcus Trescothick unbalanced not only the side's batting order but their collective mental state.

Whether Flintoff was the right man to lead the side is something that will be debated *ad nauseam*. He had enjoyed some success against India and was promised the job when he returned to fitness after his ankle operation. Andrew Strauss, meanwhile, had done a fine job as locum. Hindsight suggests Flintoff might have benefited from not having the extra responsibility while ultimate responsibility for team performance might have curbed some of Strauss's batting excesses. More pertinent, though, was the impact of what is believed to be a lukewarm relationship between captain and coach on the rest of the side. Fletcher, a pragmatic man-manager, has in his seven-year tenure forged strong bonds with both Nasser Hussain and Michael Vaughan but, so it is said, has found Flintoff less receptive. Friction causes heat: Fletcher would have had an easier time with Strauss.

Of the bowlers Harmison got better as the series progressed, serving to illustrate the amount of hard work he needs to get him right for the start of a series, while Flintoff and Matthew Hoggard bowled manfully. But the key to the 2005 success had been that England possessed four pace bowlers –

arguably the best pace attack they have ever fielded – each at the top of his game and offering no respite. Unlike Simon Jones neither Anderson, another returning from injury, nor Sajid Mahmood proved capable of prosecuting any promising situations created by others.

Much of the criticism that has been heaped on Fletcher has been unwarranted. Memories are short. When he took over the side they were a laughing stock and he managed them to an Ashes success and a ranking as the world's second-best side. If there is culpability, then he, as the top man, has to accept it, but by no means is it all down to him. However, as with many jobs, there is a natural shelf-life, after which things begin to go stale, the message losing its freshness. Fletcher has been a brilliant England coach but now the time is right to move it on.

The Wisden Cricketer, February 2007

Mike Selvey is cricket correspondent of *The Guardian*

Fred and buried: Captain Andrew Flintoff feels the pressure as England sink at Adelaide

Kevin Mitchell experiences the Australian victory through both the eyes of the partisan local press and the more sympathetic local public

ONE OF THE perverse pleasures of touring Australia when England are rubbish is to witness the local media rise to something like hysterical, curtain-tearing orgasm. It is not exclusively an Australian trait, of course. Few newspapers anywhere in the world can match Fleet Street in full, overblown, flag-waving mode. And, in 2005, maybe England did go over the top with the open-top parade, the Trafalgar Square celebrations and the MBEs. That was a populist and spontaneous expression of relief. Give 'em a break; it'd been a long time. Now it's the Aussies' turn. Again.

The support of the national team, in the street and the bars, is touching. It is heartening to see a whole nation pulling together. But there is a gap now between the supporters and the media who claim to represent them in what is, essentially, a petty propaganda war.

I don't quite know what to make of the excesses such patriotism generates, except maybe enjoy them for their grossness. These words, for instance, deserve a wider audience than the one originally intended for them.

"This time, the last time, there'll be no relief until the shell of the English cricket team lays on the SCG turf, picked bare of wings, legs and barely squirming, a chorus line of Aussie Terminators dancing around the torso, singing:
Under the Southern Cross I stand
A squashed bug in my callused hand
A giant in a giant's land
Australia, you bloody beauty."

They could have been written by Matthew Hayden in one of his less measured victory celebrations, Australian flag draped around those broad Queensland shoulders. (Or by *The Sun* or *Daily Mail* in polar opposite circumstances.) No, they appeared in the *Sydney Morning Herald*, normally a sober organ, the weekend before the Boxing Day Test in Melbourne. They were unapologetically cruel. You can almost taste the triumphalism. There is not a hint of mercy.

But that is not the mood I detected around Australia this southern summer. I saw and heard a lot of goodwill. I heard some crassness but not a lot. The Fanatics, shouted off the park by the Barmy Army, were generous in those few circumstances when it was warranted. They did not strike me as bug-crushers. There was lightness in their laughter, not ugly superiority. And the travelling supporters appreciated it.

One of the major debates in the Australian media before the start of the Ashes tour was that between old hardline lags from the uncompromising 1970s and their supposedly softer, liberal heirs who, according to the 'crushed-bug theory', were too friendly with their conquerors in 2005. There were plenty of Australians, inside and outside the team, who would not be content with just winning back the Ashes, went the dictum. They wanted total humiliation.

The trouble with such angry thoughts is they do not allow for the human quality common to all of us: fallibility. It is a philosophy that sees no merit in losing nobly. No prisoners. No excuses. Never declare (unless sick of batting), never apologise. Once they laughed at our sitcoms. Now they laugh at our cricketers. Come on, they say. At least give us a fight. What's the point of grinding you into the ground if you don't at least make us sweat.

Condescension was once a trait of the British upper classes. Inevitably it would be rendered irrelevant and absurd as the fabric of that system unravelled, and now it has been taken on by sections of the country Douglas Jardine openly admitted he despised. Revenge, for those of such a cold bent, has taken time coming but now seems entrenched.

Everyone loves a fight. What's the point of going head to head if you don't strive for victory with all sinews stretched? Equally, though, there is surely more satisfaction in a win gained smilingly, rather than one dressed in a sneer. The sweetest memories are those that lift the heart, not the ones that leave a bad taste. ◪ *The Wisden Cricketer, February 2007*

Kevin Mitchell is chief writer of *Observer Sport Monthly* and writes a monthly column in *The Wisden Cricketer*

2006-07

1st Test November 23-27, Brisbane **†Aus 602-9d** (RT Ponting 196, MEK Hussey 86, JL Langer 82, MJ Clarke 56; A Flintoff 4-99) and **201-1d** (Langer 100*, Ponting 60*); **Eng 157** (IR Bell 50; GD McGrath 6-50) and **370** (PD Collingwood 96, KP Pietersen 92; SR Clark 4-72, SK Warne 4-124). **Aus won by 277 runs.**

3rd Test December 14-18, Perth **†Aus 244** (Hussey 74; MS Panesar 5-92, SJ Harmison 4-48) and **527-5d** (Clarke 135, Hussey 103, AC Gilchrist 102*, ML Hayden 92, Ponting 75); **Eng 215** (Pietersen 70) and **350** (AN Cook 116, Bell 87, Pietersen 60*; Warne 4-115). **Aus won by 206 runs.**

4th Test December 26-28, Melbourne **†Eng 159** (AJ Strauss 50; Warne 5-39) and **161** (B Lee 4-47); **Aus 419** (Hayden 153, A Symonds 156; Mahmood 4-100). **Aus win by inns and 99 runs.**

5th Test January 2-5, Sydney **†Eng 291** (Flintoff 89; Clark 3-67, McGrath 3-67, Lee 3-75) and **147** (Lee 3-39, McGrath 3-38); **Aus 393** (Warne 71, Gilchrist 62) and **46-0. Aus win by 10 wkts.**

Letter to the editor

With apologies to Robert Browning:

Woe to be in England
To endure the Aussie
grin
The batting's bad,
the bowling poor
We didn't bloody
win.

With Dame Edna
in theatre
And Neighbours
on the screen
The Aussies have us
conquered
And Rolf Harris
paints our Queen.

Clayton Goodwin
Barnehurst, Kent

Where we came in: Australia celebrate a 5-0 win, their first whitewash since 1921

The unrivalled rivalry

Before the start of the 2006-07 Ashes **Simon Barnes** examines
what drives two nations to care so much in sporting conflict

SVEN-GORAN Eriksson got a bad press for his crime of being Swedish. People said his lack of Englishness compromised his job as England football coach: he lacked the passion, lacked the commitment, lacked an understanding of the English game. Most of this was xenophobic rubbish but there was one occasion when he made a mistake no English manager would have done.

That was when England played Australia. When England play Australia at anything, even football, everything is different. The English know it and the Australians know it but the Swedish don't. And you cannot explain that to any outsiders, let alone Swedes. So Eriksson, in his innocence, sent out not one but two teams against Australia – one team to play the first half, the other team to play the second.

Thus he spelt out the situation with pedantic clarity: we are the lofty English and we despise and patronise all you unfinished colonial hobbledehoys, so much so that we will use you as mere practice material, so confident are we that you will not be able to give us a proper game.

With stunning predictability Australia won 3–1. They won because they played the match like a match. They won because they wanted to beat England, even in a friendly. It was a great leap forward for Australian football and it took them on to a series of stunning performances at the World Cup. I was there when they scored three in the last seven minutes to beat Japan in as fine a display of never-say-die sport as I have seen. And it all began with beating the Poms.

There is a great difference between a rivalry and a feud. A feud is destructive to both parties. But a rivalry is something

that enhances both parties. We saw that with Bjorn Borg and John McEnroe, and with Chris Evert and Martina Navratilova. In a rivalry each party constantly forces the other to strive beyond himself, beyond herself. In a rivalry each person seeks and occasionally finds greatness.

I was in Sydney for two weeks during the [2003] Rugby World Cup. It was a time in which the Anglo-Oz rivalry was initially carping and strained and bitter. But over the final week, when we knew England and Australia would play the final together, the banter grew more and more jocular and added to the pleasures of the occasion.

The newspapers summed it up rather well, for once. One of the Sydney papers ran a picture of Jonny Wilkinson's boot and asked in enormous type "Is that all you've got?" The *Daily Mirror*, of all papers, got the response absolutely right: the same headline and a picture of Kylie Minogue's bottom. This was cheerfully reprinted in the Aussie papers. It captured the spirit of the occasion to perfection.

[When England won the World Cup] could [Martin] Johnson,

could [Matt] Dawson, above all could [Jonny] Wilkinson have found such greatness within themselves for any other opponent? Was it that it was Australia that brought the best out of them at the moment when it most mattered?

We all recall the last act of the Ashes series [in 2005], not just the cricket and madness of Kevin Pietersen but the nature of the banter – England supporters putting up umbrellas when no rain fell, Australians putting on their shades when no sun shone. The Anglo-Oz rivalry is almost uniquely satisfying in sport and its essence is something deeply important. Every English person has a small but genuine envy of the Australians. But – and this is the clincher – it is also true that every Australian has microscopic but inescapable envy of the English.

The English almost invariably love Australia as soon as they touch down. In Australia there is a sense of freedom, a sense of newness, a sense of renewal. This is a country that is almost without a past. Certainly its inhabitants bear a featherweight burden of history compared with the millennia we English are used to carrying about on our backs.

I have always been haunted by a line from *Voss*, the great Australian novel, by Patrick White. Voss remarks: "But in this disturbing country, so far as I have become acquainted with it, it is possible more easily to discard the inessential and attempt the infinite."

Even into the 21st century there is a newness about Australia, a sense that the

> **66** A Sydney paper ran a picture of Jonny Wilkinson's boot and asked in enormous type 'Is that all you've got?' The *Daily Mirror* ran the same headline and a picture of Kylie Minogue's bottom **99**

process of discovery and of self-discovery is incomplete. You feel that you could do anything here, that anything is possible. You have a feeling of being made new, of being set free from all that is most onerously English – the past, the weather, the class system. "Do I stink or something?" as the Australian taxi-driver might remark to the traveller who attempts to sit in the back seat.

And I have always found that intoxicating. There is the feeling that there is a great adventure about to begin, that life has a new and thrilling intensity, a new and thrilling meaning, that the infinite is almost within your grasp.

The English are, on the whole, happy to admit

this. But it works the other way as well. The Australians envy the English, though they will naturally hush this up. But, if this were not the case, the cultural cringe would not work. The cultural cringe is something the Australians are still struggling to rise above – the notion that, as a crass and callow country, they have contributed nothing to world culture beyond Kylie's bum and Crocodile Dundee's Akubra hat.

The Australians do not envy English class or manners or climate but they do envy England's oldness. The English have a sense of identity that has something to do with time. It is a sense of belonging, a sense of permanence, of rootedness.

Now these two things are in flux. English society is changing before our eyes while Australian life is more sure and settled than it was before. But even as these changes take place, the ancient, atavistic relationship between the old country and the new country still affects us.

And this strange state of affairs has its finest expression in sport. Let us not romanticise it. There have been plenty of tensions and problems along the way and plenty of nastiness and ghastliness as well. The baiting of Phil Tufnell in Australia was

vicious and the taunting of Shane Warne in 2005 – "Where's your missus gone?" – did not strike me as an honourable and amusing response.

But there is a unique relish in the winning of these Anglo-Oz contests and sharp pain in losing. The Australians turned on their own during the bad years of the 1980s when England had the upper hand. And the English profoundly resented the bullying and patronising attitude of the great Australian sides of the 1990s.

However, this is a rivalry that has brought us some stupendous sport. Prime examples: Andrew Flintoff in the summer of 2005 (or, if you prefer, the England team ethic of that summer). Then there were the Ian Botham Tests of 1981. And again you wonder if such performances would have been possible against another side.

Australia inspires. Australia inspires as a place, Australia inspire as an opponent. Get an Australian in a hammerlock and he might just say the same thing about England. And Anglo-Australian sport regularly brings from its players performances beyond their usual capacity.

John Snow, Botham, Flintoff are all players who have gone beyond their own limitations and found a level of genuine sporting greatness. And for these things they have to thank their opponents.

These two countries are linked by history, by envy, by resentment. They are bound together by adamantine ties of humour and beer and sport. In sport we express our rivalry, our mistrust, our striving for greatness, our search for identity, our insecurities, our sense of self-worth. Above all we express the complex symbiosis between our two nations, between the old and the new, between the past and the future. In sport we express our deep and unquenchable rivalry and in that rivalry we conceal a strange and perplexing form of love. But do not tell anyone – not for the next two months anyway. **⚡**

The Wisden Cricketer, December 2006

Simon Barnes is chief sports writer of *The Times*

FACTS IN FIGURES

The Ashes in numbers

The battles have raged for over 130 years and since the start the scores have been counted, calculated, revised and reworked to gain a statistical understanding of exactly what has happened. **Rob Smyth** gets his nose in a spreadsheet to figure out those figures

Highest totals

903-7 dec	Eng, 5th Test, The Oval, 1938
729-6 dec	Aus , 2nd Test, Lord's, 1930
701	Aus, 5th Test, The Oval, 1934
695	Aus, 5th Test, The Oval, 1930
659-8 dec	Aus, 2nd Test, Sydney, 1946-47
658-8 dec	Eng, 1st Test, Trent Bridge, 1938
656-8 dec	Aus, 4th Test, Old Trafford, 1964
653-4 dec	Aus , 4th Test, Headingley, 1993

Largest victories

Inns & 579 runs	Eng, 5th Test, The Oval, 1938
Inns & 332 runs	Aus, 1st Test, Bris, 1946-47
Inns & 230 runs	Eng, 3rd Test, Ade, 1891-92
Inns & 225 runs	Eng, 4th Test, Mel, 1911-12
Inns & 217 runs	Eng, 3rd Test, The Oval, 1886
Inns & 200 runs	Aus, 5th Test, Mel, 1936-37
Inns & 180 runs	Aus, 5th Test, T Bridge, 1989
Inns & 170 runs	Eng, 4th Test, Old T, 1956

Smallest victories

2 runs	Eng, 2nd Test, Edgbaston, 2005
3 runs	Aus, 4th Test, Old Trafford, 1902
3 runs	Eng, 4th Test, Melbourne, 1982-83
6 runs	Aus, 3rd Test, Sydney, 1884-85
7 runs	Aus, Only Test, The Oval, 1882
10 runs	Eng, 1st Test, Sydney, 1894-95
11 runs	Aus, 3rd Test, Adelaide, 1924-25
12 runs	Eng, 4th Test, Adelaide, 1928-29

Lowest totals

36	Aus, 1st Test, Edgbaston, 1902
42	Aus, Only Test, Sydney, 1887-88
44	Aus, 3rd Test, The Oval, 1896
45	Eng, 1st Test, Sydney, 1886-87
52	Eng, 5th Test, The Oval, 1948
53	Eng, 1st Test, Lord's, 1888
53	Eng, 1st Test, Lord's, 1896
58	Aus, 1st Test, Brisbane, 1936-37

Most appearances pictured

		TESTS	CARREER SPAN
1	**SE Gregory** (A)	52	1890-1912
2	**AR Border** (A)	47	1978-1993
3	**SR Waugh** (A)	46	1986-2003
4	**MC Cowdrey** (E)	43	1954-1975
5	**WW Armstrong** (A)	42	1902-1921
6	**GA Gooch** (E)	42	1975-1995
7	**DI Gower** (E)	42	1978-1991
8	**RW Marsh** (A)	42	1970-1983
9	**C Hill** (A)	41	1896-1912
10	**JB Hobbs** (E)	41	1908-1930

Series results

The Ashes timeline: Overall results: Played 316, England 97, Australia 131, Draw 88 In England: Played 151, England 43, Australia 46, Draw 62

2-1 ENG WIN 1882-83	1-0 ENG WIN 1884	3-2 ENG WIN 1884-85	3-0 ENG WIN 1886	2-0 ENG WIN 1886-87	1-0 ENG WIN 1887-88	2-1 ENG WIN 1888	2-0 ENG WIN 1890	2-1 AUS WIN 1891-92

PAGES 6-15

BATTING

Leading run-scorers pictured

		R	AVGE
1	**DG Bradman** (A)	**5028**	89.78
2	**JB Hobbs** (E)	**3636**	54.26
3	**AR Border** (A)	**3548**	56.31
4	**DI Gower** (E)	**3269**	44.78
5	**SR Waugh** (A)	**3200**	58.18
6	**G Boycott** (E)	**2945**	47.50
7	**WR Hammond** (E)	**2852**	51.85
8	**H Sutcliffe** (E)	**2741**	66.85
9	**C Hill** (A)	**2660**	35.46
10	**JH Edrich** (E)	**2644**	48.96

Highest scores

364 L Hutton (E), 5th Test, The Oval, 1938
334 DG Bradman (A), 3rd Test, Head, 1930
311 RB Simpson (A), 4th Test, Old T, 1964
307 RM Cowper (A), 5th Test, Mel, 1965-66
304 DG Bradman (A), 4th Test, Leeds, 1934
287 RE Foster (E), 1st Test, Sydney, 1903-04
270 DG Bradman (A), 3rd Test, Mel, 1936-37
266 WH Ponsford (A), 5th Test, The Oval, 1934
256 KF Barrington (E), 4th Test, Old T, 1964
254 DG Bradman (A), 2nd Test, Lord's, 1930

Highest averages*

		R	AVGE
1	**DG Bradman** (A)	5028	**89.78**
2	**E Paynter** (E)	591	**84.42**
3	**SG Barnes** (A)	846	**70.50**
4	**H Sutcliffe** (E)	2741	**66.85**
5	**KF Barrington** (E)	2111	**63.96**
6	**BC Broad** (E)	708	**59.00**
7	**SR Waugh** (A)	3200	**58.18**
8	**M Leyland** (E)	1705	**56.83**
9	**L Hutton** (E)	2428	**56.46**
10	**AR Border** (A)	3548	**56.31**
14	**K Pietersen†** (E)	963	**53.50**
18	**MJ Clarke†** (A)	724	**51.71**

*min 10 innings †highest averaging current players

Most hundreds

	100s	50s	50+
DG Bradman (A)	**19**	12	31
JB Hobbs (E)	**12**	15	27
SR Waugh (A)	**10**	14	24
WR Hammond (E)	**9**	7	16
GS Chappell (A)	**9**	12	21
DI Gower (E)	**9**	12	21
AR Morris (A)	**8**	8	16
H Sutcliffe (E)	**8**	16	24
AR Border (A)	**8**	21	29
M Leyland (E)	**7**	3	10
MJ Slater (A)	**7**	4	11

Most runs in a series

	S	R	AVGE
DG Bradman (A)	1930	974	**139.14**
WR Hammond (E)	1928-29	905	**113.12**
MA Taylor (A)	1989	839	**83.90**
DG Bradman (A)	1936-37	810	**90.00**
DG Bradman (A)	1934	758	**94.75**
H Sutcliffe (E)	1924-25	734	**81.55**
DI Gower (E)	1985	732	**81.33**
AR Morris (A)	1948	696	**87.00**
DG Bradman (A)	1946-47	680	**97.14**
GA Gooch (E)	1993	673	**56.08**

Most ducks

SE Gregory (A)	11
GD McGrath (A)	10
SK Warne (A)	10
IT Botham (E)	10
D Gough (E)	9
AFA Lilley (E)	9
J Briggs (E)	9
JV Saunders (A)	8
PCR Tufnell (E)	8
R Peel (E)	8
DL Underwood (E)	8
C Hill (A)	8

| 1-0 ENG WIN 1893 | 3-2 ENG WIN 1894-95 | 2-1 ENG WIN 1896 | 4-1 AUS WIN 1897-98 | 1-0 AUS WIN 1899 | 4-1 AUS WIN 1901-02 | 2-1 AUS WIN 1902 | 3-2 ENG WIN 1903-04 | 2-0 ENG WIN 1905 | 4-1 AUS WIN 1907-08 | 2-1 AUS WIN 1909 |

PAGES 6-15

BOWLING

Highest cumulative partnerships

	R	AVGE	100s	50s
JB Hobbs & H Sutcliffe (E)	2452	84.55	11	9
MJ Slater & MA Taylor (A)	1735	57.83	5	7
ML Hayden & JL Langer (A)	1413	54.34	4	5
ME Waugh & SR Waugh (A)	1249	65.73	5	3
WM Lawry & RB Simpson (A)	1229	55.86	5	3
MA Atherton & GA Gooch (E)	1219	48.76	2	9
JB Hobbs & W Rhodes (E)	1209	60.45	4	4
GR Marsh & MA Taylor (A)	1168	58.40	3	4

Leading wicket-takers pictured

		W	AVGE
1	SK Warne (A)	195	23.25
2	DK Lillee (A)	167	21.00
3	GD McGrath (A)	157	20.92
4	IT Botham (E)	148	27.65
5	H Trumble (A)	141	20.88
6	RGD Willis (E)	128	26.14
7	MA Noble (A)	115	24.86
8	RR Lindwall (A)	114	22.44

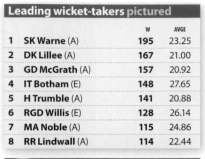

Partnerships

WICKET		
1st	329 GR Marsh & MA Taylor (A), 5th Test, Trent Bridge, 1989	
2nd	451 WH Ponsford & DG Bradman (A), 5th Test, The Oval, 1934	
3rd	276 DG Bradman & AL Hassett (A), 1st Test, Brisbane, 1946-47	
4th	388 WH Ponsford & DG Bradman (A), 4th Test, Headingley, 1934	
5th	405 SG Barnes & DG Bradman (A), 2nd Test, Sydney, 1946-47	
6th	346 JHW Fingleton & DG Bradman (A) 3rd Test, Mel, 1936-37	
7th	165 C Hill & H Trumble (A), 4th Test, Melbourne, 1897-98	
8th	243 MJ Hartigan & C Hill (A), 3rd Test, Adelaide, 1907-08	
9th	154 SE Gregory & JM Blackham (A), 1st Test, Sydney, 1894-95	
10th	130 RE Foster & W Rhodes (E), 1st Test, Sydney, 1903-04	

Highest by average

	R	AVGE	100s	50s
DG Bradman & WH Ponsford (A)	1012	168.66	2	1
DG Bradman & AF Kippax (A)	553	138.25	2	2
MEK Hussey & RT Ponting (A)	502	125.50	2	1

 4-1 ENG WIN 1911-12

 1-0 ENG WIN 1912

 5-0 AUS WIN 1920-21

 3-0 AUS WIN 1921

 4-1 AUS WIN 1924-25

 1-0 ENG WIN 1926

 4-1 ENG WIN 1928-29

 2-1 AUS WIN 1930

 4-1 ENG WIN 1932-33

 2-1 AUS WIN 1934

 3-2 AUS WIN 1936-37

PAGES 6-15   PAGES 18-21   PAGES 24-25   PAGES 26-28   PAGES 29-31   PAGES 32-37   PAGE 40   PAGE 41

Best bowling in an innings pictured

1	10-53	**JC Laker** (E),	4th Test, Old Trafford, 1956
2	9-37	**JC Laker** (E),	4th Test, Old Trafford, 1956
3	9-121	**AA Mailey** (A),	4th Test, Melbourne, 1920-21
4	8-31	**FJ Laver** (A),	4th Test, Old Trafford, 1909
5	8-35	**GA Lohmann** (E),	2nd Test, Sydney, 1886-87
6	8-38	**GD McGrath** (A),	2nd Test, Lord's, 1997
7	8-43	**AE Trott** (A),	3rd Test, Adelaide, 1894-95
8	8-43	**H Verity** (E),	2nd Test, Lord's, 1934
9	8-43	**RGD Willis** (E),	3rd Test, Headingley, 1981
10	8-53	**RAL Massie** (A),	2nd Test, Lord's, 1972

Best bowling in a match

19-90	**JC Laker** (E),	4th Test, Old Trafford, 1956
16-137	**RAL Massie** (A),	2nd Test, Lord's, 1972
15-104	**H Verity** (E),	2nd Test, Lord's, 1934
15-124	**W Rhodes** (E),	2nd Test, Melbourne, 1903-04
14-90	**FR Spofforth** (A),	Only Test, The Oval, 1882
14-99	**AV Bedser** (E),	1st Test, Nottingham, 1953
14-102	**W Bates** (E),	2nd Test, Melbourne, 1882-83
13-77	**MA Noble** (A),	2nd Test, Melbourne, 1901-02
13-110	**FR Spofforth** (A),	Only Test, Melbourne, 1878-79
13-148	**BA Reid** (A),	2nd Test, Melbourne, 1990-91

Best averages*

	W	AVGE
GA Lohmann (E)	77	**13.01**
JJ Ferris (A)	48	**14.25**
JB Iverson (A)	21	**15.23**
W Barnes (E)	51	**15.54**
W Bates (E)	50	**16.42**
CTB Turner (A)	101	**16.53**
R Peel (E)	101	**16.98**
RM Hogg (A)	56	**17.00**
SR Clark (A)	26	**17.03**

*min 1,000 balls

Most five-wicket innings

12	**SF Barnes** (E)
11	TM Alderman, CTB Turner, DK Lillee, CV Grimmett, SK Warne (A); T Richardson (E)
10	GD McGrath (A)
9	MA Noble, H Trumble (A); IT Botham (E)

Most 10-wicket matches

4	FR Spofforth, DK Lillee, SK Warne (A); T Richardson (E)
3	WJ O'Reilly, H Trumble (A); GA Lohmann, J Briggs (E)
2	HV Hordern, RM Hogg, GE Palmer, CTB Turner, AA Mailey, MA Noble, CV Grimmett (A); JC Laker, AV Bedser, DL Underwood, IT Botham (E)

Most wickets in a series

	S	W	AVGE
JC Laker (E)	1956	46	**9.60**
TM Alderman (A)	1981	42	**21.26**
RM Hogg (A)	1978-79	41	**12.85**
TM Alderman (A)	1989	41	**17.36**
SK Warne (A)	2005	40	**19.92**
AV Bedser (E)	1953	39	**17.48**
DK Lillee (A)	1981	39	**22.30**
MW Tate (E)	1924-25	38	**23.18**
GD McGrath (A)	1997	36	**19.47**

1-1 DRAWN 1938	**3-0 AUS WIN 1946-47**	**4-0 AUS WIN 1948**	**4-1 AUS WIN 1950-51**	**1-0 ENG WIN 1953**	**3-1 ENG WIN 1954-55**	**2-1 ENG WIN 1956**	**4-0 AUS WIN 1958-59**	**2-1 AUS WIN 1961**	**1-1 DRAWN 1962-63**	**1-0 AUS WIN 1964**
PAGE 42	PAGE 43	PAGES 44-45	PAGES 48-49	PAGES 50-51	PAGES 52-53	PAGES 54-57	PAGES 58-59	PAGES 62-63	PAGE 64-65	PAGE 66

ALLROUNDERS

Great allrounders*

		M	R	AVGE	W	AVGE
1	**KR Miller** (A)	29	1511	**33.57**	87	22.40
2	**W Rhodes** (E)	41	1706	**31.01**	109	24.00
3	**MA Noble** (A)	39	1905	**30.72**	115	24.86
4	**WW Armstrong** (A)	42	2172	**35.03**	74	30.91
5	**IT Botham** (E)	36	1673	**29.35**	148	27.65
–	**A Flintoff**† (E)	10	656	**34.52**	35	32.45

*Players with bowling averages lower than batting average. Min 50 wkts; 1,000 runs. †Top current allrounder

Most runs scored by wicketkeepers pictured

		M	R	AVGE	100s	50s
1	**APE Knott** (E)	34	**1682**	32.98	2	11
2	**RW Marsh** (A)	42	**1633**	27.21	1	9
3	**AJ Stewart** (E)	51	**1338**	29.08	0	10
4	**IA Healy** (A)	33	**1269**	30.95	2	6
5	**WAS Oldfield** (A)	38	**1116**	23.25	0	3
6	**AC Gilchrist** (A)	20	**1083**	45.12	3	6
7	**AFA Lilley** (E)	32	**801**	20.02	0	4
8	**TG Evans** (E)	31	**783**	17.79	0	1

Most dismissals by wicketkeepers

	DIS	CT	ST
RW Marsh (A)	**148**	141	7
IA Healy (A)	**135**	123	12
APE Knott (E)	**105**	97	8
AC Gilchrist (A)	**96**	89	7
WAS Oldfield (A)	**90**	59	31
AFA Lilley (E)	**84**	65	19
AJ Stewart (E)	**78**	76	2
ATW Grout (A)	**76**	69	7

Outfield catches

GS Chappell (A)	61
IT Botham (E)	57
AR Border (A)	57
MA Taylor (A)	46
H Trumble (A)	45
ME Waugh (A)	43
WR Hammond (E)	43
MC Cowdrey (E)	40

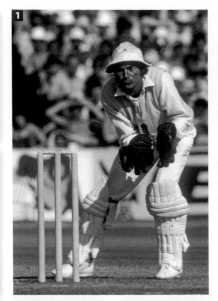

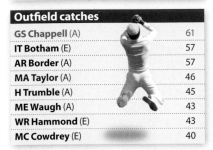

1-1 DRAWN 1965-66	1-1 DRAWN 1968	2-0 ENG WIN 1970-71	2-2 DRAWN 1972
PAGE 67	PAGES 68-69	PAGES 70-73	PAGES 74-75

4-1 AUS WIN 1974-75	1-0 AUS WIN 1975	3-0 ENG WIN 1977	5-1 ENG WIN 1978-79	3-1 ENG WIN 1981	2-1 AUS WIN 1982-83	3-1 ENG WIN 1985
PAGES 76-77	PAGES 78-79	PAGES 82-83	PAGES 84-85	PAGES 88-93	PAGES 96-97	PAGES 98-100

SPECIALIST KNOWLEDGE

Is longer better?

The switch from six to five Ashes Tests didn't really suit England: they have never lost a sixth Ashes Test. Or, indeed, a seventh. But Australia have a superior head-to-head record in the first, second, third, fourth and fifth Tests

	E	A	D
Only Test	2	4	2
1st Test	20	28	18
2nd Test	21	31	14
3rd Test	15	24	22
4th Test	19	20	15
5th Test	14	24	14
6th Test	5	0	3
7th Test	1	0	0

Lord's hoodoo pictured below

Since the turn of the 20th century Australia have lost only one of 26 Tests at Lord's. England's only victory came when they won the toss and batted but they have lost five times and drawn seven in such circumstances. On the one occasion they won the toss and fielded the match was drawn

	ENG	AUS	DRAW
1876-1899	4	1	12
1900-2009	1	12	13

Other Ashes 2009 venues*

	A	E	D
Edgbaston	3	5	4
Headingley	8	7	8
The Oval	6	15	13

*The first Test at Cardiff is that venue's inaugural Test

When it matters most ...

Since 1989 England have won only three 'live' Ashes Tests (when the Ashes are still at stake); two of them in 2005

	E	A	D
'Live' Tests	3	25	8
'Dead'* Tests	6	9	2
Overall	9	34	10

*'Dead' means Ashes rather than series no longer at stake (if Australia hold the Ashes and go 2-0 with two to play, the Ashes are not at stake)

Cashing in

Australia's dominance in that period has largely been the consequence of their vastly superior conversion rate of fifties to hundreds

	100s	50s	CONVERSION RATE
England	33	104	24.09%
Australia	72	101	41.62%

Bat first, lose less

In the last 20 years England's chances of winning, and avoiding defeat, have increased considerably when they have batted first

	W	D	L	WIN%	LOSS%
Eng (bat first)	7	5	16	25	57
Aus (bat first)	18	5	2	72	8

The importance of the toss

Both sides are more likely to win if they bat first and score under 200 than they are if they bat first and score between 300 and 399. Amazingly Australia are nearly three times as likely to win as England when the sides respectively bat first and score between 200 and 299

	W	D	L	WIN%	LOSS%
Win toss	122	88	106	39	34
Win toss and bat	107	75	81	41	31
Win toss and field	15	13	25	28	47
England win toss & bat	46	44	44	34	33
England win toss & field	3	5	14	14	64
Australia win toss & bat	61	31	37	47	29
Australia win toss & field	12	8	11	39	35
England bat first score 400+	21	15	5	41	12
Australia 400+	27	14	5	59	11
England 300-399	12	17	6	34	17
Australia 300-399	13	15	8	36	22
England 200-299	10	13	28	20	55
Australia 200-299	22	4	11	59	30
England 0-199	14	7	17	37	45
Australia 0-199	13	3	16	41	50

Wagging tails

Since 1989 Australia have also benefited greatly from lower-order runs and partnerships, with their bottom five averaging 10 runs apiece more than England's equivalents

	E	A
Nos. 1-6	32.67	46.63
Nos. 7-11	14.49	24.05
First five wickets	61.84	79.42
Last five wickets	26.62	37.00

Wickets or runs?

So what's more important: a batsman who scores 500 runs or a bowler who takes 30 wickets? Ashes history suggests you are more likely to win with a bowler who takes 30 wickets but also more likely to lose

	W	D	L	WIN%	LOSE%
500 runs	31	6	11	65	23
30 wickets	24	1	9	71	27

2-1
ENG WIN
1986-87
PAGES 101-103

4-0
AUS WIN
1989
PAGES 106-109

3-0
AUS WIN
1990-91
PAGES 110-111

4-1
AUS WIN
1993
PAGES 112-113

3-1
AUS WIN
1994-95
PAGES 116-117

3-2
AUS WIN
1997
PAGE 118

3-1
AUS WIN
1998-99
PAGE 119

4-1
AUS WIN
2001
PAGE 120

4-1
AUS WIN
2002-03
PAGE 121

2-1
ENG WIN
2005
PAGES 124-131

5-0
AUS WIN
2006-07
PAGES 134-137